PEACE WORKS

PEACE WORKS

America's Unifying Role in a Turbulent World

Ambassador Rick Barton

ROWMAN & LITTLEFIELD
Lanham • Boulder • New York • London

Published by Rowman & Littlefield
A wholly owned subsidiary of The Rowman & Littlefield Publishing Group, Inc.
4501 Forbes Boulevard, Suite 200, Lanham, Maryland 20706
www.rowman.com

Unit A, Whitacre Mews, 26-34 Stannary Street, London SE11 4AB

British Library Cataloguing in Publication Information Available

Library of Congress Cataloging-in-Publication Data Is Available

ISBN 978-1-5381-1300-4 (cloth: alk. paper)
ISBN 978-1-5381-1301-1 (electronic)

♾ ™ The paper used in this publication meets the minimum requirements of American National Standard for Information Sciences Permanence of Paper for Printed Library Materials, ANSI/NISO Z39.48-1992.

Printed in the United States of America

For Kit
Te Amo Mucho

CONTENTS

ACKNOWLEDGMENTS

Thank you to friends and family, guides and leaders, practitioners and scholars, colleagues, and most of all, the people who forge ahead in the midst of conflict to produce hope, trust, and peace. You made my work and this book possible.

Almost everything improves with teamwork. Given the complexity of our global problems, it is hard to imagine progress without it. In my own case, I have been fortunate to have a number of dedicated, loyal, and demanding bosses and to be part of their teams. In my public life, here are some of the leaders and close associates who created constructive and affirmative teams and gave me the opportunity to do the same. While I mention many, my gratitude extends to more whose names do not appear—you are valued as peers. Please remember what a significant mark you make.

Less than a year out of college, I was fortunate to start out in Maine politics working for then congressman Bill Hathaway on his 1972 Senate campaign. He ran a positive and respectful effort and was able to defeat a national icon, Margaret Chase Smith. His self-confidence and native independence always sought out a better way and his top aides, Al Gamache and Angus King, made sure that the youthful team was encouraged to be creative and productive. When we won, they asked me to open the senator's new offices in southern Maine, which Dot Harmon and I did. People wanted the senator to help solve problems. Traveling throughout a third of the state on a daily basis alerted me to the concerns of individuals and localities in a practical way.

A year of hosting a Maine public television show reinforced the importance of clear and fair mass communications. Rob Gardiner was a superb coach, objective and caring.

When I ran for Congress in Maine's First District in 1976, a stellar group of family and friends lifted up my candidacy and gave of themselves. The daily contact with voters suggested endless opportunities to improve our system. John Smart was the first person hired and I miss his verve every day. Owen Wells, Gene and Carol Waters, Duke and Dot Dutremble and their families, David and Jackie Verrill, Joan McGovern and her family, Leila Bracy and hers, Vin DiCara, Darryl Kemp, Dodo and Paul Stevens, Barbara Turitz, Steve Russell, Cynthia Flickenchild, Joe and Marie Gray, Paul Weeks, Deede and Jack Montgomery, Mike Ferring, Ed Matney, Jim Doyle, Tom Jones, Dick Mersereau, Jay Ketover, Bob Rand, China Lash, Ruth Lapointe, Mary O'Connell, Peggy O'Neil, Stephen and Daphne McDonald, the Slavicks and dozens of other students, Mark Millar, Jamie Weggler, John Jensen, and so many others encouraged me from the start. Lifelong friendships resulted. More than 40 years later, I still cherish the closeness of Jean Todd and Fraser Jones, Bill and Amabel Allen, Nancy and Kevin Russell, and those who came into our lives through the campaign.

More than a year after my general election defeat, the secretary of Health, Education, and Welfare (later Health and Human Services), Joe Califano, offered me a job interfacing with the press and public in the New England Regional Office in Boston. Gail Corey of Senator Ed Muskie's staff, John Gardner, Bill Hathaway, and Gene Eidenberg made it possible. My Washington boss was Eileen Shanahan who had just left the *New York Times* and she championed openness and preparation with a fierce purpose. The talented New England leadership of Jack Bean, Kevin Boyle, and Warren McFague reinforced the core principle that we must represent the people first every day, as did Herb Fowler in Washington, DC.

The great generosity of my Maine business partners—Art Gingold, David Eaton, Dick Anderson, Elizabeth Swain, and Connie Gemmer— allowed me to continue a wide civic involvement even as we grew an enterprise. We all believed in providing a public benefit and the culture of our organization reflected that commitment. My partners inspired many of the creative solutions I champion in war-torn places; Joe Sudbay, Pat Eltman, Laurie Whitney, Mildred Owens, Maggie Murray, Melissa Reynolds, Ann Kerry, and many others brought them to life.

During that time, I was able to volunteer as Maine Democratic Party chair thanks to my predecessor Tony Buxton, U.S. senator George Mitchell and his aide Larry Benoit, and Governor Joe Brennan. So much of my work throughout the world involves practical politics and promoting talented can-do individuals—essential elements of running a political party, which Sue Ellen Bordwell and Dennis Gray executed on a daily basis.

For many years in Maine, I imagined working on international issues and several mentors offered regular encouragement. Among those who helped were Buzz Fitzgerald, Dick Wolfe, David Mallery, Kay White, Glenn Cowan, and Lionel Johnson. When the opportunity arrived in 1994, I had the good fortune to work for and with an inspirational group at USAID (United States Agency for International Development).

USAID Administrator Brian Atwood was among the first people in Washington to recognize the need for a new approach to conflict and fragile situations. It was his vision that gave birth to the Office of Transition Initiatives (OTI) and his engaged support made all the difference in those first years when bureaucratic habits might have killed the idea. Brian's integrity and dedication to public service are inspiring. His deputies, Carol Lancaster and Hattie Babbitt, and senior staff Dick McCall and Jill Buckley gave us every chance to succeed.

My boss, Doug Stafford, deserves special mention. Now deceased, Doug makes me think of a small painting by Maine's Robert Shetterley that hangs in our kitchen. In it, the artist interprets one of Blake's *Proverbs from Hell*: "He whose face gives no light shall never become a star." Doug was radiant and shared the light. He loved us and yet never held too tight. He let us know that to work on the earth's toughest human problems is a blessing. As we faced crises all over the world, Doug believed that risks are worth taking and that progress is possible. He was a disruptive spirit who always sought to improve the lives of those in need. To do that he built teams.

His leaders, Len Rogers, Lois Richards, and Mike Mahdesian, anchored our bureau at USAID and proved indispensable to OTI's success. My closest collaborator was Mike, a constant source of inquiry, inclusiveness, and wisdom. His skillful hand steadied troubled waters and his gentle encouragement helped to move mountains. It still does.

My co-founders of OTI, Steve Morrison and Johanna Mendelson Forman, brought endless creativity, fierce determination, and intellectual breadth to everything we tried. They remain close friends.

A formative time for the field of peacebuilding, USAID bustled with talent and purpose. Deputies Bill Yaeger and Chris Phillips anchored for Elizabeth Kvitashvili, Chris Dicken, Rob Jenkins, Cathy Haberland, Heather McHugh, Chris O'Donnell, Nisha Desai Biswal, Carrie Goux, Philomena Thomas, Eric Baranick, Karma Lively, Jim Lehman, Dina Esposito, Nick Cox, Marc Scott and dozens more to create a Washington institution. Juanita Jones held it all together. Paul Randolph, Steve Siegler, David Costello, Sylvia Fletcher, Ray Jennings, Jason Aplon, Mike Stievater, Chuck Brady, Greg Beck, Buddy Shanks, Bob Kramer, Tim Schimpp, Albert Cevallos, Tom Stukel, and hundreds of local citizens in war zones pioneered model fieldwork. Partners from the International Office for Migration (IOM), Bill Hyde, Luca D'Alloglio, David Whittlesey, Stephen Lennon, Marco Tulio Boassa, and Fernando Arocena made great contributions. So did colleagues from Creative Associates, led by Danuta Lockett; DAI, with the guiding hands of Tony Barclay, David Pottebaum, and Bruce Spake; Internews, with Anthony Garrett and Jeanne Bourgault; Larry Cooley at MSI; Nancy Lindborg at Mercy Corps; and dozens of others.

We thrived because of the support of so many vital USAID forces of that time: Anne Van Dusen, Jennifer Windsor, Janet Ballantyne, Mark Schneider, Larry Garber, Aaron Williams, Toni Christiansen, Don Pressley, Carol Peasley, Nan Borton, Bill Garvelink, Margaret Carpenter, Mike Walsh, Dave Eckerson, Paige Alexander, Patrick Fn'Piere, Susan Reichle, Tom Beck, Tony Gambino, Greg Gottlieb, Anne Convery, John Wasilewski, Tim Knight, Lisa Doughten, Dayton Maxwell, Roy Williams, Sally Shelton Colby, Diana Ohlbaum, Valerie Dickson-Horton, Cindy Gire, Michael Miklaucic, and more. Successors have made OTI a force and an example.

In 1999, the U.N. High Commissioner for Refugees (UNHCR), Sadako Ogata of Japan, selected me as her last deputy. She was another global leader of great range with a catalytic impatience. Sadako always pushed to get things done and showed that the United Nations could be a center for solutions as well as debate. Kolude Doherty, Yacoub el Hillo, Filippo Grandi, Shoko Shimozawa, Thomas Albrecht, Peter de Clercq, Beverly Cole, Eric Morris, Greg Wangerin, and others throughout UNHCR brought global talent. Ambassador George Moose, Linda Thomas-Greenfield, and Nance Kyloh at the U.S. Mission in Geneva provided constant support.

Teaching at Princeton began in 2001 and has allowed me to refine many of the lessons of the past decades. Thanks to the deans I worked with at the Woodrow Wilson School, Michael Rothschild, Anne-Marie Slaughter, and Ceci Rouse; Michael Doyle, who provided the initial introduction; and James Trussell, who offered the post. The engaged public servant from Florida, Fred Schultz, gave the original bequest that funded my professorship and he continued to invest in social change throughout his life. Nate Scovronick invites me to teach and always offers clear advice. Many other colleagues deserve special thanks—especially Linda Taylor, who helps us to lead the Scholars in the Nation's Service Initiative (SINSI), and the Ullman Fellowship; Renee Weist, Karen McGuinness, David Wilcove, Barbara Hampton, Ann Corwin, Todd Bristol, and the librarians at Stokes. My students and our fellows inspire.

Under the mentorship of John Hamre, those of us at the Center for Strategic and International Studies (CSIS) produced affirmative contributions to solving the world's complex problems. His insistence that we do more than observe and criticize forced us to grow. Working alongside two dynamic co-directors, first Sheba Crocker and then Karin von Hippel, was a source of real pleasure. So many colleagues appear in the reports we authored from 2002 to 2009 that I will refrain from naming them all here, since many appear in the bibliography. Still, I should single out Kurt Campbell, who brought me to CSIS, and my closest peers, Jennifer Cooke, Tony Cordesman, Andrew Schwartz, Neal Urwitz, and Louis Lauter. Jim Dunton has provided invaluable publishing guidance on this book and for years prior.

Working on the Obama USAID transition team in 2008–2009 for Gayle Smith and Aaron Williams provided a unique overview into the entire agency. With plenty of time for laughter, they brought together a refreshing group of insiders and outsiders to produce an objective and forward-looking review of America's development efforts.

Our ambassador to the United Nations in New York, Susan Rice, invited me to join her team as the U.S. ambassador to ECOSOC (the Economic and Social Council) in 2009. Susan is a relentless force for improvement, a great competitor, and an imposing advocate. Her senior team of Rosemary DiCarlo, Salman Ahmed, Alex Wolff, Brooke Anderson, Elisabeth Cousens, Jeff DeLaurentis, Joe Torsella, Joe Melrose, Dave Dunn, Mary McLeod, Rexon Ryu, Mark Kornblau, John Sammis, Alex McPhillips, Corinne Graff, Meredith Webster, Laurie Phipps, Lynne Gadkowski, Hugh Dugan, Peggy Kerry, Erica Barks-Ruggles, and many not named here brought the highest levels of public service forward. Special thanks to my most trusted associate, Hillary Schrenell, and assistant Connie Padovano, as well as longtime partners in peacebuilding Mike Pan, Doug Mercado, and a predecessor at ECO-SOC, Betty King.

In the fall of 2011, Secretary of State Hillary Clinton (through her close associates Cheryl Mills and Heather Samuelson) recruited me to start the Bureau of Conflict and Stabilization Operations (CSO). She understood that a successful secretary of state must be strong on policy, adept at getting the department's 90,000 people to work in a common direction, and a global communicator. Her reintroduction of the United States to the world after our stumbles in Afghanistan and Iraq was skillful and successful. In addition, she supported her team and touched us when there were personal matters. After my father's passing, Hillary called our home, shared her own feelings from her mom's death earlier that year, and made us all feel better. She deserves thanks for the support she offered to CSO along with other State Department leaders, Secretary John Kerry, Bill Burns, Maria Otero, Tara Sonenshine, Melanne Verveer, Heather Higginbottom, Wendy Sherman, Jake Sullivan, Tom Nides, Tom Shannon, Pat Kennedy, Doug Frantz, Cathy Russell, Rob Goldberg, Anne Richard, Esther Brimmer, Anne Patterson, Johnnie Carson, Linda Thomas-Greenfield, Bob Blake, Dan Benjamin, Tina Kaidanow, Steve Rapp, Bill Brownfield, David McKean, Steve Dietz, Luis C. deBaca, Elizabeth Richard, Bill Taylor, Roberta Jacobson, Tori Holt, Mike Posner, Tom Malinowski, Tom Melia, Jane Stromseth, Beth Van Schaack, David Robinson, Stephen Mull, Bob Godec, and more.

Equal gratitude goes to my team at CSO. From 2011 to 2014, I loved working with our leaders, Bob Loftis, Karin von Hippel, Pat Haslach, Dolores Brown, Jerry White, Tod Wilson, Chuck Call, Erin Barclay, and Ben Beach. It was an ambitious undertaking in most every way, and with boundless energy, this committed group generated grounded ideas and desirable changes. Angela Wunderli sat close by, brought the CSO family together, and made every day more fun. Justin Tull, Greg Ventresca, Kelli Ross, Lyla Combs, Meghan Lavoo, Devin Mack, Matt Cordova, Brian Pharr, Sara Mangiaracina, Dawn Sears, Kerry Wiener, Chris Wendell, David Greenlee, Debbie Lingwood, Curtis Bowden, and Jeremy Richart created a trusted front office. Here the names and numbers grow exponentially, so I thank my caring and committed teammates. You have made the difference—and my gratitude is deep and constant.

The writing of a book brings so many of these relationships together. With the backing of Marin Strmecki, Nadia Schadlow, Allan Song, and the Smith Richardson Foundation, steadfast believers in the promise of the United States to make the world more secure and peaceful, I moved ahead. A favorite colleague, Craig Cohen, at CSIS reviewed the initial proposal, made valuable suggestions, oversaw administrative details, and provided an office to write in when I started in the summer of 2016.

Adam Graham-Silverman, a talented writer and editor, helped to improve the organization, clarity, arguments, and language of the manuscript. His constant nurturing, collaboration, and strong edits made an immense contribution. It is hard to imagine this book without his help.

Many provided writing and publishing insights, including Ben and Carol Beach, Derek Chollet, Julie Smith, our cousin Michael Thompson, George Gibson, Cynthia Barrett, Bob Reich, Roger Williams, Patrick McCarthy, Dane Smith, Chip Hauss, Robert Downey, Jim Schear, Bob Polk, Lou Goodman, Jerry Hyman, Stewart Patrick, Paul Stares, Tim Noonan, Peter Bradford, David Himmelstein, John Ratcliffe, Alyssa Bernstein, Teresa Barker, and more going back a decade. Working with a great agent, Carol Mann, took the mystery out of the exercise and led the book to Jon Sisk, Kate Powers, and Lisa Whittington, skilled and welcoming editors at Rowman & Littlefield.

Friends and colleagues served as readers of initial chapters and the final manuscript. It is hard to imagine a better reviewer than Bill Allen, with a world-class disposition and sharp instincts—and the great love of his family, Amabel, Sarah and Bob, three wonderful grandchildren, and our goddaughter, Kate. My brother Bill Barton offered his ever steady insights—at just the right times. Chuck Call, Carter Malkasian, and Cecily Brewer gathered early with numerous improvements. Mike Mahdesian, Lynne Shook, Geoffrey Wilson, and James Allen reviewed chapters and sharpened the language and the arguments. I sought title ideas from friends Jeff Marshall, David Wold, Raymond Preston, Michael Gray, Lewis Rasmussen, much of the Barrett family, and anyone I could engage. In the end, I am responsible for the copy you are reading.

Thanks are due for the daily encouragement of friendships—and the sanity they offer. College roommates Bruce Price, Tom and Lynne Shook, Don and Peggy Lents, Jim and Wendy Heldman, and Doug Allen and Lisa Fulweiler remain close, as do classmates Larry DiCara, Jeff and Yuki Laurenti, and Dan and Mayo Morgan. Dave and Kathy Van Note insist on "lots of laughs" and Maine's Tom and Lynn Hallett, Neal Allen, Bob Lynch, Bill and Julia McCue, and Joe Tacka generate many. Ben Rowswell, Angus Twombly, Jamie Metzl, John and Marcia Diamond, Matt Epperly and his family, Kirmet Lipez and Nancy Ziegler, Jean and John Gulliver, Bill Kayatta, Tom and Diana Allen, Janice Cooper, Nancy and David Nyberg, Hazel Reitz, Paul Violette, Arnie Miller, Mary Tydings, and more keep offering support. My DC tennis buddies of two decades, Jeff Dearth, John Manougian, Leo Fisher, Roger Williams, Bob and Lauren Archer, Scott Driscoll, Alan Weinberger, Cam Funkhouser, and the now-distant Fritz Edelstein and Tom Brunkow, lift up my spirits with a mix of games and life's lessons. The grace of the Palisades Community Church is ever-present, now led by the inspiring pastor, Elizabeth Hagan and chair Linda Schierow, among others. Deerfield Academy continues to extend its gracious encouragement.

Optimism is revived by newer friends and promising talent I remain in touch with: Nicole Bibbins, Jeff Thaler, Crystal Nix, Richard Paisner and Christy Weiner, Paul and Judy Bendheim, Ted and Kim Higgins, Owen Sanderson, Cindy Huang and Andrew Mayock, Hardin Lang and Alyse Nelson, Andy Rabens, Nazanin Ash, Steve Ross, Andrew Billo, Anita Sharma, Cynthia McCaffrey, Bill Nash, Noam Unger, Jason Lewis-Berry, Rebecca Linder Blachly, Morgan Courtney, Liora Danan, Milan Vaishnav, Melanie Greenberg, Bob Berg, Dick O'Neill, Julia Roig, Sandra Melone, Greg Nickels, Dan Welborn-Sanborn, Ken Frankel, Gail Morgado, Andrew Hyde, Andy Loomis, Seema Patel, Dar Vanderbeck, Justine Fleischner, George Hamilton, Karen Larsen, Brian Keane, Amir Bagherpour, John Jaeger, John Schroder, Lindsey Doyle, Neal Kringel, Doug Henry, Jeff Martini, Jennifer Hawkins, Vanessa Kulick, Will Meeker, Linda Jamison, Jonas Wechsler, Chris Corpora,

Eythan Sontag, Jessie Evans, Christine Cheng, Claire Sneed, Mark Irvine, Annie Bird, Shannon Hayden, Sundaa Bridgett-Jones, Dennis Sheahan, and Patti Washburn. Again, many more fill my heart and mind.

Childhood friends (and their parents and siblings), including Gregg and Julie Petersmeyer, Chris and Vicki Bastis, Hallie Thorne, Leni Fleming, Gretta Doering, Mark, Jacque, Donna and Dan Hazelton, Tom and Lynn Lenhart, Dave Peterson, Evan Haynes, Jeff Marshall and Donald and Shawna Barrett, made years of hanging out together a joy. Chris, Liz, and Isabel Dorval embrace us with their hospitality, David and Jil Eaton could not be more loving, and Jo and Lynn Dondis, Drew Himmelstein and Aaron Britt, Jamie Studley and Gary Smith, Jackie Potter and Bill Black, and Diane Robertson bring out the best. Our neighbors Rob and Karen Whale, Pat and Cherie Nichols, Halcy Bohen and Gerry Slater, Mike Sandifer and Rhonda Taylor, Margie Palm and John Heffernan, Charlie and Mary Lanman, Stephen and Lauren Lennon, Phil Rockmaker, and Laurie and Pat Coady envelop us in warmth. The same is true of cousins Amy Thompson, Stuart, Susan, Jean and Peggy Smaha McGillivray, Peter and Mary Kay Tobin Thompson, Chub Whitten, Amy Whitten and Dennis Ryan, Bonnie Bryant, Rob and Robin Whitten, and the broader Whitten, Barton, and Lunney clans.

The recent loss of dear friends Rick Crockett, Tom Stemberg, Patricia Cepeda, George Elsey, Scott Dolley, and Bobbie Greene McCarthy leave gaping holes and rich memories. Lifelong family friends Lola O'Byrne, Lee Leonhardy, and Molly Tully remain close.

All of this richness begins with a loving family. The surviving elders, George and Naomi Whitten and Barney and Elsa Barton, are on both sides of 90, and still full of character. The Lunney clan is Wisconsin strong and a source of deep affection. With our daughter Kacy now in California, we are enjoying the great company of our West Coast tribe including Julie Ball and Theresa Canizzaro, Lisa and Mike Derezin, Rick and Alexandra Taketa, and Sarah Barton. Closer to home are Brigitte and Marc Mansourian, Robert and Teresa Barton, Will Barton and Kate Peterson, and Jeremy Ball and Amy Wlodarsky, and the next generations.

Inspiration starts with those who love you first, and my parents, Bob and Nancy, lifted us up every day. My father's Marine service on Iwo

Jima led to a lifetime commitment to making the world more peaceful. Mom's incredible talent and empathy had no borders and was the direct inheritance from her own mother, Marion Whitten—my first boss and a beacon of warmth, wisdom, and affection.

It is hard to imagine two more loving and encouraging older brothers than Brad and Bill, and adding to that love is their wives Julie and Lisa. They have lavished enthusiasm, dedication, and games from my first memories. Jesus and Jorge Mendoza expanded our family and offered constant support. Our daughter's best friend from elementary school, Cherise Alexander, has become a "bonus daughter" as has Liv Lehmann, America's friend in Geneva.

My wife of 43 years, Kit Lunney, is a constant source of love, generosity, and good company. She cares more than anyone I know and brings flavor to every day. We share an unbounded love for our daughter, Kacy, a teacher who is making the world better one student and class at a time.

It is not always easy for an extrovert to spend hours alone, writing in a back room. A friend encouraged me with this reminder: "Writing is easy. All you have to do is sit down at a keyboard and bleed." Kit has cajoled me in every way. As usual, that brings forth a story.

When I ran for Congress in 1976, I wanted to build the Maine public's enthusiasm for the political process. One idea was to let voters know that I would be grateful, win or lose. My commitment was to thank them at their work places for a week after the election, whatever the result. On the Thursday after the general election defeat, I awoke at 5:30 a.m. on a gloomy November morning that matched my post-defeat spirit.

Kit, no early riser, sensed my lack of desire when I turned off the alarm and crawled back into bed. She inquired in a croaky voice, "What are you doing?" My response, "I don't feel too well." For the only time in our then first year of marriage, she bellowed out, "You are blowing it!" I jumped out of bed, drove off to the pay shed at the S. D. Warren paper mill in Westbrook, and started thanking the surprised workers.

They seemed as awkward with my presence as I was, but then a response jumped into my head: "Hey, I'm not here for my funeral. Just want to say thanks." Most laughed, we found a comfort zone, and a narrative was in place. The transition to the next stage was underway— thanks to Kit. She makes progress and so much else possible.

These are my foundations. People matter and relationships fuel progress. That is why I am able to dedicate myself to advancing peaceful democratic change. Thank you for joining in this journey. You are needed.

INTRODUCTION

I.

As the Arab Spring protests spread into Syria in 2011, the collapse of Bashar Assad's hated regime seemed inevitable. Repressive governments in Tunisia and Egypt had fallen overnight and nonviolent demonstrators jammed Syria's streets. Military defections would quicken and the Free Syrian opposition took charge of local governments everywhere. It was just a matter of time before Assad would step aside.

Encouraged, the United States sought ways to support Syria's nascent revolution. With the violent repression of Assad's totalitarian state, few knew how to govern. Over decades, promising political figures had been jailed, tortured, killed, or exiled. In the State Department's Bureau of Conflict and Stabilization Operations (CSO), we began an overt program to bring opposition groups together. In Southern Turkey, just across the border from Syria, activists would meet and learn about basic governance and secure communications, while receiving "nonlethal" assistance of food, medical supplies, satellite phones, and laptops.

At the conclusion of a 2012 training session with thirty talented "Free Syria" local leaders, participants stood to thank our team. We heard the usual courtesies and appreciation. Then one man stepped forward. As he walked to the front of the room, he grabbed a laptop computer from a table and raised it over his head. Holding it flat, like a shield, he cried out, "This won't save my life when the barrel bombs fall!"

Faced with growing resistance, Assad chose to put down the peaceful protests and divide the opposition forces by bombing his own people. As the death toll neared 12,000 and refugee flows accelerated, Syrians told us, "We will win, but if the United States does not stop the bombing, 100,000 will die." Optimism would give way to bravado and then despair as the bombing continued and the suffering increased.

We sought to encourage the deep Syrian desire for change and survival. Within six weeks of the laptop incident, our State Department office began to offer a new kind of training: search, rescue, and triage. In that first session, we trained 23 people from North Aleppo. Two days after their return to Syria, they rescued a family of four from a bombing site. This was the beginning of the White Helmets, who by mid-2017 had mobilized an all-volunteer force of 3,350 in 135 locations and saved more than 92,000 lives. The United States spent about $750,000 to train the first 78 groups, though demand quickly outstripped our ability. Annual international support would reach $20 million.

The White Helmets remain one small point of light in a stubbornly intractable conflict.[1] They may have saved tens of thousands, but the death toll in Syria stands at more than 400,000. The torrent of 12 million refugees strains Syria's neighbors and threatens to crack the liberal European order. The bombings ended the peaceful protests, sowed chaos among opposition factions, and created space for extremists like the Islamic State to flourish. At the United Nations, Russia blocks attempts to intervene, furthering Assad's impunity. Meanwhile, 168 White Helmets have died, with more than 500 injured—often in targeted airstrikes.

On a visit to an Istanbul earthquake-training site in 2013, I saw a Syrian team preparing for the destruction they faced at home. Surrounded by collapsed concrete and rubble, a Syrian pediatrician and 20 colleagues searched for missing people. Under the glare of generator-powered lighting, they shifted huge chunks of debris, shouting out, cursing, and encouraging each other, sweating under the strain. This was the doctor's new reality in Idlib: with little warning, aerial attacks killed, maimed, and chased neighbors from their homes. Relentless bombing terrorized cities and other liberated areas.

The doctor wanted to save lives, but not this way. Only in his mid-30s, the Syrian's sensitive face bore the fatigue, sadness, and worries of war. He saw little reason for hope. Tears streamed down his cheeks as he spoke of his inability to take care of the children. "I cannot even find the simplest medicine. Illnesses that I could once treat within minutes are now a chronic problem."

The enormity of the conflict in Syria overmatched everything America and its allies were willing to do. Parts of the U.S. government tried innovative ideas and yet the situation kept getting worse. From my office within State, we asked, could any of our plans address a brutal air campaign, growing extremist terror, and a fleeing population desperate for change? Or, were we just another fig leaf, saving lives but unable to alter the facts on the ground?

2.

Syria is like so many of today's proliferating complex conflicts. It is part of America's dilemma. The United States has the resources to do nearly anything to try to make the world more peaceful—from a tiny investment in White Helmets to the reconstruction of Iraq and Afghanistan. Much of the world will follow our lead or respond to our economic or political pressure. At least on paper, we dearly value the freedom that so needs defending in many of these conflicts. Yet our record in the last 25 years—Rwanda, Bosnia, Somalia, Yemen, Iraq, Afghanistan, Libya, and Syria—is a powerful argument for humility.

In Iraq and Afghanistan, we continue to put lives at risk and spend billions of dollars for questionable gains—in security for America and stability for the people of those distant lands. We have tried other ways with no better luck: In Libya, we looked to allies and the United Nations to own the post-invasion political transition, and chaos ensued. In Syria, where the West left the war to worsen, it ate away at the hope of Syria's people, at Middle East stability, and ultimately at the Western vision of openness. We must acknowledge that the conflicts where we have invested the most money and attention torment us. Why is this? Can it change? Our record of accomplishment in Syria, Iraq, Afghanistan, and so many others suggests that we do not know how to help. This has been true for decades, in both Republican and Democratic administrations.

Each president of the past 100 years engaged the United States in a foreign intervention. By choice, of necessity, desired, or accidental,

American forces took part in full-scale wars, occupations, stabilization, or rescue operations in every part of the world. Since the 1990s, Bosnia, Afghanistan, Iraq, and now, to a lesser extent, Syria consumed America's national security community. Former Secretary of Defense Robert Gates often points out that he did not predict even one of these events in the past twenty years.

This is not an argument for a flawed practice to continue; rather, it's an acceptance that threats overseas will continue to produce fresh challenges. Wars in distant places have a way of becoming American priorities.

Despite President Donald Trump's "America First" bluster, this may be truer now than ever. Trump is contradictory and unpredictable, which only increases the odds that we will find ourselves, by choice or not, in a mess somewhere overseas. As volatile as the world may be, the United States cannot risk burying its head or striking out in erratic ways. Trump's emphasis on military strength and distaste for other parts of our national security mean that we will be unprepared, with fewer tools at our disposal. Trump's plans are not tailored to the instability, war, and "problems without borders" that dominate our national security. Trump calls for *more*, when *better* is the greater need.

Still, a restless American electorate presents an opportunity for serious reform. Our public believes that the current approach is failing. Thousands of lives and billions of dollars went into the conflicts of the past 20 years, yet the dominant practices of the key institutions barely changed. Intelligence, defense, diplomacy, and development remained disconnected from local people—weak on the ground and slow to react. Humanitarian aid's steadfast apolitical posture produces short-term relief but not change. The number and complexity of conflicts have grown, but our record remains poor. There is a chance for sensible change—if fresh thinking, thoughtful experiments, and renewed public attention supplant traditions, tired habits, and vested interests.

What's more, the world's conflicts will not wait around for our political dysfunction. Those conflicts are the fundamental reason we need change. If we do not build a clearer understanding and better solutions, we allow threats to grow and thus we become more vulnerable, to say nothing of the suffering we abet from the sidelines.

3.

My interest in this work is a gift from my parents. My dad was a Marine captain in the maelstrom of Iwo Jima and in Japan at the end of World War II. His tale was one of survival, not heroism. His experience led him to a commitment that he and my mother made to each other to dedicate the rest of their lives to a more peaceful world. They chose to do that work as American diplomats.

My parents, two brothers, and I became a Foreign Service family, honored to represent the United States in Uruguay, Argentina, Spain, the Dominican Republic, Bolivia, and Mexico. From a young age, our parents sought to expand our appreciation of other cultures, insisting that we go to local schools, speak Spanish, and have friends from the host country. They built my interest in public service and taught me to seek out and understand people, wherever I went. Their example was full of respect for the people of our host countries, belief in America's ability to make a difference, and humility in the face of large challenges. Two lifelong values derived from their example anchor this book.

First, I argue for an approach that makes local people our primary concern. Often the United States overlooks a country's greatest strengths—the ingenuity of its own people—in favor of a do-it-our-selves approach. Without local partners, this work will not succeed or carry far into the future.

Second, America must remain catalytic. Our assistance is most valuable when it arrives early, supports local initiative, and jump-starts promising changes. America should think of itself as a venture capitalist, not a pension manager: provide seed funding and accept longer odds, with the possibility of greater rewards. Within that outlook, there is an inherent humility and risk tolerance, because success is infrequent. That is appropriate for dangerous places and fits our taxpayers' commitment.

This book will provide a principle-driven guide for citizens and practitioners that is consistent with these two core values—which I believe reformers can use to pursue a better way forward. Among the foundational beliefs that will appear throughout the book are the following:

- Every situation is complex, so listen, stay curious, and learn.
- There is too much to do, so focus on the truly important.

- We do not want to take over, so trust local people.
- Improvement is always possible, so measure progress.
- Public support matters, so communicate tirelessly.
- Institutional practices may not fit the circumstances, so find innovative ways to work.
- If we keep these core principles in mind, America's conflict work will fulfill its promise.

It is possible to save lives and taxpayer dollars and produce a more stable world for trade, travel, and peaceful exchanges. I recognize that there will be many failures and still believe that the United States must "lean in." Risks may be high, but great returns are also possible. The people I have seen coming in and out of violence have transformed me: a Bosnian translator, a Syrian pediatrician, a Rwandan orphan, Haitian women, Pakistani bloggers, Nigerian filmmakers, and Kenyan farmers. War is not a dry policy question; real lives are at stake.

Since 1994, I have been at the center of several efforts to make the U.S. government, the United Nations, and our allies more agile and effective in fragile and conflict countries—some of the most marginal and difficult in the world. Brian Atwood, the administrator of USAID under President Bill Clinton, asked me to lead a new Office of Transition Initiatives (OTI) in March 1994. With the former Soviet Union in full collapse and a world of countries in distress, Brian had an idea for a "political development" program to ease the transitions.

Frustrated by six months of institutional inertia and resistance, Brian wanted an outsider's perspective—and even optimistic naiveté. In a chance visit to his office, he saw those qualities in me. For my part, I loved building organizations and soon found the challenge to be among the most stimulating on earth. Brian gave me a start on what became my life's mission: to advance peaceful, democratic change.

OTI was the right place at the right time. The competition with communism defined the work of those who came in the decades before. Post-9/11 Afghanistan and Iraq consumed those who came after. At the end of the 20th century, when I started, we faced an outbreak of wars and atrocities and few limits on how we could seek to solve them. From Angola to Indonesia, I was able to test ideas and build experiments in dozens of conflicts. That immersion produced innovation and a sense of promise. We saw that it is possible to build peace.

Five years later, I became the Deputy High Commissioner for Refugees in Geneva, a frontline U.N. agency that was stuck in political quagmires like Bosnia. Fighting would break out, hundreds of thousands would leave their homes, suffering would spread, and the primary response was "call in the humanitarians." Then they stayed, and stayed and stayed. My boss, High Commissioner Sadako Ogata, saw "the gap" between humanitarian assistance and development aid and wanted to address it. We could help refugees subsist, but to help them thrive—to resolve the conflict's roots—required a different approach. I worked on Kosovo, Sierra Leone, and West Africa, and sought to pull together new coalitions with the World Bank and the U.N. Development Program (UNDP).

After that post, I spent most of seven years teaching and learning at Princeton's Woodrow Wilson School and at the Center for Strategic and International Studies (CSIS). It was a liberating environment that allowed me to imagine new frameworks and policies. I studied reconstruction in Iraq and Afghanistan, the role of religion in conflicts, the use of new technologies, and the emerging crises in Pakistan and elsewhere—always challenging the status quo and suggesting constructive alternatives.

When President Obama took office, I went back to the United Nations as the U.S. ambassador to the United Nations' Economic and Social Council (ECOSOC), where I saw a world waiting for the reengagement of American leadership. In October 2011, Secretary of State Hillary Clinton asked me to lead the new Bureau of Conflict and Stabilization Operations, a second opportunity to start a new part of the U.S. government. She wanted to increase State's agility in global hot spots. Over the next three years, we worked on a huge range of issues in every part of the world. From gang violence in Northern Central America to ethnic reconciliation in Burma, we created a culture to improve U.S. effectiveness and coherence. We made clear that the United States needed to focus on a few places, develop a deep understanding, and catalyze local promise. Much work remains.

The United States has not become appreciably better at dealing with these crises even as they have consumed American military and diplomatic attention. My role has been only one among many, but I have been in the privileged position to see how specific obstacles and patterns have impeded American effectiveness. These problems are not solely American. Similar systemic and bureaucratic challenges plague the United Nations, the European Union, and our partners in places like the United Kingdom and Canada. We also share serious challenges in fragile states.

In the coming chapters, I will look at several major cases where I worked to see what we did right and wrong to build a how-to guide for improvement. The first section will look at the state of the threats and America's history of interventions and successes. Then a review of the wars of the 1990s in Bosnia, Rwanda, and Haiti; the missed opportunities to build the peace in Iraq and Afghanistan in the early 21st century; the more recent case of Syria; and how future challenges are playing out in Nigeria, Pakistan, Burma, and Kenya. A chapter is then dedicated to how our own dysfunctions make this work even harder. The book ends showing how a fresh approach could make America more successful in conflict situations. *Peace Works* brings together history, stories, policy, and local insights to apply pragmatic lessons.

The enormity of constant 21st-century conflict and our own lack of preparation for it are two addressable challenges. We can learn from experiences—many of them described in this book—and chart a new course. We are not powerless to change the situation on the ground—or in Washington. We must do it better—from how we prevent these conflicts to how we help countries recover. Violent breakdowns in civilization will not go away. In 23 years working in more than 40 war-torn places, I have seen conflicts arise, return, and abound. Whether we want to or not, we will have to engage. As we have learned, conflicts will come and find us.

I

Matching Threats and Resolve

Each Sunday, our local church invites the congregation to ask for prayers.

On the morning of August 21, 2016, the minister spoke of the prior night's attack on a wedding party in Gaziantep, Turkey. First reports said it was a twelve-year-old suicide bomber and that 30 died and 120 were injured. We prayed for the victims.

These were not my memories of Gaziantep. As a safe and convenient place to hold talks with a range of the Syrian opposition, I had been in this thriving, agricultural center on two recent visits. For the Syrians, this historic border citadel offered welcome relief from the terror of their own war. While there were rumors of Syrian secret police and spies, our expansive exchanges took place without fear. We wove our way through the narrow streets and bustling populace. In the welcoming bazaar, we admired the silver, spices, nuts, and flowers.

The bombing in Gaziantep was one more jarring reminder of the dissonance of today's violence. Rash and unpredictable, conflict and chaos assault the conscience with a sudden ferocity. Sometimes it is years in the making; at others, there is a sudden, shocking surprise. The complexity produces a range of awkward responses.

There are choices beyond prayer. First, we must improve our understanding of what is happening.

I

IS THE WORLD GOING TO HELL?

I.

Religion, tribes, feuds, ethnicity, economic distress, income and wealth divides, traditional alliances, historic divisions, colonial patterns, social pressures, ideology and separatism contribute to today's conflicts. So do failed political leadership and corruption, broken systems of justice, and large populations of youths with too few prospects and too much idle time. Then there is also the urgency of the moment—that now is the time to address the inequity or to settle the score.

The speed and exposure of communications further compound today's complexity. In the most remote places on earth, cell phones make instant contact possible. The transfer of funds, offering of opinions and reinforcement of alliances is easy. The Internet speeds manuals, instructions or provocative videos, increasing the sophistication and capacity of even the simplest fighter. "Anyone with a keyboard is a cyber warrior."[1] Because of satellites and the global web, television and radio continue to capture the imagination of millions and now reach audiences way beyond their original markets.

Technology has made weaponry ever more lethal. An inexpensive drone is now a delivery system. Miniaturization and automatic fire turn individuals into couriers of mass destruction., while 3-D printers allow anyone to engineer sophisticated designs.

Our system cannot deal with individual threats. The trust that makes a society function depends on thousands of daily actions of respect for others. When a car stays in its lane, a business pays taxes, or a classroom listens to a teacher, progress is possible. The chaos of "every person for themselves" is daunting. When threats are weaponized their influence over the lives of others and the intimidating effect on thousands is paralyzing. A renewal of the broader community responsibility, such as Boston embraced after the Patriots' Day bombing of 2013, appears to be our most promising response. It is hard to imagine a free society where there are enough concrete stanchions, tracking cameras, cyber monitoring, or bulletproof vests to contain the phenomena. Vigilance without vigilantism is achievable. Some will come back to the spirit of our grandparents, "caring for the neighbors."

Of even greater concern is when countries choose to act outside of accepted conventions. "Taking back what is ours," such as the Russian seizure of Crimea, or the assertion of new territories, like China in the South China Sea, show the limitations of a global response. For years, outlaw leaders like Slobodan Milosevic of Serbia, Charles Taylor of Liberia, Muammar Gaddafi of Libya, Saddam Hussein of Iraq, and Bashar al-Assad of Syria operated in their own space—and often copied each other. Now the practices are more mainstream and our institutions appear neutered. Sovereignty will need rethinking and responses will have to move beyond sanctions and force. Taking advantage of the system for our own gain, something that America has done, is subject to instantaneous global disapproval—often with market consequences. Pronouncements of "America First" will ring hollow as our interdependencies expand.

Borders will be permeable by people and political groups. Holding territory will continue though it may be anachronistic or even dangerous. The seizure of large swaths of land and cities by the Islamic State of Iraq and Syria (ISIS) may have been both its greatest achievement and its demise—making it vulnerable to conventional military force. Even as ISIS's holdings and economic underpinnings deteriorate, there is still a sense that the ground they occupy is not the heart of their strength—that we will need to find a better way forward to deal with them.

Each place is unique, but some features are recurring. Official political violence threatens to surge out of control (as in Kenya, Nigeria, or Bangladesh). Political movements emerge and challenge long-stable rule (e.g., the Arab Spring). Small factions use extreme measures to establish outsized impact and international reputations (e.g., the Lord's Resistance Army or Boko Haram). All in a context of greater global awareness and concern.

Why do these places and conflicts matter? Instability threatens our allies, entire regions, and our homeland. It has a way of becoming personal, whether we are there or not. If we reach out, these countries are potential or actual trading partners, home to markets of more than two billion people, more than a quarter of the world's population. Global power vacuums have a way of attracting terrorists or incubating longer-term problems.

While state-on-state violence has declined, there has been a proliferation of other conflicts. They erupt faster, with a greater ease and diversity of violence, with less control by political elites. Popular revolts are expanding, driven by emotion and commitment and spread by narrative resonance and all manner of media. Often, neighbors fuel the violence. Where the 20th century saw large conflagrations that killed nearly 100 million people, the 21st century has started with hundreds of smaller, less ordered, yet frightening events that kill dozens on most days and create a broad sense of insecurity.

Instability is everywhere. A range of indicators suggests that about one-third of the world's 193 U.N. member states are at risk of social unrest.[2] The 2017 Global Peace Index found "that the world became more peaceful in the last year, however, over the last decade it has become significantly less peaceful."[3] Ninety-three countries improved and 68 deteriorated according to the annual survey of countries, covering 99.6 percent of the world's population. Multiple other sites confirm the same news[4] using different data, such as the record number of refugees and internally displaced people, now totaling more than 60 million. "The number of armed conflicts in the world increased by 25 percent from 2012 to 2014" and "the estimated battle deaths of 2014 are the most in any single year since 1945. . . . [T]he world has become a more dangerous place."[5]

The dilemma of the "new world disorder" has stymied global policy makers and America's national security establishment for most of the past 30 years. The problems "are convoluted, and often inscrutable," exhibiting "the characteristics of 'wicked problems,' as enumerated by Rittel and Webber in 1973: they defy definitive formulations; any proposed solution or intervention causes the problem to mutate, so that there is no second chance at a solution; every situation is unique; each wicked problem can be considered a symptom of another problem. As a result, policy objectives are often compound and ambiguous. The requirements of stability, for example, in Afghanistan today, may conflict with the requirements for democratic governance. . . . Indeed, the law of unintended consequences may be the only law of the land."[6]

The concept of "mutual assured destruction" (MAD) comes to mind. For years, MAD has been the sane logic that kept nations with nuclear arms from using them. The gravity of the threat required deterrence. Lesser forms of violence did not enjoy such rational thought.

Now we are entering a period where there are multiple forms of mutual assured destruction. Cyber warfare has that quality: if you take out my electrical grid system, I will incapacitate your transportation hubs. So does terrorism: yes, you can attack my capital with seeming anonymity, but can't anyone retaliate? Global warming also is MAD: one country can pollute to its heart's content, spurring others to be less responsible, but we will all pay the price. Lowering the international standards of governance will likewise produce a more threatening world. And on.

Some will hide behind sovereignty, while others will claim that a government does not back the attacks. Rogue actors are now everywhere, especially since the destructive weaponry is so easy to purchase or build off the Internet. Is *Lord of the Flies* our future?

Do we accept this? Will fortress America be so secure that the craziness of a Mad Max world will not reach our shores? It is incumbent on the world's adults to engage and to break these cycles of irresponsibility and inevitable violence.

The conflict world in which I have worked demands our attention. Not in a way that suggests America has all of the answers or that our mere presence will make things better, but as an example of how anyone who wants to help should comport themselves. We have not always done this well but we should have learned—after all, the United States has been the most regular player. Between our soldiers and civilians who have worked in war-torn places, we should have an alumni association of millions with personal experience.

Since 2002, there have been more than 20 high-level panels, distinguished-leader reports, and major studies examining challenges such as atrocity prevention, fragility, post-conflict reconstruction, and state building.[7] A broad consensus has emerged: We must "substantially improve our ability to address the crises and conflicts associated with state weakness, instability, and disasters, and to support stability and reconstruction following conflict."[8]

A compelling potential ally, civil society, is suffering repression. Since 2012, "120 laws constraining the freedoms of association or assembly have been proposed or enacted in 60 countries"—many being U.S. partners.[9]

As the United Nations enters its eight decade, a new U.N. Secretary General promises to work on the prevention of conflict, saying that it has not received the attention it needs or deserves. There is a powerful argument for saving billions on war and trillions on reconstruction—but our institutions have changed so little that it seems more like lip service than the dawn of a new age or outlook.

David Brooks describes a "contagion of chaos" that consumes much of the world in "violence, theft and radical uncertainty." He describes a large number of people governed "by raw fear . . . without functioning institutions" where "predatory behavior and the passions of domination and submission blot out economic logic." Until cruelty is tamed and order created, progress is impossible.[10]

2.

How do we find a people's peace among the chaos?

We do not want to inure societies to constant violence. Throughout history, entire cultures and families are set back for generations by the violence they have suffered. Studies of the "siempre hay mañana" (there is always tomorrow) culture of Mexico suggested that it was the result of the total exploitation and suffering of the indigenous people at the hands of Spain's conquistadors. The low value that the French put on the lives of their African slaves in Haiti redounds to this day. The grotesque destruction that the Portuguese lavished on Angola as they bitterly departed at independence in 1975 colored the following decades. My conversations in the Balkans often drifted back a millennia to recount a historical humiliation.

George Mitchell, in the midst of his Northern Ireland negotiations, would tease with this insight: "I have never been anywhere like this, where a person will drive 100 miles to receive an insult!"[11] And of course, we still encounter deep divisions in America, 150-plus years after our civil war. Phrases like "violence exposure" and "mortality salience" are not common, but they shape so many of the toughest places on earth—even more than poverty, injustice, and poor governance.

It is also harder to get people to pull together to build a community and a nation if they have little confidence that there will be a tomorrow. Or, if the hurt of losing a family member is recent. As we met with members of the Syrian opposition, I was shocked that almost everyone I spoke with had suffered physically at the hands of the Assad regime. Was it any wonder that so many had fled, been lost forever, or just did not want to engage in any civic activity?

While at UNHCR, we found that several of our best people had spent too much time going from one disaster to another. Some suffered post-traumatic stress disorder and others were hardened. Most had major family complications, including divorce or long-term separations. Several friends have spoken to me about their own great sadness. While easier to discuss today, there is a general lack of appreciation for those who come in and out of these places, without family.

Reflecting on his own 1994 work in Rwanda, a former colleague titled his TEDx Talk "The Day My Heart Cracked."[12] His memories went back to the genocide, the pain, and his own efforts to keep getting up and making a difference.

After returning from World War II, Bill, our dad's middle brother, committed suicide in the Barton home in Foxboro, Massachusetts. A Phi Beta Kappa scholar at Brown, he was preparing to attend Duke Law School. Bill had served in Army Intelligence in Germany with the 104th Infantry Timberwolves and we think was among the first to liberate the notorious Mittelbau-Dora Concentration Camp in Nordhausen in April 1945. The family felt that had broken him. He died from the gas stove in the family kitchen.

My dad's exposure as a Marine to the deaths of so many, especially on Iwo Jima, marked him in a different way. He only spoke about the war in response to a question and never idealized it. Once we went to see Clint Eastwood's *Letters from Iwo Jima*, an interpretation of how the Japanese might have felt in that bloody battle with almost 30,000 U.S. casualties. I thought it was a sensitive and thoughtful view. Dad, who never expressed prejudice or spoke in generalizations about any group of people, did not like it. He could not find a soft spot for the Japanese on Iwo Jima—even decades later. I wondered if the arbitrariness of death had perhaps diminished his ambition. It surely made his settling back into a "normal" life, which had grown to include his first son, more challenging.

This all colors my own reactions. Every so often, a person will ask, "How do you process the rawness of the experiences that you witness, hear about, and live through?" Joking, I will sometimes say, "I am from New England, where we make denial a calling." But that does not tell the tale. While I am in the places, I so focus on how we can help to make it better that it creates a busy safe spot. Back in the United States, I try to understand the context and dig deeper into the motivations of the parties. Still, at times, I will find myself describing what I have witnessed to a friend or gathering, and suddenly, emotion overcomes me. A simple story, such as the one about the Syrian doctor, will be too much. Most of us who do this work just do the best we can—and that does not compare to those who must live through a conflict.

You can go anywhere on earth today and encounter mass violence— Paris, Orange County, Islamabad, a Texas military base, a South Carolina church, a Colorado movie theater, or a New York City bike path. Some are connected, others are random, and all are fearsome. Our test is how to deal with it. The data are mixed.

Some argue that the world is going to hell and that the "carnage" must stop. [13] Others see a more hopeful era. In *The Better Angels of Our Nature: Why Violence Has Declined*, Steven Pinker shows that the arc of history is bending in a more peaceful direction. Using history, psychology, science, polling, and data, he describes a world that is less full of threats. With this baseline understanding, he argues that "the past seems less innocent; the present less sinister." There is less violence, Pinker says, because our ancestors worked to reduce it—and we must improve even further. [14]

My view is balanced and passionate. I am no fan of violence. Yet I can see how we must be ready for war. How we think about it matters. Moral justifications for war do not end with "Just War" theory. In the early colonial days of America, Benjamin Franklin and the pacifist Quakers of Pennsylvania faced extinction. From the 1740s through the French and Indian Wars, they chose to pursue self-defense, despite resistance from their religion and opposition to new land taxes from the

Penn family.[15] I have seen too many situations where bullies must be countered in a way they understand. Violence begets violence, for sure. It also can preclude greater violence.

Even in the aftermath of war, I can see there are benefits. A professor in college talked of the millions who died in the Mexican revolution and then spoke of the long peace that often follows such loss. "Children Will Listen" was Stephen Sondheim's description of learning. Evil forces have been stopped and millions of lives saved by the use of well-timed violence. I might not be here but for the use of nuclear weapons in Japan and my Marine father's survival of what would have been a campaign of attrition.

Scholars have shown that wars spur the expansion of democracy. Voting rights grew from the mid-19th century on,[16] as elites required soldiers to fight wars and then faced publics seeking their rights: "During wartime, when governments are desperate for manpower to help them fight more effectively, they may be forced to pay more attention to the common man."[17] But today's wars might not do that:

> War has stopped functioning as a democratizing force. Among the great powers, expensive technology that substitutes for manpower has made the draft redundant or even troublesome. Within insurgency groups that otherwise would have to be democratic to attract as many fighting men as possible, control of mineral wealth or religious orthodoxy allows them to run autocratically. Insurgencies that do not need to win the hearts and minds of the populations in which they operate bring all of the blights of bloodshed and destruction without the benefits of accountability. Democracy is not out of reach for these societies, but the path will be hard and war will not help them get there.[18]

Is there any reason to hope?

There is. For me it starts with human resilience and the feeling that people will persevere with encouragement. In path-finding interviews of 60,000 "Voices of the Poor," the World Bank concluded that individuals want three things: opportunity, empowerment, and security. My experience confirms these three basic desires—irrespective of class, with personal safety as the precondition for progress. As long as people are being shot, physically intimidated, and starving, do not expect progress in other areas. Once conditions are safe, building trust and pluralistic self-governance will foster opportunities in a peaceful, democratic environment.

To fulfill our promise, America needs to develop the political will. Ours is a time where a number of issues are converging and competing for our attention: the feeling that many of the world's conflicts are just part of a hopeless mess, the ever-present sense that we should do more about our domestic problems, and the global threat of terrorism. Western democracies, especially the United States, must be convinced of the importance of this work, and must believe that they can make a difference if they do it well.

Our most effective leaders have struggled to motivate us for years. In his third State of the Union speech, Franklin Delano Roosevelt argued for the expansion of American influence, observing, "I suppose that every realist knows that the democratic way of life is at this moment being directly assailed in every part of the world." He went on to say, "I find it unhappily necessary to report that the future and the safety of our country and of our democracy are overwhelmingly involved in events far beyond our borders."[19]

That has not changed. With a new president in another reality, Americans must redouble their efforts to expand world peace. "America First" has a ring to it, but the central role the United States plays in larger events renews our strength.

Legitimate peacemaking efforts matter. Scholars have pointed out that "since 1945 settlements of civil wars that have lasted about five years have seldom later collapsed into future violence."[20]

3. PAKISTAN

Pakistan is a worthy poster child for a more unpredictable world. A rambunctious young country, Pakistan harbors a combustible mix of nuclear weapons, conspiracy theories, booming population, backward-looking religious movements, long-standing insecurity with India, and terrorism. America's military campaign in neighboring Afghanistan compounds the complexity. It is also a bundle of contradictions, with modern infrastructure, global links, established institutions, burgeoning media, and grander aspirations.

When I started working on Pakistan in 2005–2007, it was careening along almost out of control. One of only four countries in the world where every form of U.S. assistance[21] was in play, Pakistan was deteriorating. Despite providing billions of dollars of assistance, the United States did not have a current view of the country or a coherent sense of what might help. That accumulation of ignorance prompted our 2006 CSIS study. Fearing that it could become the world's next great disaster, we sought to understand Pakistan's drift into violence. In meetings with hundreds of Pakistanis in the four provinces, we saw a country that is full of potential—unfulfilled and often disrupted by violence.

A surge of bad news confirmed a growing reputation as "the world's most dangerous place."

As we studied Pakistan, the regime of military leader and President Pervez Musharraf was collapsing and the Pakistan Taliban was within 60 miles of the capital in Islamabad. Army, border guards, and police were taking substantial losses as they fought in the Northwest Provinces. Terrorist bombs had exploded in the primary cities of Lahore, Karachi, and Peshawar. American drones and missiles were a first response to al-Qaeda in the northwest tribal areas and decried by many for being indiscriminate. After years in exile, former Prime Minister Benazir Bhutto's return to Pakistani politics ended in her assassination.

Everywhere we visited in Pakistan had some form of violence in the months and years surrounding our missions. On June 9, 2009, Peshawar's Pearl Continental Hotel was bombed with 17 people killed and 46 more injured amid massive destruction. We had stayed there just months before. A short walk from our Sheraton in Karachi was the Marriott parking lot where a suicide car bomb had targeted the neighboring United States consulate killing four and injuring 30. Many friends and colleagues used the Marriott in Islamabad, attacked by an explosives-full dump truck on September 20, 2008, killing 54 and injuring more than 250. A Lahore landmark, Iqbal Park was the site of an Easter morning bombing that killed 14 Christians and 64 Muslims and left more than 340 injured. Most personal was the kidnapping of our UNHCR host in Quetta, John Solecki, in February 2009 on his way to work. Killed in the ambush was his U.N. driver, Syed Hashim Hazara, a gracious, middle-aged Pakistani father who had shown us the Baluchi capital. Two harrowing months later Solecki was free.

Moments of promise arose, only to go away. When lawyers marched from around the country to plead for a return to the rule of law, there was hope. When the legal system seemed to pursue a military leader, there was a sense of justice. When a devastating 2005 earthquake killed 87,000 people in the north, the entire country rallied together. America's humanitarian response, which included important assistance from the U.S. military, lifted the Pakistani view of our country—though not for long.

Surprises marked each day. At dinner with two prominent jurists and their wives, we heard that the United States had arranged the 9/11 attacks on the Twin Towers as a reason to invade Pakistan and Afghanistan. These national level leaders had adult children living, studying, working, and thriving in the United States. They loved their prolonged annual visits with their families in America and yet subscribed to this gigantic conspiracy theory. We heard the same elsewhere—at every level of society.

Distractions, conspiracies, and public demonstrations were commonplace—along with a sense of normalcy.

In the garden city of Lahore, filled with universities, religious schools, and parks, we met with authors, scholars, think tanks, and students. On a Friday afternoon drive to Fort Lahore, a memorable Mughal-era citadel and UNESCO world site, we passed a raucous rally of thousands in neighboring Iqbal Park. Young men, bused in from the countryside to protest the Danish cartoons of the prophet Muhammad, bellowed the threatening sounds of amplified exhortations into our car. We drove through with purpose.

Minutes later we were at the fort, choosing a world-class guide and engaging in a series of informal conversations with a range of Pakistani youth. Our fascination was mutual and we spoke of their schools, hometowns, and views of America. They were curious and open, if skeptical about the United States.

At the end of our tour, we began to walk across an imposing courtyard toward the iconic Badshahi Mosque, one of the world's largest. Suddenly we were merging with hundreds of the demonstrators as they headed to prayer. Their anti-West protest was a combustible mix of a stimulated and large, youthful, all-male crowd and we reversed course and returned to our cosmopolitan hotel. There, a beauty pageant was underway and young Pakistani models were everywhere. Later that night, we ate at a wonderful barbecue place overlooking the mosque, our dinners cooked on the street and cranked by pulley to the rooftop deck, as if nothing had happened.

Dissonance surrounded us. A well-run, underused toll highway sped our journey from Islamabad to Peshawar. While there, we met with the impressive police chief, a high-level, career civil servant, inside of his fortress-like station. In the heart of an unruly city in the Northwest Frontier province, the chief found his own movements curtailed by daily threats.

On the rooftop of Peshawar's Pearl Hotel one evening, we had a cosmopolitan dinner with a most engaging leader of the Pashtun-dominated Awami National Party—regular targets of attempted assassinations.

At sunset on the Punjab border between India and Pakistan, we witnessed a ceremony in Wagah where elite troops of both countries march with intense and competitive martial fanfare toward each other—and then open the gate between the two rivals to lower and fold their respective country's flags. An exchange of polite handshakes followed and the gates reclosed for the night. Cheered on by hundreds of bleacher-seated partisans on either side, the historic battleground is now a theatrical event[22] as they tone down the more aggressive elements of the pageant. Still in 2014, a young suicide bomber killed 60 and injured more than 100 as the event ended on the Pakistani side.

We felt the divisions in Sindh province too—between the historic residents and those Muslims who arrived from India at Pakistan's independence 60 years earlier. It is a fractious relationship with frequent violence. When one group is in power, the other suffers—with the police and authorities involved in acts of retribution.

One evening, I had a chance to interview a leader of the more recent arrivals. A physician and former mayor of Karachi, he now ran the city's dominant political organization, the Muttahida Qaumi Movement (MQM). Distrusted by the large Sindhi population, the MQM is a disciplined and ruthless personality cult. Whenever we mentioned the MQM, the reaction was "you shouldn't talk to them," and then, "but you must." After all, they provide a major piece of Karachi's organizational core.

Karachi is a hot mess. One of the world's mega-metropolises, a sprawling port city of 20 million, it is a mixed bag, host to a range of political forces, the scene of frequent violence, and still, a functioning economic engine. Despite an unpredictable feel and oft-stated fears of violence, it works.

At his invitation, I met the doctor at a public gala, the 25th anniversary dinner of the Karachi Marriott. As we walked to his table at the front of a full, seated ballroom, the stares left me with one feeling: who is that with the local Mafia boss? While the MQM ran the city, the gathered elites did not like it.

From that conversation and subsequent visits, it was clear that the MQM intended to hold onto power in every way possible. For the moment, they would retain Karachi's rule with a combination of basic municipal services, technocratic competence, and strategic alliances with the national government. Politics was an existential matter for the MQM. When not in charge, they lost jobs and lives. They would always find a way to side with the winners. Few other parties had as clear a purpose.

In April 2008, we visited Quetta, the capital of Baluchistan province. Remote and disconnected, Quetta harbors Pakistan's West Point, the families of Afghanistan's Taliban leaders, and a long-standing independence movement. Our brilliant Pakistani-American guide would not join us because of her family's security fears, so there was some trepidation.

As we drove along a pleasant creek, we looked at the large houses of the Quetta Shura—Afghanistan's Taliban leaders—behind whitewashed walls. It was as tranquil a sun-filled spot as you would find in Southern California. Minutes away, we passed through the gates of the military academy with its more formal security and manicured grounds. Then to the bustling downtown with time-worn infrastructure. All coexisting peacefully.

The next day, a mysterious high-speed drive accompanied by a bearded tribesman toting a Kalashnikov rifle took us into the heart of the city to a meeting with a political party leader. Our host, a former member of the national Senate, was under a constant threat of assassination because of an unsettled, multi-decade family "blood feud."

After a hurried drop-off at a discreet row house, our urbane host spoke about historic divisions, a range of local justice, and his son's attendance at Colby, a leading liberal arts college in my home state of Maine. We discussed the presence of the Taliban's Afghanistan command center, the disappearance of hundreds of Balochi civilians at the hands of Pakistani security forces, and the disregard for Baluchistan by the Punjab state elites. In a country where the Punjab province politicians have dominated, the distrust runs deep. While the grievances were familiar in a way, the constant references to violent outcomes were defining.

But the dissonance continued.

Even the basic dimensions of the violence were in dispute. After dozens of interviews, the range of contradictory information made it impossible to describe Quetta's situation. We heard that there were 800 foreign fighters or 10,000; that they integrated into the community and married locals or were violent outsiders who were beheading people. That the Uzbeks were the most extreme, or were part of a multigenerational group that had a row of car mechanic shops in Quetta. Or, that the military and the ISI were double-dealing and actually responsible for most of the attacks. Also that once-objectionable drone strikes were now hitting more foreign fighters (an acceptable result in the view of those we spoke to).

The stories went on. Most had valid personal insights, but only small pieces of a complex puzzle. Without hundreds of local sources and constant cross-checking of information, it would be impossible to understand the violence in the region.

Historic wrongs kept surfacing. Too many conversations with Pakistanis started out with a painstaking review of Pakistan's brief history since breaking with Britain in 1947—a narrative full of missed opportunities, grievous acts, and victimization. Many cited "the establishment"—a three-headed conspiracy of the military, the intelligence services, and the United States—and its vice-like grip. Still others kept a wary eye on India, an opponent in three major wars since 1947, as a constant threat. It was hard to find a Pakistani party or institution that felt responsible. Yet, Pakistanis wanted to be in charge of their country.

We recognized that a reversal of Pakistan's extremist violence would start with a societal sense of responsibility. No one else cared as much and the domestic capacity existed.

As Pakistan became younger, more media centered, and less controlled by traditional forces, America was missing the changes. Because of the burning of our Islamabad embassy in 1979, bombings of our Karachi consulate in 2002 and 2006, and regular security threats, our country team was isolated. Foreign Service Officers served one-year rotations without being able to get around. So much was happening in a vibrant nation of 170 million and we were not keeping up.

How might the United States help most?

4.

It starts with our outlook. Do we care enough about Pakistan to develop a constant partnership? Pakistanis do not think so. "Because of its sense of vulnerability, Pakistan has always been on the look-out for big-power friends. . . . Pakistan's efforts to ingratiate itself with the United States have never produced long-lasting dividends. . . . When in the mood, the United States would overwhelm Pakistan with loving attention and generous gifts. But the tempestuous relationship was never steady."[23] America must decide that it cares.

Second, how will we approach Pakistan? Is it the embodiment of our fears or a place of real opportunities? Do we want to interpret it as the home of thousands of madrasas that are producing armies of backward-looking, violent, Islamic, radical youth or as the country where the anti-modernist Muslim political parties have seldom broken out of single digits in any election? On our visits, we saw hope springing forth all over the country. After the assassination of Benazir Bhutto by a suicide bomber in late 2007, support for al-Qaeda in the North-West Frontier Province "plummeted from 70 percent to 4 percent in just five months. . . . In elections that year Islamists won 2 percent of the national vote."[24]

America must dedicate itself to helping Pakistan's silenced majority achieve a peaceful future. To do that, Pakistan will need assistance to address a centralized political establishment that has tolerated corruption for decades. It will need a justice system that is reliable. It will have to educate its children. Progress in these areas will reduce the threat of terrorism and strengthen the hand of those who seek a less violent way in Pakistan.

These are epochal struggles between modernity and tradition and the outcome is in doubt. Pakistan will need friends to advance reformist changes. America will be of little value if we go about our business in a familiar way.

One challenge is that the presence of U.S. troops in Afghanistan distorts America's view of Pakistan. With so much analysis of the Afghan war—and how that is progressing—there is a natural twinning of the two countries. The result is a view of Pakistan in an Afghan context. For an outsider, it was striking how much the analysis differed from Kabul to Lahore. That is inconceivable to Pakistanis and they recoil from our use of an Afghan prism.

We complemented our fieldwork in Pakistan with some data collection back home. It turned out there was no single place in Washington that could articulate what America was doing or even the amount we were spending. With no single repository for that information at the Office of Management and Budget (OMB), the Appropriations Committees, or the national security agencies, we set about identifying that number, exclusive of secret intelligence accounts.

At a gathering of regional experts, we asked for estimates of the figure and the consensus was $750 million per year. An initial howl of rejection greeted our conclusion that the number was closer to $2 billion per year.[25] A similar exchange occurred with our ambassador in Islamabad, who wondered why we included the $100 million per month that was going to the Pakistani military for use of bases and other Afghan war support.

Our analysis showed that 90 percent of the U.S. funds were going through Pakistan's military, long thought to be the country's most stable institution. Multiple coups and a broadening of the military's reach into businesses, education, and other parts of Pakistani society, something we saw on our visits, elevated public suspicion in Pakistan. America's preponderant relationship with Pakistan's military and intelligence sectors became a large part of a popular alienation.

The detailed release of the data altered the debate in Washington.[26] Despite a GDP of $150 billion, America's $2 billion of assistance per year remained a major focus of Pakistani concern. America would need alignment with the people of Pakistan if we sought to increase our effectiveness.

"For American assistance to be effective in a large-aid-recipient state such as Pakistan, it must go beyond transactional, quid pro quo deals and address the country's main drivers of conflict, instability and extremism," our report stated.

Despite more than $10 billion in U.S. assistance since September 11, 2001, distrust, dissatisfaction and unrealistic expectations continue to undermine the official goal of developing a strong, strategic and enduring partnership.

Pakistan's main drivers of conflict, instability and extremism include: a culture of impunity and injustice, discontent in the provinces, ethnic and sectarian tensions, a rapidly growing and urbanizing youth population, and extremist views among traditional allies. Militant groups exploit these underlying conditions to recruit followers on the basis of a narrative of shared suffering and injustice and the failure of the state to provide stability or prosperity.[27]

"We worried that the U.S. government was neither prepared for an unexpected turn of events nor focused on Pakistan's long-term stability and prosperity. . . . Our underlying assumption was that for U.S. assistance to be effective, it must address what matters most to Pakistanis—and yet we found that current policy does not focus enough on the Pakistani people's most pressing concerns or aspirations."[28]

We characterized America's policy as "reactive," "short-term," non-strategic, dominated by our relationship with the military, and often, interrupted.[29]

Having seen a range of prior reports fail to capture the attention of decision makers, we set out to hold dozens of meetings around Washington. We recognized that people are busy dealing with the day's business and often do not have the time to step back, dig deeper, and think strategically. Those most responsible for Pakistan in Washington welcomed the breadth of our inquiry and envied our freedom to move around the country.

We found a single overstretched individual at the State Department trying to process the range of intelligence reports for Secretary Condi Rice, while also tracking two other countries. He had visited Pakistan once in the prior two years—and then mostly the embassy. At the Department of Defense (DOD), a vital regional post turned over three times in less than a year.

The Senate Foreign Relations Committee staff was already engaged on Pakistan and the report fed into a bipartisan review by Senators Richard Lugar, Joe Biden, and John Kerry. In turn, that produced legislation that would attempt to redirect the imbalance and change the direction and emphasis of U.S. policy.[30]

Pakistan has held together better than expected. It is still an attention-getting political mess with many functioning parts. The United States is not a determinative player, but we can contribute to a more peaceful future.

5. LESSONS APPLIED

Even in a world going to hell, there are plenty of opportunities for action. Whether the situation is promising enough to take the significant risk involved depends on understanding the place, the nature of the violence, and if there is an opening.

Few cases will be as sprawling as Pakistan, but each country requires the same diligence and patience to sort out the intricate puzzle of conflict.

Three principles for this chapter follow.

I. Accept the Impossibility of the Task and Then Expand Your Understanding of the Chaos, Violence, and Conflict.

Do not feel as if you have to come up with a solution or answer.

These are tough places to work. The qualities that have brought a country to conflict are intimidating at most levels, including physical danger, closed societies, mafia-like infestations, oppressive and exploitive leadership, and widespread corruption. All of these elements conspire to produce a noxious blend of misinformation and disinformation and a diet of anecdotes that are heavy on rumors and conspiracy theories. Be ready to say that it is beyond your ability to dissect.

How serious are you about improving your understanding? Are you able to strike a balance between rigor, curiosity, and creativity? How do you manifest that? A wide breadth of contacts often leads to the depth you need to be effective. Spend the time and get the competing views.

America's analysis of countries in conflict is not good, and there are not many nations that do it better. Examples of inadequacy abound: the U.N. Department of Political Affairs is notoriously understaffed and also reluctant to provoke a collapsing member state with gloomy reports; lead countries, such as France in Cote d'Ivoire, seem to be more proprietary than analytical when a crisis looms; even Israel, with its sophisticated systems and thousands of human contacts, can still be surprised when it ventures into a tiny geographic area like Gaza.

Wherever we encounter violence, creative people are applying fresh multidimensional and interdisciplinary approaches. Conflict is a wicked witch's brew of human failings and depravity, so expand the references well beyond economics, power politics, ethnic groupings, religion, and many of the other shorthand explanations. Recognize that the chaos of conflict will require the application of history, politics, economics, religion, anthropology, science, sociology, psychology, and more. Start with a broad canvas.

Be open to those who are expanding the tools of peacebuilding. Pursue exciting practices that are treating violence as an epidemic, expanding the role of women in peace negotiations, using social and traditional media to circumvent roadblocks, applying neuroscience to conflict dynamics, and interpreting information through new datafication tools.

II. Remember that It All Comes Back to Local Responsibility.

The United States must know that it is not the answer in a foreign land. We should never be more than a catalytic force. If we adhere to that role, we accelerate local responsibility and curtail the blame games that are so characteristic of conflict places.

Former president of Ireland Mary Robinson makes a compelling argument about her country. She says that Ireland's future turned when it moved from England-centric to thinking of itself as being strategically located between the United States and Europe. These changes are necessary—and historic.

Focus on the domestic rejection of violence as a key building block. See what steps are available locally and how they can be encouraged or expanded as the starting point. International intervention is much more complicated than providing a boost to a positive local opening.

Know your existing portfolio and the implication of your current partnerships. America's lack of perspective on the billions going to Pakistan's military weakened our efforts to connect to the broader public. Even though $2 billion a year was not transformative in a country with a $150 billion GDP, it was of great significance to a Pakistan military with an annual budget of $5–10 billion. For those who wanted a return to civilian-led government, the U.S. aid was a status quo abettor.

III. Build a Culture of Anticipation.

Why are we constantly surprised? Conflicts start as slow-cooking cauldrons that deserve more than a few concerned experts hovering in a lonely vigil, joined by a mass of others when it boils over.

There is a reluctance to anticipate. Almost all experts failed to see the rapid collapse of the Soviet Union before the Berlin Wall fell in 1989, despite academies full of Sovietologists. Hamas's success in the Palestinian elections of 2005 shocked another set of experts. The global economic collapse of 2008 and the start of the Arab Spring in 2010 also came as surprises. When Pakistan's Taliban advanced to within 60 miles of Pakistan's capital, Islamabad, it produced a shock and then a crisis mentality.

Not only are there numerous early warning systems and reports,[31] but also much of the daily international news highlights disturbing trends. My USAID boss, Doug Stafford, would say, "Give me the Reuters wire and I will be able to tell you where the next humanitarian crisis will be." Today, there are blogs, e-mail, and cellular communications, but these resources have not initiated a rush to prepare. The trail of Google searches spell out broad, sweeping trends. Overload may now be another reason to miss the obvious.

Denial remains the norm. While many will embrace the longer-term predictions of massive and expensive studies by the intelligence community,[32] or rush to the emergency of the day, there is a seeming inability to take the next step and prepare for the crisis of tomorrow. A conversation with one of the wisest U.N. officials about developing problems in Pakistan around 2002 serves as a good example. "Pakistan cannot collapse," he said. When asked "Why not?" his response was, "Because it would be too awful!"[33]

Of course there are numerous other reasons to resist a thoughtful approach, including the usual refuge of scoundrels, the shibboleth of sovereignty. By playing that card, miserable leaders can deflect international attention and rally nationalist zeal behind their destructive patterns. Americans can use the inverse argument to say it is outside our jurisdiction.

Equally distressing are more mundane hazards: a lack of imagination; overly busy scheduling of policymakers; and a cloying possessiveness by those responsible for a place or problem within the bureaucracy. As a colleague recently wrote, "Both parts are debilitating; first the principals are so time-pressed that they are often tempted by the meretricious call of the glibbest arguments, if argued forcefully enough; and, the bureaucratic infighting is endemic."[34]

Efforts to address these patterns have not gained the upper hand. When USAID Administrator Andrew Natsios founded the Office of Conflict Mitigation and Management (CMM) in 2002,[35] it began a series of conflict assessment reports that detailed the volatility of 20 countries. A valuable innovation, the reports were seen to be too controversial, ended up being tightly held, and have been cut back to a few per year. Their wise intent was to guide future programming to address the central political development challenges facing many nations. The State Department's best diplomatic reporting should do this too, but it often addresses the more immediate time horizon. Similarly, the often-touted country war plans of the Pentagon are unlikely to have the granularity or political insight that helps with anticipation.

The U.S. government is far too reactive. Too often, the U.S. government operates like an old-fashioned fire department, ever-ready to rush to a crisis with a shining red truck and pour water on the flames. Our crisis-watch capabilities should be regular, interagency, and less classified. Ambassadors should convene country teams to worry about what can go wrong and to prepare plans. Integrated Washington teams could then refine them. For example, if a 90-plus-year-old authoritarian, like Robert Mugabe of Zimbabwe, runs a country we should prepare America's next steps. I seldom saw this kind of work.

Red teams that question your conclusions are always useful and seldom found in the civilian side of government. More common in the Pentagon as "war games," they still need broader application. A well-known example was a $250-million, two-year, 13,500-service-member exercise called Millennium Challenge 2002 (MC '02) that was designed to test new weaponry and ways of fighting in an Iraq/Iran-like setting. After the red team pre-empted the planned attack by sinking the Navy fleet with a chaotic mix of suicide speed boats and nondoctrinal attacks, the game needed a reset. Popularized by Malcolm Gladwell in *Blink* as an example of a resourceful red team leader finding a way to neutralize a Goliath, the exercise still had value for showing how vulnerable the United States can be even when it has almost every advantage. That it cost so much and took ten years to report the outcomes in an honest way is not desirable.[36] That it popularized the use of smaller, regular red team exercises in the U.S. military was a positive outcome.

With a situation as complex as Pakistan, I believe that assigning the analysis to two or three competing teams of integrated U.S. government officials (e.g., State Department, USAID, CIA, DOD, and others) would have value. Each would have full access to all existing programs and could commission polls, reports, and analysis as needed—plus the ability to travel around Pakistan. Within a few months, all the teams would present their findings and strategies for a high-level review. The winning team would lead in the implementation of the plan, which might incorporate some of the best recommendations from the other competitors.

If the United States is going to spend $2 billion on a place, having a contest for good ideas is a small and wise investment. Challenging core assumptions might forestall a rush to false consensus—and the process could identify some fresh talent to lead the difficult work.

The world may be going to hell, but America can be much more coherent and effective. Finding new ways to offer assistance is essential.

2

WHY SHOULD WE ACT AND WHEN?

I.

As conflicts unfold around the world, the United States is in constant demand. Despite a range of mixed experiences and current shortcomings, America is a first stop for bilateral and multilateral assistance. "I can tell you for certain, most of the rest of the world doesn't lie awake at night worrying about America's presence—they worry about what would happen in our absence,"[1] then secretary of state John Kerry offered in 2014.

Central questions for the United States remain: Why should we act and when? The reasons vary but there is usually a combination of threats and national values, local suffering, the involvement of allies, and the inevitable spread of violence. Often there is a reluctant American public, skeptical of the purpose of U.S. engagement, doubtful of the import, and wary of the costs.

One myth that must be addressed is of the self-made nation. "One of the roadblocks to our reaching a sustained commitment to the objective of helping other countries develop in freedom is the haunting question 'We did it all by ourselves; why can't they?'" wrote Federal Appeals Court judge Frank Coffin of Maine. "The short answer is that we didn't do it 'all by ourselves.' To begin with, we waged a successful revolution. But one out of fifteen dollars was loaned to us from abroad. That margin of 7 percent may well have been the critical margin of resources."[2]

Coffin went on to detail the "lenient" loans and international credit that made America's growth possible, including a foreign bond of $11 million to finance the Louisiana Purchase. "We were not always model debtors," Coffin wrote and described the repudiation of debt by several states "while nine others defaulted on interest during the lean years of 1841 and 1842."[3]

America benefitted from the help of others and has often been generous. We have advantages and opportunities that no other nation enjoys. Yet American exceptionalism collides with a national reluctance, producing significant hesitancies.

At my core I believe in expanding freedom and giving people a fighting chance to make it on their own—with great humility. Coffin, who served in all three branches of our federal government, called for us to sustain our "historic efforts to assist in the evolution of free, responsible, and prospering nations."

He wrote, "It is a levy on the American spirit, understanding, and will. It is a call to this generation to sense a new extension of the spirit of the Declaration of Independence in an interdependent world. In responding to this call, the people of the United States will be doing far more than giving this nation the ability to endure in its leadership. They will have rediscovered their national purpose. They will be serving their deepest national interest."[4]

It is time for a full-throated call for America to give local people, wherever they live, a fair chance to thrive in peace. At the same time, we must balance this ambition with a constant search for improvement.

2.

Our history is instructive, both for its restraint and for activism.

Suffering from the exhaustion of eight years as America's first president, George Washington sent a farewell letter to the nation in 1796. Assisted by James Madison and Alexander Hamilton, he sought to address the perils he most feared for our country. Intervention in the affairs of Europe and "foreign entanglements" featured prominently. Fully one-quarter of this correspondence reinforced that "it must be unwise in us to implicate ourselves, by artificial ties, in the ordinary vicissitudes of her politics, or the ordinary combinations and collisions of her friendships or enmities." Washington counseled, "Just and ami-cable feelings towards all should be cultivated. The Nation, which in-dulges towards another an habitual hatred, or an habitual fondness, is in some degree a slave."[5]

Jefferson's inaugural address of 1801 spoke of "entangling alliances with none," and that sentiment dominated for most of the century.[6] On July 4, 1821, then secretary of state John Quincy Adams addressed the Congress and explained the nation's early noninterventionist foreign policy. "[The United States] has abstained from interference with the concerns of others, even when conflict has been for principles to which she clings. . . . [S]he goes not abroad in search of monsters to destroy. She is the well-wisher to the freedom and independence of all. She is the champion and vindicator only of her own."[7]

In the late 1800s, the grounding for America's role in the world became the "expansionist impulse."[8] The onset of the Spanish-American War marked a clear change, though challenged by many. Among the doubters was Mark Twain, who characterized the Philip-pine-American War as a colonialist adventure: "I cannot for the life of me comprehend how we got into that mess."[9]

Motives and behaviors mattered as the world stumbled into World War I. "Even open societies . . . are not immune to the appeal to honor and the fear of humiliation. The relentless emphasis on shame and face, on position and credibility, on the dread of being perceived as weak sounds an icy note through the rhetoric of 1914. . . . The prospect of being discredited, 'reduced to a second-rate power,' was what drove the war forward."[10]

Coming to the world's rescue in World War I and then stepping back from the next stage of responsibility led to further U.S. interven-tions. Stopping evil in World War II and the successful post-conflict rebirths of Germany and Japan further emboldened political leaders. In a memorable series of lectures at the National War College, George Kennan struck a note of realism: "Today you cannot even do good unless you are prepared to exert your share of power, take your share of responsibility, make your share of mistakes, and assume your share of risks."[11]

The Korean War was more muddled but the dramatic post-conflict progress of South Korea emboldened nation builders.

U.S. policymakers often underestimated the enormity of the task. In Vietnam the United States intervened in order to prevent the loss of a distant country to communism. As we expanded our ground forces in Vietnam in May 1965, Clark Clifford warned President Johnson about "a quagmire." American political pride, hostile terrain, and an enemy that believed more in its cause[12] became our foundational failures. The sacrifices of Vietnam led to considerable self-examination, reforms, and a greater reluctance to intervene in distant wars, but there remained a feeling that the United States could solve a complex problem if it just set its mind to it.

Political theorists raised concerns that the United States did not have a current or correct understanding of the changing world. In his 1969 path-breaking *Political Order in Changing Societies*, Samuel Huntington described the shortfalls: the absence of political community, the inability to build societal trust, and the inattention to politics by the development community.[13]

The brushfires of the 1980s, from Grenada to Libya and Panama, did little to enlighten future U.S. engagements. We learned more from the furtive support we gave to anti-communist forces in Central America.

A growing confusion marked the 1990s, as David Halberstam described in *War in a Time of Peace*. He wrote about America's finest diplomats no longer being able to define the global struggle as one that was Moscow or communist centered: "In this new era, evil was simply evil, albeit localized. It no longer bore a recognizable brand name that would cause Washington to spring to readiness, and where there would be large domestic American political constituencies pledged to counteraction. The talents and the experiences of the last forty years had left many senior national security people somewhat slow to spot a very different kind of crisis and ill-prepared to respond."[14]

Many argued "the botched Somalia intervention (in 1992–3) . . . obliged" a full re-evaluation and retrenchment that tempered the international response just at the moment that there was a "sharp increase in domestic conflicts."[15] Karin von Hippel's *Democracy by Force: US Military Intervention in the Post–Cold War World* noted a developing "democracy rationale" and "non-interventionary norm" that lessened the likelihood of force. Bosnia, Rwanda, and other conflicts confirmed that sense.

Dissatisfaction with the ambiguity of the prior decade produced a millennial change in Washington. Harvard's Joseph Nye worried about "declinism" in the 1990s and now "cautioned against triumphalism."[16] Following the 9/11 attacks on Washington and New York, the "global war on terrorism" became the rallying cry for a heightened presence in more than 100 countries.

During research for his prescient pre–Iraq War article "The Fifty-First State" in *The Atlantic*, James Fallows spoke to retired Air Force General Merrill McPeak, who addressed the limitations of "human imagination about the long-term consequences of war" and what follows. "Wars change history in ways no one can foresee," McPeak told Fallows. He also mentioned how well the U.S. military had performed, with the exception of "fighting not organized armies but stateless foes, [where] we have underestimated our vulnerabilities."[17] The Afghanistan and Iraq wars confirmed those strengths and weaknesses and stimulated a strong counteraction.

"America may have lost its stomach for military intervention," columnist Charles Blow wrote in the *New York Times* in the late summer of 2013 when the Obama administration was considering the appropriate response to the use of chemical weapons by Syrian President Bashar al-Assad.[18] Citing a range of poll numbers, Blow spoke of the "war-weariness" of the American public and attributed it to the "sinkholes" of Iraq (nine years) and Afghanistan (then in its 12th year) and the involvement of the United States in military action in places that Americans did not know for all but "7 of the past 30 years." As he raised central challenges for the president and our body politic, Blow said, "Convincing Americans that a place they hardly know about poses a security threat may prove difficult." It did in Syria.

Now, the Trump administration is trying to brand a driving threat as "extremist Islamic terror." These simplified prisms offer focus, but not strategies or solutions.

The new world disorder does not lend itself to comfortable interpretations. In 2014, Henry Kissinger spoke of America's "increasingly ambivalent role on the world stage" and asked, "Are we facing a period in which forces beyond the restraints of any order determine the future?"[19] The late Zbigniew Brzezinski emphasized U.S. engagement with others, even as it must sort out its own challenges: "Today, with distance made irrelevant by the immediacy of communications and the near-instant speed of financial transactions, the well-being of the most advanced parts of the world is becoming increasingly interdependent. In our time . . . the West and the East cannot keep aloof from each other: their relationship can only be either reciprocally cooperative or mutually damaging."[20]

Theories for moving ahead abound. Ethicists are attracted to "just war." For others, the hope that thousands of deaths will never again happen lives in the language of the Genocide Convention. In the international community, there is now R2P, the "right to protect" civilians who are subject to attacks from their own governments. Concepts such as "Positive Peace" are more recent, suggesting that rational arguments and defining economic data might carry the day.

Without U.S. leadership, the resulting vacuum is painful to behold. In the turmoil, international institutions lose credibility, mutual ignorance fuels rifts, and the so-called civilized world cowers behind private security, gated communities, and Maginot Line–like walls or Star Wars fantasies. People everywhere fear attack, and nativists exploit it.

The lessons from our history make clear that the United States needs a united, affirmative agenda for conflict response in the 21st century. As the complexity and impact of far-flung conflicts grow, we must respond to help countries resolve the top issues driving violence and provide the right tools only when cases are ripe for our help.

3.

What have we learned from our successes?

Since the fall of the Berlin Wall in 1989, the United States has militarily intervened in 20 countries.[21] The United Nations currently has 16 further ongoing peacekeeping missions across the world that the United States supports financially but without troops.[22] Interventions are frequent but seldom completely stabilize a conflict zone.

America has a mixed record. Naturally, the most recent experiences of Afghanistan, Iraq, and Syria are prominent and merit deeper attention in this book. Most cite the successes of Japan and Germany. Karin von Hippel mentions three advantages encountered in those cases: "unconditional surrender after World War II gave the Allies *carte blanche* to do what they wanted"; "highly literate industrialised societies—favoured and facilitated change"; and there was a "serious commitment on behalf of the Allies to create democratic states."[23]

The deep histories of self-governance in Japan and Germany shaped their postwar journey, even as U.S. representatives led the drafting of new constitutions with decentralized authorities. "The occupation worked," Edward Peterson wrote, "when and where it allowed the Germans to govern themselves."[24]

Yet, strong American leaders with outsized authority had the final word. "Never before in the history of the United States had such enormous and absolute power been placed in the hands of a single individual,"[25] described General Douglas MacArthur's role as the Supreme Commander for the Allied Powers in Japan. He was seen as "more important than Confucius."[26] John Kenneth Galbraith, the economist, spoke of "an arrogant certainty of high purpose."[27] Many feared that ours was an authoritarian versus democratic model and a Japanese song of the time asked, "How can we have a democracy with two Emperors [MacArthur and Hirohito]? The great democratic teacher was as unassailable as the emperor himself."[28]

Still, the United States set a principled direction emphasizing individual liberties and respect for human rights, "the freedoms of religion, assembly, speech, and the press. They shall also be encouraged to form democratic and representative organizations," a Presidential Policy statement declared for Japan.[29] At one point, MacArthur asked for a new constitution within a week. As John Dower, author of *Embracing Defeat*, recounted in a lecture: In one of those exchanges, a young woman drafter asked to include the phrase "men and women are equal before the law." When told no, she cried. The men said, "Let's give her this one," and Japan now has the Equal Rights Amendment that never passed in the United States.[30]

Dower spoke of the "culture of defeat" that existed in Japan. At its heart was the death of two million soldiers and one million civilians. Urban devastation destroyed 66 cities. Liberation from the militarist politics that consumed the prior 25 years of Japan's politics fed a pent-up demand for change. Happiness came back into Japanese life. "Glenn Miller and Betty Grable probably did more for Japanese liberation than any number of high-minded lectures on *demokurashii*."[31]

Adjustments abounded in each nation. Initial expectations of a few months of occupation turned into years, with the bulk of U.S. troops staying in Germany until 1955 and Japan until 1952. Both countries still house large U.S. bases and forces. Shortages of food reached famine levels and became the priority. Significant purges of officials took place with many bureaucrats staying in office to keep things moving.

America saw the Japanese as "an obedient herd"[32] and MacArthur "saw himself as a reformer of the Japanese soul."[33] "Sex, screen, and sport" helped to carry the message. Movies introduced kissing scenes and baseball became the democratic game.[34] While he abhorred the actions of both Germany and Japan, MacArthur was dismissive of what he perceived to be the childlike qualities of Japan's civilization versus the "mature race" of Germany.[35]

Alliances developed with conservatives in Japan as we sought out capitalists and anti-communists. Censorship and control grew more stringent, proceedings less transparent and accountable, and our own leadership dominated by white, military men. In Japan, war crimes trials followed with 920 executed—but the emperor stayed. Dower saw a "suppression of memory" that remains to this day in corrupt ties to conservatives, a failure to make a clean break from the past, and re-vanchist militarism.[36]

Whatever the shortcomings, most agree that true friendships resulted between America and Japan and Germany. Seventy years later, they are among our most steadfast allies, buttressed by irreversible reforms and the early support of the United States. These U.S.-led interventions provide valuable lessons, salutary and cautionary.

4.

Other successes are South Korea and Colombia.

With the surprise invasion by North Korea on June 24, 1950, South Korea, America's ally, suffered a string of defeats and defections. Three days later, President Truman ordered U.S. military forces to assist the South. Within two months, the Congress appropriated $8 billion for the effort. A U.N. force, anchored by an unprepared, though determined, United States, pursued a seesaw conflict for the next three years. Of 1.2 million full-battle deaths, more than 33,000 were Americans.

Initially cornered, the South Koreans displayed profound local commitment. "Success or failure, life or death, for the southern regime, led after August 1948 by President Syngman Rhee, hinged ultimately on the loyalty, strength, and fighting capability of its army, which in turn, relied on its American advisors and trainers."[37] Over a five-year period, the South Korean military built its resilience backed by 2,000 U.S. advisors. It underwent a "strategic revolution" and displayed a "will to fight" that was decisive.[38]

While most commentators agree that U.S. economic assistance in the 1950s helped sustain slow growth, some believe that America's pro-agriculture focus delayed the eventual industrialization of South Korea—which fueled the "Asian model" of development from the 1960s to today.[39] Land reform mattered and the United States played a key role in those changes. Of less value was our support for a corrupt regime and "dependent capitalists."

The commitment and confidence that the United States showed in the alliance, combined with the direct security and economic benefits of a long-term military presence and the huge demand for Asian production during the Vietnam War, contributed to this historic turnaround. Yet to be resolved is the continuing presence of the U.S. military.[40]

Another U.S. success was Colombia, where a 50-year internal conflict cost 220,000 lives, 45,000 disappeared, and seven million displaced from their homes.[41] By 1999, Colombia was in a "state of emergency." After a series of failed efforts, Colombians had reached a collective conclusion that, if the deteriorating conditions remained unchecked, the viability of the nation was in question.[42] The government was incapable and sympathy for the largest rebel group, the FARC, collapsed as they pursued assassinations, kidnappings, and drug dealing.

Colombians were ready for a change and recognized that their ownership of the challenge was essential. Massive, social media–generated street demonstrations called for peace, a restoration of public safety, and freedom of movement. The U.S. role was focused and complementary.

Plan Colombia, wherein the United States provided $8 billion from FY 2000 to FY 2012, helped. Directed mostly to the professionalization of Colombia's military and police, the U.S. assistance leveraged domestic commitments. Both forces grew in size and competence and improved intelligence and commando strikes had a damaging effect on the rebels, increasing defections.[43] Economic growth returned to robust levels, safe travel around Colombia became possible, and the justice system began to deal with militias and other elements of the war.

Successive Colombian presidencies offered solid partnerships. Colombia's native prosperity targeted the common challenge and insider/elite enabling of the war declined. Still, progress on a full and formal peace would determine future economic growth. With the tacit support of the United States, four years of peace talks in Cuba produced a "state of the art" agreement between the government and the FARC in 2016.

Despite rejection in an October 2, 2016, popular plebiscite, the national legislature accepted the 300-page peace agreement with the FARC later that year. Of note were innovative sections on transitional justice, which sought to deal with the "crime of rebellion" with "calibrated conditionality."[44] These included multilevels of punishment, some "restrictions of liberty," and a large set-aside fund for victims of the violence. The U.S. aid in the justice area and beyond mattered.[45] With Colombia a stable and prosperous country, many elements of the turnaround are now models for Central America.

5.

In all of these U.S. engagement successes, certain things were in place: a driving purpose, deep public support and involvement, and pent-up demand for change in the countries we sought to help.

None of these experiences argues for isolationism or constant meddling. Rather, they argue for something more subtle: enlightened self-interest and an informed opportunism, complemented by a strong sense of responsibility—America as a constructive player that is not just prone to act.

At home, public opinion has shifted away from support for foreign interventions. A December 2013 Pew Research Center survey showed that 52 percent of Americans say the United States "should mind its own business internationally and let other countries get along the best they can on their own." Just 38 percent disagree with that statement— the most lopsided outcome in nearly 50 years of measurement—while 51 percent say the United States does too much in helping solve world problems.[46] Of course, when a crisis arises, public opinion shifts, as it did right after the Paris attacks.

Consider, however, that these polls take place after a decade of war that produced what we might describe as mixed results. Few hold up the extraordinary, military-dominated efforts in Iraq and Afghanistan as a model for how we should approach conflict or our engagement with the world. Vast intelligence operations have focused on terrorism to the exclusion of critical local knowledge. Fortress-like embassies and armored caravans deny diplomats rich, country experiences. And the development community focuses on needs such as health and food on which it can make measurable impact, sometimes regardless of those programs' connection to broader, more political priorities.[47]

Today there is a broad consensus that we need to intervene more wisely, with greater coherence and effectiveness. The agreement is greatest on the hazards we face and on the need to know more about the places where we engage. In contrast, there are serious differences of opinion on when we should take action, whether the United States is best suited to play an active role, what we might do when we get there, and who should take the lead within the government.

6.

What guidelines should America follow in making a decision to act?

If the world produces a crisis every two-and-a-half weeks,[48] then we must build a better way to deal with this dynamic mess. The United States must not enter into conflicts without rigorous preparation and understand how to improve the results. A practical guide, something that policymakers and citizens alike can revisit to confirm our decision making, will help. It starts with: Why should we get involved in a conflict outside of our borders? When is the right time? What role might the U.S. play?

Many American leaders have created their own formulations and there are striking similarities.[49] The Powell Doctrine[50] for military engagement is among the best known and it offers eight questions.

1. Is a vital national security interest threatened?
2. Do we have a clear attainable objective?
3. Have the risks and costs been fully and frankly analyzed?
4. Have all other nonviolent policy means been fully exhausted?

5. Is there a plausible exit strategy to avoid endless entanglement?
6. Have the consequences of our action been fully considered?
7. Is the action supported by the American people?
8. Do we have genuine, broad, international support?

Derived from a 1984 version by then secretary of defense Caspar Weinberger, it "reflected a dominant strain in the U.S. military culture, a wariness about incompetent civilian leaders too carelessly employing America's sword for dubious causes in protracted or ambiguous contingencies."[51] Though oft-criticized for simplicity and rigidity, the various guidelines force policymakers to review their premises in a pragmatic and thoughtful fashion.

Looking back at America's military engagement in Afghanistan and Iraq, it is difficult to answer more than half of the questions in the affirmative for each case. In both cases, questions 3, 5, and 6 are troublesome. A "might makes right" mindset may have overridden common sense.

"The fundamental nature of war precludes precision," but decision makers should minimize catastrophic miscalculations. If we are left with the predictable vagaries of wars, so much the better. Winston Churchill told us to expect "Antiquated War Offices, weak, incompetent or arrogant Commanders, untrustworthy allies, hostile neutrals, malignant Fortune, ugly surprises, awful miscalculations—all take their seats at the Council Board on the morrow of a declaration of war."[52]

Careless adventurism, both military and civilian, marks too much of American history. Disaster tourism is objectionable on multiple levels— and it should not take the loss of young lives to confirm. Striking the balance between the desirable and the achievable is our pragmatic goal.

My preference is a commonsense *ladder of progression* that forces us to answer four sequential questions:

First, does this truly matter to the United States? How much do we care? Does it fit into our priorities? Are we primarily responsible? Do we feel connected to it? Suffering in another part of the world moves us, but at what level? This is a particularly agonizing process for Americans.

A favorite narrative is that the United States is an indispensable nation[53] with unmatched levels of empathy and generosity. While our political debate may veer between full engagement and isolationism, the difficulty lies in the broad space between these polar descriptors. What should we do in most of the cases we face versus those clearly defining moments where there is a direct attack or the barbarity of the situation awakens all of the world?

There are priorities and we must acknowledge them. When an explosion of physical assaults and homicidal violence in north Central America led to an overwhelming flow of unaccompanied children into Texas in 2014, the stabilization programs of CSO in Honduras took on greater importance. At the same time, when we reviewed the chaos in the Central African Republic we assumed that the French or the United Nations would take the external lead.

A tougher call was the Syrian civil war. "In August 2011, President Barack Obama issued Presidential Study Directive 10 (PSD-10), which declared the prevention of mass atrocities and genocide to be a 'core national security interest and core moral responsibility' of the United States."[54] Syria was the first serious test of the new Atrocities Prevention Board (APB). Massive human suffering, regional instability, and the resulting flow of refugees into the front yards of vital U.S. allies challenged the idea.

President Obama cared about the amassing of human deaths, but also faced broad public opposition, the possible shutdown of the U.S. government, an economy that was slowly coming back, and a health care plan that was off to a rocky start. I felt that greater U.S. involvement was inevitable, but that the president was not ready to make Syria a top priority. The APB would take a pass on Syria though we would raise the principles in planning meetings with the Pentagon and others.

Often, the first decisions are the most important. We have proven ourselves capable of restraint, skilled on occasion, and deeply flawed in a wide range of interventions, so our discussions about how much we care need to be fulsome.

If we decide to do *something*, then the following questions matter. A positive answer to each triggers the sequence.

Second, is there an opening or opportunity to pursue? The second decision we must make is to answer the question of timing. Is it an opportune moment? Is there a promising opening? Has the conflict produced a ripeness?

Once again, this is a highly subjective discussion. Still, we must be willing to be cold-blooded in our assessment. Lives are at risk. If we take action, we know that America's body politic will inevitably be distracted.

What is changing, either more worrisome or more positive, that suggests an opportunity to make a difference? Is one party seemingly more vulnerable or agreeable to a change? Are we well-informed?

In the mid-1990s, President Clinton's delayed entry into the Bosnian War was criticized by his leading Republican opponent, Bob Dole. Still, the right moment for a broader U.S. action did not appear. Finally, Clinton acted when Serb forces compromised French and British peacekeepers, there as part of the United Nations. This was his personal interpretation of "ripeness." Thousands of U.S. troops would deploy without a loss of life.

A hardheaded assessment of whether this is the right time is required before moving ahead.

Third, is there a unique role that we can play? If we are still hopeful, then the United States must address whether it can make a difference. What is the greatest need? What will the level of effort we are likely to exert and the attention span we will devote/produce? Is there a unique role for the United States? What are others capable of doing? Will any outsider's help be welcomed in the midst of the struggle? Who is best positioned to be in the lead?

Too often America starts with the threat or the challenge by asking, "What can we do?" That beginning reflects our empathetic concern and problem-solving nature but overstates our self-importance and sense of centrality. The first steps must be more calculating and dispassionate, a cool measurement of the situation. There is always something we can do—but how much and for how long should reflect our level of caring.

America's wealth and liquidity is a great advantage. So is our nearly universal diplomatic presence, military might and modernity, humanitarian breadth, and institutional history. Our values matter. Which combination of these is most appropriate for the given situation?

Once again, this is no time for sentimentality. However wonderful, America is not the answer to everyone's problems. And remember, if we were so good at this, why wouldn't we have solved some of our own society's violent behaviors? Will it be any easier to do this work in Kosovo or Kenya than it is in Kansas City?

As the homicide rate soared in Honduras, the United States sought out ways to improve local investigations and prosecutions. We found that the introduction of a few talented individuals from police departments in Dallas, prosecutors from Seattle and Philadelphia, and governance experts from Costa Rica, Mexico, Colombia, and the region could provide Hondurans with needed coaching. America was in the right place at the right time with the right people to help.

Whether it will be with a "light or heavy footprint," this soul searching puts us at the precipice of moving into someone else's country or backyard.

Fourth, are there local partners? We want to make things better but our role should be limited and always in support of the initiative of others. For success, the people of a place must care more than we do. Believing in their native potential is the vital gift of an outsider. Evidence of our trust is a transferable asset. When we deliver our assistance in a confidence-building way, America helps those at war embrace their ultimate responsibility for rebuilding lives and communities.

In Honduras, our enlightened U.S. ambassador Lisa Kubiske led to an alliance of local civil society groups organized by the rector of the National Autonomous University, Julieta Castellanos. Motivated by the highest murder rates in the world and the slaying of Dr. Castellanos's son and a friend by eight police officers, the *Alianza Paz y Justicia* was credible and dedicated. Their focus on police and judicial reform and fighting official corruption and drug cartels resonated. The United States helped the Hondurans develop a political agenda that included mass communications and legislative lobbying so that the number one concern of average Hondurans, the lack of personal safety, dominated the presidential campaign.

Identifying potential partners, even if they are broader categories of people, is an essential early step. Among the most promising are women, youth, and others who are seldom in charge. Combined, they always represent demographic majorities—and often have significant pent-up energy.

This step also helps with the challenge of a graceful exit. Inherent in the search for partners is this inevitable conversation: "You have a viable future. Thank you for letting us help. We are your steadfast friends and will do our best to help you succeed in the challenges of the next few years." Overstaying our welcome need not be America's default position in conflict cases.

7. LESSONS APPLIED

Three key lessons to take from this chapter follow.

I. Force Answers to the Most Fundamental Questions about Care, Commitment, and Timing.

What we must avoid is rash responsiveness—the United States taking action without having debated the most basic questions.

A thoughtful process need not be slow and inconclusive. War is humanity at its rawest and most complex moment. I do not believe that people begin to kill their neighbors without multiple motivations, so I prefer to analyze each situation through as many prisms as possible. It is not enough to say that the conflict is economic, religious, political, territorial, ethnic, or about powerlessness. In my experience, it is an unholy mix. Measure these elements and then be ready to answer the four key questions in the ladder of progression.

II. Make the Ambition Fit the Context.

Each conflict offers a special promise. Few countries are at the same point in their social, political, or economic advancement, so customize.

America must avoid trying to turn every place where we intervene into "a shining city upon a hill."[55] Yes, the basic freedoms of speech, movement, and assembly should grow. Without those, nothing is sustainable. Most often, basic security and survival are the cornerstones of progress.

Beyond that, the United States should be careful to avoid nation, or even state, building. We should have plenty of good ideas to offer, but we cannot slide into long-term occupations or 21st-century colonialism. It does not work nor does it fit our traditions or culture.

III. Engage the Public.

Greater involvement of the public and the Congress will force every part of our political system to step up and take responsibility.

Seldom does the American public participate or engage in the early stages of the discussion or preparation for a crisis response. Most damaging, America has moved away from direct responsibility. The Congress does not vote on wars. Debt rather than taxes pay for them. Without a draft, our citizens are sheltered from the direct sacrifices of lives lost and damaged. Daily coverage is scant and public debate muted. Often we use civilians in combat roles, "gathering military intelligence, building and guarding infrastructure, transporting fuel and equipment, de-mining and destroying explosives, and training and supporting police. Private security companies now typically guard U.S. diplomats and embassies, including the diplomatic post in Benghazi that militants attacked on September 11, 2012."[56]

Our native ability to question authority and forge consensus from a difficult and challenging dialogue is a great asset. Often, our citizens are "informed" of the choices that have been made and expected to provide support with taxes, their sons and daughters, and great patience. "National security matters" and the need to act quickly prevent public involvement.

Our people's beliefs are the foundations of America's influence and effectiveness. When we are faithful to them we are capable of helping to build a more peaceful world.

II

A New Hope in the 1990s

1.

Optimism flourished around the globe as the Cold War ended in 1989. The long and often dirty struggles of superpowers, with their proxy wars, disinformation, and puppet regimes, appeared to be over. Better days and a move to democracy and free markets awaited.

It was not long before a harsher day emerged. Dormant and repressed tensions resurfaced in the early 1990s and conflicts proliferated. Before long, the scholars and journalists reached for the view that we were entering a new world of disorder.

At any one time, there were 25 ongoing wars, often too small or remote to garner much attention, but with hideous consequences. Civilian deaths outnumbered soldiers' by nine to one in these conflicts, which were mostly internal and not state to state.[1] Humanitarian disasters morphed from 90 percent nature driven to 90 percent man-made, "complex emergencies." Refugee and internally displaced populations soared into the tens of millions and xenophobia flared in the heart of Europe.

Facing three crises (Kurds fleeing to Iran, Ethiopians repatriating and Somalis to Ethiopia, and Albanians to Italy) in her fourth week as the new U.N. High Commissioner for Refugees in 1991, Sadako Ogata spoke of "enormous geopolitical changes without effective and up-to-date means to counteract them."[2] She bemoaned the absence of "effective formulas to deal with uprisings dominated by nationalism and localism."[3] One change she offered to the traditional orthodoxy was her oft-quoted statement, "There are no humanitarian solutions to humanitarian problems." Contained in that statement was a full-bodied recognition that every refugee situation was the result of political problems—and that the solutions must also be political. Ogata called the response to the conflict in Bosnia a "humanitarian fig leaf," meaning that emergency aid and medical supplies were not what the crisis truly needed. Instead, she sought ways to address the underlying issues, what she called "the gap between humanitarian relief and development."[4]

2.

Despite America's military success in the first Gulf War, we would remain chary.

In the most prominent case, Somalia, America swerved between military-backed nation building and negotiation. On October 3, 1993, an aggressive humanitarian response to starvation turned into disaster. In a hellacious gunfight in downtown Mogadishu, 18 elite U.S. soldiers died and 74 more were wounded while as many as 1,000 Somalis also perished. Through CNN, Americans watched Black Hawk helicopters shot down and American bodies dragged through the streets.[5] The scars of that experience still color our debates about foreign intervention. Remindful of Vietnam, Somalia produced a further caution in the United States and a syndrome, labeled "Vietmalia" by Richard Holbrooke.[6]

The Cold War view that we should be willing to "pay any price, bear any burden" for liberty was now tinged with reluctance.

In her memoir, Madeleine Albright wrote, "With the possible exception of ancient Rome, no society has ever auditioned for the role of world policeman. Certainly the United States—at least through the end of the twentieth century—never desired that part."[7]

That would capture U.S. reluctance to act in the former Yugoslavia, a war that involved our closest allies, and Rwanda, a conflict where we would avert our eyes. Even Haiti, in our immediate neighborhood, generated substantial doubt about a U.S. role.

As Ogata pointed out, the United States needed new ways to approach these emerging challenges. Change was a necessary but controversial concept. USAID's traditional development experts focused on economic and social programs that might take decades to show results. On average, an idea would take more than two years to reach on-the-ground implementation, with turgid "assessment missions" and ever-more-complicated contracting mechanisms. That would not work in places where a bad night at a saloon could produce a change in government.

State Department diplomats were more transactional, motivated by immediate political concerns. Their preference was to deal with their governmental counterparts, negotiate, and draft understandings. In culture and practice, they offered analysis and discussion, not action.

Humanitarians were effective at providing immediate relief in crisis. Political neutrality was the lubricant for their work, offered in exchange for access to all victims.

The U.S. military had the labor to do nearly any job, but its youthful soldiers had no training for political or development work. Furthermore, making places safe was already a huge undertaking. The Pentagon's size, deep pockets, and positions all over the world eventually led it to take on traditional aid and reconstruction tasks, with mixed results.

Nongovernmental groups (NGOs) remained wary of the military, and the optics of uniformed Americans in civilian roles made them uncomfortable. Constant financial pressures constrained NGOs as they expanded their reach in conflict settings.

That configuration left a gap. We needed tools to meet new conflicts, such as those around elections, government transitions, and post-conflict reconstruction. We needed an organization that operated on political insight, long-term strategy, and immediate impact in global hot spots.

Brian Atwood, President Bill Clinton's nominee to head USAID, pointed out this gap at his Senate confirmation hearing in 1993. Atwood said that he would make the agency more relevant to the dramatic changes that were arising everywhere.[8] He presented an affirmative argument for political development and the promotion of democracy with the creation of two new offices dedicated to those purposes and features. When I arrived in Washington in March 1994 to start one, the Office of Transition Initiatives (OTI), there was considerable debate within USAID about what we should do and whether a tiny office could be valuable.

Even in my initial job interviews, I heard the doubts. Brian's initial description was of "a $30-million office with ten people." When I spoke to his deputy a few minutes later, the Georgetown academic Carol Lancaster, she asked me, "So, why are you the right person to run a $20-million office with four people?"

My response helped me to get the job, if not resolve the difference. "I don't know much about Washington, but I just walked 40 feet from Brian's office to yours and I lost $10 million and six people. Maybe I'm not the right guy."

Carol's response was "Did he say that????" as she picked up the phone with verve to remind Brian of the latest numbers. Others only saw the limitations. One seasoned USAID executive told me, "If the Administrator really wants this to succeed he should have given it $500 million." I remained intrigued by the chance to start something new in the midst of a large, established organization and felt that imaginative approaches and early money could make a difference.

At USAID, Brian and his idea builder, Larry Garber, hosted regular talks, weekly roundtables, and shared writings. The discussions made major contributions to our work. Mary Anderson, an expert in "complex emergencies" (the name given by humanitarians to conflict disasters) said, "Evidence is that aid more often worsens conflict (even when it is effective in humanitarian and/or development terms) rather than helps mitigate it" and cautioned that we should "do no harm."[9] Economist Amartya Sen explained the virtues of public participation and openness so that individual citizens could make wise choices in the toughest of circumstances. Ben Barber, author of a best-selling 1995 book *Jihad vs. McWorld*, argued, "Democracy grows from the bottom up and cannot be imposed from the top down. Civil society has to be built from the inside out."[10]

All influenced our thinking as we jumped into the major conflagrations of the 1990s.

3.

The 1990s mismatch between the vast number of conflicts and slim global resources to address them led to great creativity and innovation. Those who practiced in this period had opportunities to work in a wide range of war settings—experimenting, building pilots, and testing ideas.

There was a restlessness among practitioners, fueled by dissatisfaction. Some humanitarians grew frustrated by the traditional approaches of saving lives versus addressing wars' stalemates and nationalist leadership. One of the most notable was Fred Cuny, described by a biographer as driven by "an almost obsessive desire to bring order out of chaos, the dream of forging a unique strategy in tackling the messy problems of the world."[11] Cuny believed that the end of the Cold War would produce a fresh round of complex emergencies and he pushed the military, governments, and humanitarians to adapt.[12] To do that, he would take on the vaunted traditions of "neutrality" and "sovereignty" and the "advocates of caution."[13] He was a "bomb thrower" and even had a spat with Mother Teresa.[14]

His Sarajevo water project was most famous. With the city's water supply controlled by the sadistic Bosnian Serb leader Radovan Karadzic and snipers killing hundreds of Bosnians seeking water at wells, Cuny sought to build a new pipeline.

Cutting deals, flying in supplies, skirting the front lines, using mountain tunnels, overcoming bureaucratic resistance, and getting it done in warlike conditions, Cuny made inroads. He generated hope. In the worst of circumstances, Cuny could produce progress. Inventing new ways of doing business in complex global politics was not without cost, however. Cuny disappeared in Chechnya in 1995, trying to negotiate a ceasefire.

We took courage from him and from others, like Julia Taft, who championed massive daily airdrops of food over strife-torn Sudan. The media and communications work of George Soros and his Open Society teams also showed how well-targeted assistance could generate popular energy. With their support for free and fair elections, groups like the National Democratic Institute (NDI) and the International Republican Institute (IRI) opened doors that we all followed. Major reviews, such as the Carnegie Corporation of New York's Commission on Preventing Deadly Violence, lifted up the issues and practices.

We also learned from honest reporting about failure and the importance of transparency. One example was a devastating U.N. report in October 1995, *The Fall of Srebrenica*. A systematic and unyielding account of one of "the darkest pages of human history," this review described how a U.N. mandate to protect safe areas collapsed and Serb forces systematically exterminated up to 20,000 mostly Bosniac civilians within one protected zone. The report gives no quarter in its riveting 100 pages describing every form of brutality, cowardice, prevarication, delay, and avoidance of responsibility that nations, organizations, officials, and individuals exhibited leading up to the "mass slaughter of unarmed victims" in mid-July 1995.

From these experiences and others, my co-founders Steve Morrison and Johanna Mendelson Forman and our leaders Doug Stafford, Mike Mahdesian, Len Rogers, and Lois Richards built OTI as an agile instrument of the U.S. government, ready to move into a conflict or crisis situation within six weeks. With a bit of liquidity and a special Congressional exemption to waive certain rules in an emergency ("notwithstanding authority"),[15] OTI leveraged modest resources in several initial hot spots: Bosnia, Rwanda, Haiti, and Angola. We instructed OTI teams to propose ideas as if our entire budget was available, thus expanding our creativity and influence. I had seen real estate developers use similar tactics in Maine. Where other offices could not find a spare person or transfer funds from other accounts, OTI recognized the immediate needs of conflict situations.

It would take a while to refine the essence of "political development" but the availability of an office that could customize solutions and pay to get them started overcame many bureaucratic obstacles. Pilots and experiments flourished in an action-oriented culture. In the early days, our boss Doug Stafford would refer to OTI as "the Peace Corps on steroids" and "a job shop for emergencies." Visitors to our State Department offices would speak of the energy in our overcrowded suite as we developed new talent, tools, and instruments to attack opportunities in a range of places.

Whereas almost every other U.S. government office had to pursue a geographic (only working in Africa, South America, etc.) or subject-matter mandate (e.g., health, energy, housing), OTI started with the premise of "what is most important and most needed?" Many times OTI would be the only party in a room in Washington with that flexibility. Alliances with other parts of USAID, State, DOD, and the National Security Council developed and Congressional support grew. Partnerships with other like-minded countries began and the foundations for a new way to deal with "the new world disorder" started.

3

BOSNIA

First Lessons

I.

The breakup of Yugoslavia had been a long time coming. At the end of World War I, the country was born from six republics and two autonomous Serb provinces, then occupied by Axis powers in World War II.[1] A charismatic World War II hero, Josip Broz, known as Marshall Tito, then held the country together for more than 35 years.[2] He pulled off a balancing act among the various republics, keeping the most populous group, the Serbs, from dominating the others.[3]

By the time Tito died at 88 in 1980, Yugoslavia, as so often happens after a strong leader, was ready to implode. Some of the political class exploited the country's divisions, and economic stagnation provided a spark. The fall of communism in Eastern Europe helped tear Yugoslavia asunder. Pent-up resentments in every part of the country became independence movements battling a violent, nationalist Serb government. The conflict would start in the spring of 1992, kill 140,000, displace 2.2 million, and send hundreds of thousands of refugees into a traumatized Europe. Many would never return home.

Slovenia left without a fight, but by 1994, Serbia and Croatia were in a violent stalemate and a savage war with ethnic cleansing centered in Bosnia. All sides committed war crimes, with the preponderance by

Serbs. Western Europe fiddled while Sarajevo burned, hoping that the parties would come to their senses.

In the United States, President Clinton had promised during the 1992 campaign to stop the violence, but delayed once in office. America mostly stood by, a witness to barbarity near the heart of its premier alliance, Europe. Humanitarian assistance and a collection of often-weak U.N. responses substituted for any direct U.S. intervention in the slaughter.

A tenuous ceasefire arrived in the spring of 1994, after two years of fighting. For the first time, NATO bombed the Serbs who had been shelling the Bosnian capital, Sarajevo, from the surrounding hills. NATO shot down four Serb fighter planes for violating a U.N. no-fly zone. This fragile moment presented an opportunity to encourage peace.

The USAID administrator, Brian Atwood, asked my new office if some form of political development assistance might help Bosnia to move beyond war.

2.

Our arrival was without incident.

We drove through side streets and checkpoints, avoiding the broader boulevards where sharpshooters could set up in deserted high rises. Near downtown, we came out on "Sniper Alley," the main thorough-fare, where the only operating hotel left in the city sat. An ugly mustard pillbox, the Holiday Inn was unwelcoming—almost one-third of the façade shot up by gunfire. The rooms facing Grbavica, now the Serb part of the city, were unsafe.

A dank and expensive refuge, it accepted only deutschmarks and offered a tiny selection of tired food to diplomats, journalists, and aid workers. At night, I pulled the rug-like curtain as tight as possible to minimize the likelihood of a bullet straying into a lit window. To escape, I would turn on the TV and through the static watch a World Cup soccer game from the United States. Gunshots and an occasional blast would ring out. There was not much relief.

This was Sarajevo in June 1994.

As the head of USAID's new Office of Transition Initiatives (OTI), I was in Bosnia, a first testing ground. NATO had created a tenuous break that needed encouragement. I was part of a three-person U.S. "delegation," though we were hardly that, arriving with the prospect of assistance beyond humanitarian goods.

There is no substitute for seeing these conflicts firsthand: the bleakness of destroyed homes and apartment houses; graveyards full of new markers, the emptiness of the Olympic stadium; the shrapnel-pock-marked sidewalks; the plastic sheeting in place of windows, and the burnt-out twin towers of an iconic modern office complex right next to the Holiday Inn. The hollowed-out city had lost large chunks of its sophisticated residents and replaced them with people fleeing from the countryside. Those who remained had a shell-shocked quality, like prisoners with no release dates.

As we walked the streets, we used the dumpsters as protection from any schnapps-drinking sniper and scurried across intersections with sight lines into the hills. Intermittent trolleys, with their windows shot out, were not an attractive alternative.

On our first morning, several Bosnian leaders invited us to an official meeting. They wanted their constituents to know that American assistance was coming—and had the government TV channel tape our ceremonial arrival for that evening's newscast with an inflated message: see, things are getting better.

By that afternoon, we found ourselves in the office of the mayor of Sarajevo. He was a dynamic force, the kind of practical politician you expect when there are many daily problems. Sarajevo, under Serb siege for months, was suffering in most every way: no water supply, fleeing residents, no funds to pay anyone, to name the most pressing.

When I asked the mayor if he could recommend someone to serve as a guide and translator, he suggested the young Muslim woman sitting just down the table. Earnest, direct, and somehow unsophisticated about the extremes of the war, Munerva[4] turned out to be key to the rest of the visit. Her sincere desire to help me understand the situation made all the difference.

If I said, "Who are those Muslim women wearing head scarves?"

She would say, "We will go tomorrow and meet with the Muslim women's association."

Likewise, "What are the children doing?"

Her response, "We will visit the rhythmic gymnasts and a schoolroom."

"What is it like on the front lines?" Within a day or two, it was coffee with fighters, in the back room of a makeshift garrison, only yards from their adversaries—and former neighbors.

During the gloom, there were also moments that suggested possibilities.

One day I asked, "Why would anyone want to have a family in the middle of this living tragedy?"

I should have anticipated Munerva's literal answer: "I will take you to the maternity ward of our new hospital."

On a sunny morning, we drove to the Kosovo Hospital and met a senior doctor. In the older part of the facility, he showed us war wounded, emergency procedures, blood supplies, and prosthetics. At the maternity ward, the doctor started looking for an expectant mother for me to interview. He opened a door and there on the bed, with her legs high in the air, was a woman in full labor. This was the closest I had been to a birthing situation since our daughter's delivery five years earlier.

Despite my recent arrival in the peacebuilding profession, I felt I was nearing a career moment. "This seems inappropriate," I demurred. The doctor insisted, "No, this will not be a problem."

With the moans and groans only a few steps away, I politely thanked him and asked, "Is there another future mother who is not currently giving birth?"

It turned out there was a roomful of five or so expectant mothers just a few doors away. As they lay on beds waiting for the contractions to intensify, their husbands paced in the courtyard outside their windows, smoking. I spent the next two hours talking with the mothers-to-be. While there was a certain absurdity to the scene, the women welcomed the distraction.

Why were they building a family in a time of war? Mostly, because they wanted it and had no idea when the fighting would stop. "Might as well do it now," seemed to be the dominant idea. Somehow, the rhythm of the place kept on.

As we prepared to leave the hospital, the ebullient chief of staff, a Bosniac doctor, enveloped us in a warm greeting. A bear of a man, he took great pride in his modern facility, one of the few institutions still working in shell-shocked Sarajevo, despite the many doctors who had fled to new lives in Germany. He told us the survival of the hospital was due to the steadfast service of the nurses, who had not been able to escape Sarajevo. They survived without pay for months.

"What level of pay would it take to reward them and stabilize your work force?" I asked.

"About $100 per month," he said.

Often, I have found that if I am not in a rush to solve a problem and keep listening, a collective wisdom begins to show up. Sometimes it feels as if a light bulb goes on. Related conversations began to converge. A former law school professor was disdainful of the "opportunists" who were filling the jobs of departed colleagues. "They never would have made the faculty in the old days," he said.

Mass departures were hollowing out the professional class that was necessary to sustain the city and even more vital to rebuild. How could we stop that trend?

In Sarajevo, a notion began to develop: if the city was going to have a future, it must stabilize the remaining middle class. The largest representatives of that group—perhaps even a critical mass—were the nurses and teachers, mostly women. What if the United States and the international community focused on these people, paid their salaries, and called upon them to reach out to the city's youth? These links might create a powerful new political force—just what Bosnia would need to renew.

Energized by this prospect, but still unsure that it could work, I spent the final few days in Sarajevo sizing it up. I sought to bring together an informal "board of directors," made up of the most capable people we had seen in our two-week visit. It was an unusual mix. The wily head of the Jewish center, who managed to evacuate all of Sarajevo's Jewish children on a chartered Yugoslav military flight just before the fighting started, and who still found a way to bring in German currency to sustain the remaining members of his small community. The middle-aged lawyer who ran the largest Muslim women's organization, an impressive operation that was publishing and distributing tens of thousands of newsletters throughout Bosnia. A young German who was organizing daycare centers in block housing throughout the city, and others. I saw the prospective board as the guiding hand that would keep our initiatives on track.

I started back to Washington energized to sell the idea as OTI's first project.

3.

Immersed in the hopes and dreams of dozens of engaging Bosnians, our overwhelming desire was to make things better. Caught up in the intensity of Sarajevo, I suppressed a larger reality: it was clear that the war was not over.

This only came into focus at my first big meeting back in Washington with USAID administrator Brian Atwood. I reported on what we found and enthusiastically offered my idea. It did not fly. Congress, he said, disliked paying salaries in other countries. As the first offering for a new office, he thought it would not send the right signal.

The decisive factor came when I told him that we would often run the 50 yards from the parking lot into the Holiday Inn. He asked, "What do you think are the chances of the cease-fire holding?"

I answered, "Somewhere around 10 percent. Most people are still talking about the 'aggressors,' their enemies, or using inflammatory descriptions. They expect that there will be at least one more round of major fighting."

Brian offered a comforting response: "I think that OTI should be a post-bullet program." Although I felt pressure to build a successful, first test case for OTI, and worried that our new friends might not survive more fighting, I was flooded with relief. As I would learn, little more than humanitarian assistance is possible during violent conflict.

Whether battle-tested or a conflict rookie like myself, it is hard to get a true measure of the potential of a conflict. I have come to believe that it takes a lucky balance of mind, heart, and gut—intellect, empathy, and instincts. Keeping those in balance is never easy, but it is essential when thinking about what to do in a war-torn place.

Two of my bosses' reactions to the meeting reflected different strains of thought within the U.S. government. One boss, my closest colleague, lauded my honesty. The other, a senior careerist at USAID, called the meeting "disastrous." She believed that you should always do something—even if the evidence argued for delay or inaction. It is hard to do nothing, especially when you have the ability and face heartrending challenges. This pernicious instinct is behind some of our most ill-fated interventions.

Despite my initial worry, I came to believe that activity and expenditures did not comprise progress. I encouraged OTI to take a pass on a country if, once evaluated, the conditions precluded success.

That approach is still an exception to the rule. If we say that America is spending money—or offering "deliverables," in State Department parlance—then the United States must be helping. Often, that is not the case.

At OTI, we would await a better moment and continue to plan and prepare. It would not be long before we went back.

4.

The war grew more brutal and attracted extensive Western media coverage. The British and French proved incapable of producing a peace. America began to take a more forceful role. It started with the Washington Agreement of 1994 that ended the Muslim-Croat war and created the "embryonic political blueprint"[5] of the Bosnian Federation.

As the initial Croat-Bosnian Federation struggled to come together and there were lulls in the fighting, we traveled the countryside. A team of academics and field organizers went throughout Bosnia seeking partners and possibilities.

It was a barren landscape, still dominated by violence. Random thugs stopped one of OTI's teams at a checkpoint, taking its SUV and its contents. Though our team was not hurt, their long trudge back to safer territory was a vivid lesson in the limitations of "diplomatic immunity" in the Balkans. Outraged calls from America's regional diplomats to our newfound allies in the Croat-Bosnian Federation recovered the vehicle a day later—with a fresh coat of camouflage paint applied overnight. The carjacking was not an official action, more an extension of a "spoils of war" and paramilitary culture that dominated the landscape.

As arms began moving from the United States to the Croats and the Bosniacs, the Bosnian rump state of Serbska shrunk and the reversal of fortunes began. With the Serb slaughter of thousands of Muslim men at Srebrenica in July 1995, NATO began a two-week bombing campaign that split the Serbs. Still, the Serbs seized some French peacekeepers, part of a U.N. mission, as human shields against NATO bombings. That required a response. America's reluctance was eroding.

Weakened by a string of failures, Serbian president Slobodan Milosevic embraced U.S.-brokered talks in Dayton, Ohio, in 1995, which quieted the war. The military effort in Bosnia would be significant, but only to provide policing: preventing violence and providing a reassuring presence against marauding warriors. Sixty thousand heavily armed NATO troops, a third of them American, would be dispatched to keep the peace. We would commit to a year in 1996 and stay until 2004. The broader Dayton Peace Agreement and the presence of a robust neutral force would provide much more room to work and the civilian side of the U.S. government ramped up.

5.

As the fighting neared a sporadic halt in 1995, "reconciliation" became the goal of State Department and USAID programming in Bosnia. Many of us believed that our assistance could accelerate the healing process and bring people together. We discussed a range of ideas, though economic development schemes were the norm.

We also hired a team of Americans who had worked in the Balkans for the previous few years. Several had been part of the International Rescue Committee's refugee efforts, worn down by the frustration of keeping people alive to die another day. They were eager to deal with politics and systemic change. Critically, they had existing networks of local people, including spouses and partners. That familiarity and skill was indispensable.

While a regular U.S. embassy began to take shape in Sarajevo, Ambassador John Menzies and his tiny staff were homebound—he even slept in his small office. As the fighting ceased, OTI established field offices in Tuzla, Zenica, and Banja Luka, while running the operation from Sarajevo. These forward-operating camps became vital to understanding developments throughout Bosnia and to building partnerships with the Bosnians, humanitarians, and U.S. military. Like so many who worked in the Balkans, we heard of the historic hatred between groups. What was ironic was how little often lay at their heart. Our field teams noted this in one report: "Where little apparent distinction existed, the difference is often created or resurrected from history. Styles of dress, ways of drinking coffee, spirituality, terms of greeting, architecture, the significance of certain colors, decorum in one's home, etc. have all undergone painstaking *ethnification*, making some acutely aware of whether what one is doing or saying is 'Muslim,' 'Croatian' or 'Serbian.'"[6]

Later, when OTI was able to pursue work in the Bosnian countryside, we held a team-building exercise with our staff in the town of Zenica. In my comments to the staff, I made a comparison to our work in Haiti. A bright and attractive young Bosnian-Serb lawyer from Banja Luka did not like the association. "We are Europeans," she said with disdain and puzzlement. "We used to vacation in Venice." Even in those sniffled words, there was a denial, a superiority to the conflicts of other places, a plea not to be mistaken with the barbarians of Africa or Asia or South America. In her suffering, she still managed to hold onto the conceit that seemed to dominate this conflict: because we are sophisticated people, we can settle a bunch of scores without hurting ourselves.

Every war has its own defining characteristics. Self-indulgence was the dominant feeling in Bosnia. Sure, there were centuries of disagreements and imagined wrongs, and yes, recent economic problems had increased daily pressures, but the act of attacking neighbors, blowing up houses and places of worship, and chasing thousands of people from their homes had the feeling of a lazy, convenient idea.

Most saw short-term opportunities but were clueless of the long-term consequences: "This is my chance to finally settle the score with that neighbor whose cow is always crossing onto my land. I can take care of this nagging piece of business, right that wrong, and not pay the consequences." Many of the political leaders of the time played up the bullying opportunity, but a well-educated and middle-class European community went along. It was painful to witness such societal sloppiness lead to widespread human suffering.

Suddenly, relatives were being killed or maimed and solid homes with red-tile roofs burned in the classic Bosnian way—torched from the inside with a fire-bomb destroying the timber attic underpinnings so that the hollowed concrete square structures were left with blown-out holes instead of windows and doors, looking much like a human skull.

The suffering created a born-again victimization among all groups. "The war wiped out any habit of self-scrutiny that Serbs, Croats, Muslims, Slovenes might once have possessed. Each nation has embraced a separate orthodoxy in which it is uniquely the victim and never the perpetrator."[7] Polling showed that more than 95 percent of each group felt that they were targeted and oppressed.

Immersion produced insights. In most places, people are ready to share their concerns, frustrations, and near-term wishes. Meet enough people and the weight of their testimony or collective "wisdom of the crowds" begins to settle in.[8]

This was, in a nutshell, the approach I have tried ever since: Spend time with the broadest range of people possible, build a deep understanding of a place, determine the true opportunities, and boost promising ideas. It sounds simple—even obvious—but the United States misses it. There is some risk in the fieldwork and it does take time, but there is no excuse for collective ignorance.

We are often tempted to jump to a conclusion or to offer a solution after brief contact or based on experiences, but we must resist, especially in these most complicated of settings. These cases test the extremes of human violence and suffering, so they deserve the most careful consideration. By engaging fully with people's frustrations and aspirations, it is possible to imagine a way to build trust and perhaps find a new, common direction.

6.

As America sought to encourage "reconciliation" in Bosnia, initial experiments proved too ambitious. With excellent contacts and the ability to implement ideas with "quick disbursing," venture capital–like funds, a small OTI team took the lead for the U.S. government.

Four simple criteria framed the initiative: use Croat-Bosnian Federation institutions (to strengthen the initial government experiment); resolve cross-community/divided-community tensions (to expand freedom of movement and foster interdependence); multiethnic participation; and cultivate democracy (to build some processes).[9] We saw these criteria as a way to encourage unity of effort among the various groups and within the international community of governments and private organizations.

Over the next few months, OTI initiated 25 test projects for around $650,000. Our own reviews found that none of the 25 met the criteria (or in most cases even one of the four) and that the warring parties were in no mood to do anything together.

In one case, the reconstruction of a destroyed changing room at a soccer field on a sectarian border between Croats and Bosniacs in the city of Vitez faltered. While all wanted the facility, there were many obstacles. The Croats, for example, refused to sign the letter of agreement because of five "Bosniac" words they circled. Neither side made good on its commitment to provide labor and materials, an ownership requirement of OTI. It took months to do the work, though sharing of the facility was the next challenge.

Before we tried any larger efforts, we needed a better understanding of why our test projects were not taking hold. Significant U.S. funds awaited "reconciliation" opportunities and OTI's experiments provided the best insights available. For an independent review, we brought in Bob and Cindy Gersony, noted investigators who had done breakthrough reports on Mozambique, Liberia, and Nicaragua.[10] Bob and Cindy would spend months meeting with people at every level of a society, identifying what was taking place, and suggesting a few straightforward ambitions that fit the context. More like anthropologists than political analysts, they would work with Bosnian, Croat, and Serb translators at the same time and stay in out-of-the-way hotels and guesthouses.

Their report back to Washington was telling: "I have never seen such honest reporting within the US Government, but, nothing is working."[11] The Gersonys praised our truth telling and concluded that the failure of the 25 projects meant that "reconciliation" was premature. The findings frustrated many at the State Department and USAID and disrupted the normal processes. Since regular programming would take months to design, contract, and implement, the Gersony report meant that all preparations for a bright, shining moment at war's end would need rethinking.

The Gersonys did find one small exception: an OTI initiative that was restoring a few rooms in homes in a Croat-Bosniac buffer zone. Neighbors helped each other; the municipalities cooperated and selected skilled contractors in a balanced way. There was a common interest in getting on with their lives. That $200,000 experiment with 17 homes in Bilalovac Kisaljak became a highly successful $25 million U.S. emergency shelter program that allowed residents all over Bosnia to return to their partially restored houses. People wanted to be home, though profound distrust prevented reconciliation.

Stymied by the relentless Bosnian war, we learned that our policy was premature—and yet, from a small restoration project emerged an ambitious plan to rehabilitate destroyed homes on all sides of the conflict. It was a step the United States could take beyond basic humanitarian survival aid without being naïve that we could solve the conflict. Progress was possible, just not reconciliation.

Here was a case of "learning by doing." Tests, pilot projects, and experiments should be essential building blocks. Too often in the government, there is a fear of "precedents" to justify inaction or continue with unexamined approaches. I err on the side of sins of commission versus omission: if it works, it is a precedent; if it fails, it was an experiment.

Sir Alastair Pilkington, the inventor of the process to make plate glass, once told me the key to his success: "For four years I went into the laboratory and broke glass. I set a world record for broken glass. Only then did I discover the float method which is now used around the world."[12] Wanton experimentation is a necessary learning device in conflict settings as well.

Additional benefits redound. When people in the field begin to realize that their insights are influencing events and decisions in Washington (New York or Geneva), they too become more responsible.

7.

Our second area of emphasis was mass communications. The political class perverted information and too many accepted it. How could we circumvent that system and begin to reverse the destructive trend that fomented the war?

The first thing we noticed was that in a war zone, people are desperate for the latest information. Whenever we went into a home, the televisions were on. Few now trusted the state-dominated outlets, but most could find other stations because of satellite dishes. Radio provided local information thanks to a George Soros–supported initiative that kept many stations from collapsing. All the local outlets faced partisan intimidation, but their greatest problem seemed to be economic survival. A visit to the vaunted state-controlled television station in Sarajevo made clear that the staff was going unpaid. All of these elements presented an opportunity.

On a rainy late afternoon in Sarajevo, I visited a TV station that other internationals described as a "Muslim fundamentalist" outlet. The station was in the old part of the city, across the little Miljacka River that runs through Sarajevo, in the rear, ground-floor apartment of a poorly marked building. Without a taxi, I would never have found it. Only the station manager and his assistant were still there. He told me that we only had a few minutes because he was on his way to a paying job.

As we sat in his office, the television showed a German soccer match. This pirated programming highlighted another problem: the need for material to put on the air. I asked him why his station was "fundamentalist." "Achh! That Jackie Shymanski of CNN, she spreads these lies." He called to his assistant, a modern, urban woman, dressed for an office job, and said, "Would I have a woman dressed like this working for me if that was true? No, they just say these things because we have a mullah offering prayers in the evening hours at the same time that the internationals are all turning on their TVs at the Holiday Inn." Struck that the prayer hour could be paid programming or local material, I asked him if he would consider selling commercial time.

It took about three seconds for the station manager to reach into his drawer and bring out a price sheet. "Of course, we would be honored to sell advertising on our station." The sheet was an advertiser's dream: one hundred TV spots for around $900. With no other advertising sales, the manager did not care if the spots were 30 or 60 seconds in length. Nor did he care much about their content.

From that initial visit, an idea blossomed. A young Bosnian staffer in our Tuzla office traveled across war lines and through ethnic divides to collect rate sheets from every TV and radio outlet in Bosnia. There were no one-stop ad agencies. Without exception, they were open to selling time and carrying a message of peace.

The next challenge was to find a local production company. One day we stopped at a highly regarded video documentary group in Sarajevo to admire the beautifully shot and produced pieces they made for the BBC and other international networks. Because of these global customers, the prices were high and their availability limited. Stuck, we came up with an alternative: bring in a U.S. political campaign consultant, Peter Fenn, for a week. Have him and a colleague, Sally Patterson, co-produce a series of commercials with a Tuzla station.

Peter's first-generation contribution was invaluable. Working with our local staff of a half-dozen Bosnians, he managed to develop a cohesive theme: "Make Peace Your Future." Each word mattered: it was going to take hard work (Make); there was only one choice for moving on (Peace); the responsibility was in the hands of each and every Bosnian, not NATO or Tito (Your); and if you wanted a life like other Europeans, now was the time to think ahead (Future). Within a week, they produced a handful of unartful but clear commercials, teaching the locals some tricks of the ad business in the process.

In days, the spots were running incessantly throughout Bosnia, with a USAID logo making clear our support. They had a "Please don't squeeze the Charmin" annoyance about them and after hundreds of viewings we began to hear from Bosnians all over the country: "Please stop!" It was a measure of success! With an entire population sequestered in their homes and nothing else on TV, almost everyone heard the message everywhere, all the time. The campaign, alongside shock at the war's horrors and disenchantment with its leaders, was a useful catalyst. It was a tiny foundation for peace.

8.

Even in the darkest days, the Balkans maintained a gallows humor—dry, sarcastic, and biting—that provided welcome relief. In Zenica, an industrial city with a giant, hollowed-out steel complex at its center, we found a comedy troupe that was capturing the temper of the times.

With our support, they made a series of TV commercials that ridiculed the debates among the political class about ways to establish the ethnic identity of each sliver of Bosnia. Amid the violence, officialdom fought over passports, license plates, and government documents.

In one case, the comedians' plans for a road trip ran into the complication of not having the proper license plate for each community they would drive through. One guy had a supply of Croat, Bosnian, and Serb license plates. He kept his sidekick running to the back of the Yugo to change it each time they thought of a new municipality on their route. Just before they all squeezed into the tiny car, itself a reminder of a failed national initiative, the sidekick came up with a brainstorm: why not put the plates on a rotisserie that would rotate as they traveled?

The ads addressed everyday problems within a larger, hostile environment, but the viewers liked their absurdity. As the buzz began to grow, we supported another series of ads that asked people on the streets what they thought of the Zenica troupe's spots. These testimonials showed average residents' appreciation for the implicit call to move on to weightier matters. By creating public sentiment for change where the warmongers were dominant, we felt that it might be possible to elevate the debate back to the central concerns that were destroying the Balkans.

9.

Reliable, useful information during times of great stress is vital. In Banja Luka, we found a courageous journalist, Zeljko Kopanja, publishing a weekly tabloid, *Nezavisne Novine*. In it, he often had a hard-hitting story on the merchants of war, along with the usual fare of a nearly broke publication: horoscopes, gossip, sports, and even soft-core porn.

Paper costs and state-run printing plants had constrained his operation, so we offered help in a few ways. With an election approaching, we paid to print an insert that would allow every party to publish a brief version of its platform. We then supported distribution of the paper to every house and apartment in the city. Young Serbs delivered the papers. Never before had opposing views been so widely circulated.

Zeljko continued to challenge the Serb authorities and received countless threats. On one visit to Banja Luka, I even talked to the British peacekeeping leader about protecting Zeljko. His circulation and influence grew as his paper published more frequently, and he created a radio station.

In 1999, he got into his car, turned the key, and set off an explosion that cost him both his legs and nearly his life. The October 22 UPI story from Banja Luka said,

The editor of a Bosnian-Serb newspaper had both his legs amputated on Friday after his car exploded. Editor Zeljko Kopanja had received death threats after publishing an acclaimed series of articles detailing alleged war crimes committed by Bosnian Serb officials. The newspaper, Nezavisne Novine, said in a statement it would not let the car bombing force a change in the independent publication's tough editorial policies. The newspaper is a rare example of independent media in this former Yugoslav republic that declared independence in 1992, particularly on the Bosnian-Serb side. [13]

Our last grant was to make Zeljko's office completely accessible to people with disabilities.

As American policy evolved and the leadership of Slobodan Milosevic became a central hurdle to peace, we continued to seek out media-savvy partners. The promising leadership of the student organization Otpor brought a strategic focus to the protest against Milosevic's rule. OTI became their first funder and provided open assistance. Joint strategy sessions, political conventions, and street protests combined to produce the critical mass to challenge Milosevic.

Being students, Otpor took advantage of its reach into political, military, and police families, preparing those institutions for critical events. When there might have been a violent crackdown, the machinery of the state respected the students and the people and the dictatorship tumbled. Otpor captured the same dry Serb humor we saw all over the country. In one iconic video, the students deliver a birthday cake to Milosevic. Shaped like the former Yugoslavia, the cake was broken into separate states. [14] Even in the darkest days, we must try multiple channels to bring about change.

Often, changing the dominant political will is the best effect that the United States can have from afar. Mass communications is a powerful, growing tool—one that U.S. government–run agencies do not exploit well. Our experiences in the Balkans proved the value.

10. LESSONS APPLIED

Bosnia was the first place I went in my new job and one of the first for OTI programs. It was also new territory for the U.S. government, both in our aims and methods. We took lessons into the projects and countries that followed.

First, we learned to take a pass when conditions are not ripe. If the situation is unsafe, unready, or if we are unable to address the larger conflict, it is not helpful. Just doing something can make things worse.

This was not always easy. Most keenly, I felt bad because we had met hundreds of people who wanted help to get on with their lives— and to live in peace. We had the capacity to help, but I knew that we were not likely to get very far, so we left them behind. We heard people out, observed their impossible situations, but we knew that fighting would resume. Still, we intervened where we could, starting small and building where possible. Where things didn't work, we moved on.

Second, determining whether a conflict is ready for our type of help requires an anthropological approach. In future conflicts, we tried to emulate the Gersony model with teams instead of individuals. Without the endless conversations, the home visits, and the maternity ward voices, insights and intuition would not have been anywhere near as acute.

Third, deliver reliable information and present tough choices to the greatest number of people. Bosnia was OTI's first clumsy foray into mass media, but it would not be the last. I carried its lessons for more than 20 years, when they became a part of much more dynamic efforts in Indonesia and Nigeria. How do we help reach the moment where political will shifts and the populace demands change?

Many of these insights recurred nearly everywhere I went. We were trying to provide *political* aid, aimed at contributing to a lasting end to an intractable conflict. It was most promising through a focus on local people, outside the capital and the walls of the U.S. embassy, all across the country. We moved money to promising projects quickly and measured and adjusted them as needed. Our other early experiments would also provide similar insights.

4

RWANDA

Open Wounds

I.

There were premonitions before the genocide began on April 7, 1994.

Throughout the 20th century, Europeans collaborated with a Tutsi kingdom and favored elite to run Rwanda at the expense of the majority Hutu ethnic group. The Tutsis imposed forced labor, seized lands, and took most administrative and political jobs in what Philip Gourevitch called an "apartheid system rooted in the myth of Tutsi superiority."[1]

Identity cards widened the ethnic divide at the expense of any sense of national identity. In 1957, the Hutus published their own manifesto claiming their right to democratic rule. The first episode of major political violence came in 1959, chasing tens of thousands of Tutsis from their homes before the independence in 1961, when the Hutus took power. Belgian complicity marked both the Tutsi reign and the Hutu ascent. From that point on there were mass killings of Tutsis in multiple years. There had even been "practice massacres" in the 1990s. "Killing Tutsis was a political tradition in postcolonial Rwanda," Gourevitch wrote. "It brought people together."[2]

Neighboring Burundi, with a similar Hutu-Tutsi divide, did no better. In 1993, the first free election of a president produced a Hutu winner with 70 percent of the vote. His subsequent assassination and an attempted coup led to nearly 100,000 deaths over six months. During that initial wave of violence, the United States opposed sending U.N. peacekeepers, saying that such an intervention would be too open-ended.[3] A million people would leave their homes.

In November 1993, a U.N. peacekeeping force arrived in Rwanda to monitor a negotiated ceasefire between the Hutu government and Tutsi rebels, the Rwandan Popular Front. On January 11, 1994, the U.N. commander, Canadian Brigadier General Romeo Dallaire, cabled U.N. headquarters in New York that "extremist Hutu militias were being secretly armed" in order "to attack Belgian peacekeepers, murder opposition politicians, and kill Tutsis."[4] Dallaire kept up these detailed warnings, but Rwanda never rose to the top of the U.N. Security Council's agenda.

On April 6, 1994, rockets destroyed the plane carrying the presidents of Burundi and Rwanda as it returned from peace talks in Dar Es Salaam, Tanzania.

My first exposure to the region was an early morning meeting on April 7 with the visiting foreign minister of Burundi. USAID's Africa bureau was seeking help for the two, tiny, conflicted nations and we were not yet aware of the crash. The minister, a young woman, had just received the news and was in shock. Overwhelmed with sadness and informed forebodings, she was unable to concentrate on business as usual. In my ignorance of the region's deadly modern history, I did not comprehend the enormity of the situation.

It would not take long to wake up. Roadblocks and roundups followed the crash. Within hours a full-scale genocide would be underway, with majority Hutus killing hundreds of thousands of Tutsis and scores of moderate Hutus—almost all by machetes. Burundi would see substantial but more sporadic violence, often led by the Tutsi army against the majority Hutus. Youth groups, based on soccer club models and called the *interahamwe* ("those who attack together"), led the carnage.

Later that day, assassins killed Rwanda's prime minister and the ten Belgian peacekeepers who guarded her. Facing near-certain death, desperate Rwandans reached out to their friends around the world. Academics, nongovernmental organizations, and friends of Rwanda cried out for help, but most paid scant attention.[5] Minutes mattered and nothing happened for weeks.

Outside forces did little, even as the deaths accumulated to 800,000. The French and others remained loyal to the Hutu power leaders and even continued to support the Hutu government with arms.

America was unprepared in most every regard. There was no political will to intervene in the heart of Africa and no clear way to do it. Debates centered on theory, while the killing continued. As the genocide reached its bloody conclusion on July 16, Brian Atwood asked me to join a small U.S. delegation that would look at justice, governance, and stability for Rwanda. After one of the most brutal slaughters in human history, now what?

2.

Upon landing at Kigali's small, modern airport, we found an eerie silence.

Even the 200 U.S. soldiers that had just encamped as part of the early post-genocide response lacked the normal bustle.[6] That was truer of the drive into town. We heard a single motorcycle, without a muffler, approaching from blocks away. There was no effervescence on the streets—playing children, hawking merchants, or friendly greetings.

There was an emptiness. Stores remained, without shopkeepers, products, or customers. A member of our delegation said, "It is like a neutron bomb went off in the entire country," referring to a new U.S. weapon that would kill people without destroying property.

With so few visible markings of war, it was hard to imagine the violence. The killing was fast and brutal, with minimal damage to buildings or infrastructure and few bullet holes or destroyed armored vehicles alongside the roads. It was the destruction of a people.

The 100-day genocide was intricate, rehearsed, and complete. An interim official of the new Tutsi-led Rwandan Patriotic Front (RPF) government told us about the killing of a moderate Hutu politician and his family. The murderers went from his office to the children's elementary school classrooms—to make sure there would be no survivors.

The harvest of a century's worth of division was apparent. I would often ask, "What group is that person from?" The answers seemed to follow personal likes and dislikes. We heard of tall Hutus who were mistaken for Tutsis and summarily executed.

Those who remained could hardly cry. Fear prevailed and the pain ran deep. Any gathering of even a few Rwandans was an overwhelming collection of suffering. "Are you a survivor or a killer?" was the oft-unstated opening question.

Silence prevailed and even conversations would take months. As I gently probed a surviving staffer at the U.S. embassy, Bonaventure Nyibizi, he finally said, "I have lost most of my family in the past few weeks. My own escape was pure luck. It is impossible for me to answer."

The silence from every part of the world was consistent before and during the genocide. For a meeting with the RPF-designated Hutu president, we climbed five stories to the top of a mostly deserted French hotel, the Milles Collines. While waiting in a neighboring room, we spoke with the Roman Catholic bishop of Newark, Theodore McCarrick. He too was in Rwanda to seek an understanding. How could a nation of one religion, 70 percent Catholic, turn on each other with such viciousness? "Why did our flock do this?" he asked, shaking his head.

The systemic murder would be the primary order of Rwandan life for decades to come. The tragedy would define a fractured society. Any attempts to move ahead without full recognition of the genocide would fail.

3.

We flew on to the resort town of Goma, Zaire (now the Democratic Republic of Congo), suddenly home to two million Rwandan refugees—many of them perpetrators of the killing. What we saw was raw and frenetic. Desperation and menace converged on the shores of Lake Kivu, one of Central Africa's picturesque, landlocked Great Lakes. Chaotic and noisy, it was in stark contrast to the silence of Kigali.

We wanted to understand the refugee crisis and to see what the perpetrators planned. At the overcrowded provincial airport, cargo planes full of relief supplies landed every few minutes. A burgeoning community of nongovernmental organizations (NGOs) rushed to save lives in newly arrived trucks and SUVs. A squadron of the French

Foreign Legion protected the emergency food and health packages against the surge of desolate refugees.

On narrow dirt roads, thousands of outcasts fled to one of the sprawling refugee camps that had sprung up overnight on forbidding lava dust and rocks. Men, women, and children, some carrying bundles of belongings as big as themselves, swarmed water trucks and food-distribution tents.

The air felt heavy and tense as if charged with static electricity. Any touch could provoke a shock. Hutus were on the run. Many had killed their neighbors, moderates, and strangers. Some had led the brutal assaults and feared reprisals from the "cockroaches"—their leaders' description of the Tutsis. What had been a strength—their ethnicity—was now a weakness. They left their lives behind to face near-term suffering in squalid conditions and an uncertain future.

As we drove into the tired resort town of Goma, a rotting stench filled the road. On our left was a mass, too-shallow grave with hundreds of cholera victims.

Now, the well-worn hotels were jammed with the fleeing leaders of the Rwandan genocide, some still trying to wheel and deal. In our brief exchanges, there was no remorse. We met with a handful of Hutu leaders in a motor court, where they had taken the best available shelter for themselves. They spoke as if the genocide was a mere distraction and imagined a return to dominance in Rwanda.

We drove up into the hills above the lake, feeling anonymous and protected inside a white SUV, coursing through a swarm of people, as we tried to get a sense of what was going on in the makeshift camps. None in the roadside throng waved or acknowledged us; they just kept their heads down, busy with their survival.

The hungry mob was on the move, cutting and consuming trees and bushes for fires, leaving swirling smoke hanging in the air and an acrid smell of human waste everywhere. In a sudden flurry of activity, a crowd of 15 or 20 spilled onto the road. At the center, a man, screaming, his burning red gut freshly sliced by a machete. His transgression was unknown but the punishment was swift.

For the first time, the mass of the problem became more personal. I had never seen a human being suffer so and it shook me. I was suddenly a witness to the exact behavior that had killed hundreds of thousands in the preceding weeks. My revulsion remains to this day.

4.

This was the aftermath of violence at its worst. What would be possible after the loss of so many people? How could we help the victims of the genocide, the Tutsis, now the victors, to start anew yet set aside the murderous divisions of the past? What might shape a fresh political future?

Addressing the humanitarian crisis was familiar, though the Goma airlift would be among history's most heroic. Within weeks, emergency supplies and basic shelter would accommodate the millions who had just arrived. These were just Band-Aids over the deeper wounds, which led back generations.

Now we also had additional problems: how to deal with 120,000 killers, the *genocidaires?* What of the lingering refugee camps, full of potential for a new invasion of Rwanda from rearmed Hutus? How to separate the Hutu refugees from their remaining poisonous leaders? Would these people ever be Rwandans again?

When we began to seek a way forward, one thing was clear from our travel and conversations: Progress would not be possible without prying some sense of justice out of the aftermath of the genocide. That was the first priority. While many of us understood the importance of this point, the majority of our efforts did not reflect it.

How could justice advance in a country where everyone was a victim or a perpetrator? After an early period of substantial retribution killings, the new government established calm and order, but it did not have the ability to investigate the massive number of cases or prepare and conduct trials. On a regular basis, survivors identified attackers, and Rwanda's primitive jails overflowed with tens of thousands of undocumented prisoners.

The prospective attorney general told our delegation what the new government most wanted: speedy trials, in Rwanda, with a death penalty option. The Rwandans felt that would be the truest way to deliver justice.

The response of our delegation leader, the Assistant Secretary of State for Democracy, Rights, and Labor, John Shattuck, did not satisfy our hosts. The United States sought to finesse all three Rwandan desires. In 1993, the United Nations created the International Criminal Tribunal for the former Yugoslavia, which provided a high-level venue to try these most heinous cases. This impartial court would have the highest standards, we argued, so it would only make sense to try Rwandans there. (These tribunals focused on the leaders of atrocities, not the foot soldiers.) On their second request, we worried that it would be impossible for local trials to be fair and peaceful. Finally, we knew our European allies would reject the possibility of a death sentence. There was a broad logic to our position, but it would prove to be misplaced.

By moving the trials out of the country and into international legal standards, we minimized the urgent need of Rwandans to see justice firsthand and in their communities. Adding Rwanda to the difficult docket of the Yugoslav trials was neither quick nor productive. The nascent tribunal was overwhelmed even before it took on Rwanda. In addition, the lead prosecutor, South African judge Richard Goldstone, was overloaded, and the initial investigators overwhelmed. With the selection of Arusha, Tanzania, as the trial site, the whole process required relocation and construction of new buildings for the trials and prisoners.

To mitigate Rwandans' disconnection from the trials, OTI paid for daily radio broadcasts from Arusha back to Rwanda. In addition, communities throughout the country saw videos of the trials, providing some link to the punishment of the political leadership that promoted the genocide. We also led the donors to professionalize communications between The Hague and Kigali. What could have become a distant exercise became more real to the Rwandans—and there was widespread interest.

At one point, OTI sent a prosecutor from Los Angeles to see about accelerating the investigations. The destruction of evidence was a concern. He too was overwhelmed.

Meanwhile, Rwandans ran lower-level trials in-country and proceeded to execute the guilty, dismissing the Europeans' concern with capital punishment. Our objections and designs made little sense in the midst of Rwandans' search for justice. Our cardinal mistake—perhaps the cardinal mistake in all of this work, which we never seem to learn—is that solutions driven and imposed by outsiders never stick, especially without the input of the people we claim to help.

5.

The courts were not the only way to deliver justice and safety, though none were immune to our arrogance. Among those eager to stabilize Rwanda was the U.N.'s first High Commissioner for Human Rights, José Ayala Lasso, thrice Ecuador's foreign minister. He had begun his term two days before the genocide started and felt that international human rights experts would provide comfort to the Rwandans remaining in the country.

Ayala Lasso's plan was to place 100 human rights monitors all over Rwanda as a first line of reassurance to the remaining population. Some would begin to collect evidence, but their primary purpose was to show Rwandans that the world cared; they should feel safe. It could also function as an early warning system.

The plan faced some obvious operational hurdles. First, where would we find 100 human rights professionals willing to go to Rwanda on a three-month contract right after a genocide? Second, how many of them could work effectively when the country and language were foreign to them? Third, how could we expect a U.N. policy shop in Geneva that had never deployed such a group to deliver a functioning field operation?

An American monitor later described the experiment this way: "Having the High Commissioner for Human Rights lead this effort was like asking the Library of Congress to put out a forest fire. There are plenty of references but zero experience. It was an institutionally structured mess."[7]

The United Nations had grand ambitions but no practical method, no system or model, for achieving them. We set out to bring the bold idea into practice. We argued for drafting monitors who knew the area, maybe even spoke Kinyarwanda and could be trained in some fundamental human rights practices. By definition, this was a small number of candidates. Working with the inspirational leader of the Returned Peace Corps Association, Chic Dambach, we identified several former volunteers who were eager to return to the region at this crisis point. This was a small contribution despite resistance from human rights traditionalists and U.S.-wary U.N. officials and it helped lead to future Peace Corps efforts.

When finally deployed, the monitors did not help to collect evidence—rather, they upbraided the new Rwandan government, which had no police and few prisons, for having soldiers arrest people and excess incarcerations. The genocide went unaddressed.

The monitors reported to us that their leaders were misinterpreting the Rwandan situation and constraining the fieldwork. Dispirited, they asked us to make a change. Unfamiliar with the formalistic U.N. system, we called and lobbied Ayala Lasso's office in Geneva and reported the U.S. desire for a new top person. His deputy agreed to go along if we could find another Brit to take the place of the current leader. From our work in Haiti, we had met a promising Brit human rights expert, Ian Martin, and after some calls and reassurances, put forth his candidacy. He stabilized a difficult mission by providing material and leadership support to the field.

Later I would learn that this kind of direct intervention is extremely rare. Naïve insistence led to a deal. How many practical and necessary changes never happen because of the perceived need to follow diplomatic formalities?

Building up the monitors' capacity and finding pragmatic ways forward became our work. America would end up being among the first supporters of the International Criminal Tribunal and the human rights monitors, seeking to ground these grand ideas on a daily basis.

6.

Rwandans' passion for near-term justice required a new culture of awareness and respect for the rule of law. Where impunity was the standard, we helped Rwandans find practical ways to deliver a modicum of justice.

Since there was no Rwandan statute for dealing with crimes against humanity, a talented American human rights monitor, Jane Rasmussen, worked with the attorney general's office to draft and adopt a new genocide law. It set different levels of culpability, from being an organizer down to a supporter.

With a surge of prisoners topping more than 100,000 (exceeding capacity several fold), our next concern was that trials would take decades. In an attempt to see the length of time needed to adjudicate all the cases, OTI sent an American University statistician to survey those in jail. Through a random sample of a few hundred prisoners, we believed that it would be possible to determine what percentages of the total jail population fell into each category of Level 1, 2, 3, or 4 crimes—and then determine the number of years the trials might take. After a visit to one major prison, the expert saw that most of those held did not have paperwork or charges. Made-up names, by the accused and the authorities, combined with a total lack of evidence, threatened the likelihood of justice. Unsettled, the Rwandans reversed their cooperation and did not let her complete the census in other jails. We encouraged other avenues.

In many villages, a more familiar trial method began to take shape. The *gacaca* model required local *genocidaires* to admit their crimes, face questions from victims, and express repentance in exchange for the community's forgiveness. This indigenous idea gained traction: *gacaca* courts prosecuted 400,000 genocide suspects in 11,000 communities between 2002 and 2012.[8] Those public events allowed towns to move ahead. Even in the worst circumstances, and with virtually no international funding, a local idea worked. "If one stated objective of judging mass violence is to reconcile divided communities, then victims and perpetrators must also be brought together again, and close to the scene of the crimes."[9]

7.

By March 1995, Rwandans' collective shock remained, but they also felt a growing need to build a normal life. Post-genocide Rwanda was absorbing multiple transitions, including Hutu to Tutsi government; patriarchal families to matriarchal; French language to English; native-born and raised to returnees from Uganda and elsewhere; farm-dominated to urban; and, the most basic, a decimated population. In addition, an inexperienced government was in charge of a shell of a country, fields lay fallow, small provincial prisons were overflowing with defendants from the mass murders, and depression permeated the society. Genocide destroyed the population, the workforce, and the country's culture and economy. Trust was scarce.

There could be no return to the prior ways. A new normal was necessary. How could we help salve their desperate urgency to get on with life? The answers did not magically appear. On a return trip, I once again sought the wisdom of the crowds by traveling around the country, listening and looking.

Unlike the immediate post-genocide moment of 1994, the hilly roads now teemed with a sense of purpose. Strangers earned wary looks, but people were also busy with the demands of living: returning to untilled fields, carrying crops and babies, washing clothes. Rwandans' resilience combined the need to remember and a desire to move forward.

At an orphanage in the southern university town of Butare, a truck full of relief supplies and the animated voices of dozens of children disrupted a sparkling late afternoon quiet. In a concrete former school, the young Hutu and Tutsi children, survivors of the previous year's bloodletting, played in a dirt central courtyard.

A chubby three-year-old girl, not much younger than my own daughter back home in Washington, grabbed my pinkie. A colleague and I were there to observe the humanitarian response, and as I wandered through the converted classrooms, my new friend held fast. She did not talk or smile—just grabbed on. In that tight little grip was the determination of her people. Here, in a temporary safe space, where there was an organized tranquility and heartening care, one little person was reaching out, in search of some certainty.

The reasons were obvious. As a colleague would later write, "In recent interviews at unaccompanied children centers, we asked what they hope to be doing five years from now. Most said they do not expect to be alive."[10]

Near Kibungo, on the border of Rwanda and Tanzania, the devastation of the Tutsi population was complete. The U.N. human rights monitor for the region, a South American with limited experience in Africa, seemed shell-shocked as he described the systematic killing of all Tutsis. There to offer a stabilizing influence, the monitors offered some comfort to a decimated populace. The United States funded the monitors because we believed that a reassuring presence of outsiders would help to stabilize the area. Retributive killings and other horrors remained a threat in the vacuum-like, post-genocide moment—and the commitment of the international community provided relief for the remaining Rwandans.

The U.N. official stood next to a wall-sized map of Rwanda and pointed out the pincer-like method that the Hutu-power attackers had employed. With the Rwandan military surrounding a zone, the *interahamwe* would be set free to prey upon all Tutsis inside of that defined place. When they had murdered all the Tutsis, they would move on. The monitor showed how lakes and rivers served as boundaries and how the government's documentation by group provided a clear census to track victims.

"In this village there were 2,000 Tutsis; now there is one," he said, using the map to highlight the brutal efficiency. "On this point of land, there were 1,200 Tutsis, and now just two."[11] And on. The handful who survived played dead, hid in lakes, or just got lucky.

8.

By the time we visited, the *genocidaires* had fled and a skeletal population remained. Tutsi returnees had begun to take over the homes and small farms of those now in Tanzania, but emptiness dominated.

A short way down the road we stopped to talk with a market woman. Vibrant and playful, she quickly asked about our marital status. "There are not many men around here," she flirted. That was clear. At least 70 percent of the people we saw were women and children.

This became the germ of an idea.

After a morning U.N. helicopter ride to Gisenyi, on the western border with Zaire, with a hung-over Canadian pilot who smelled of whiskey, we sought out groups of women. What had they done together before the genocide? What activities had they returned to? What did they want to do now?

We heard about getting their kids back to school, cooperative day care operations at their homes, and the enlarged burden they felt since so many of the survivor families were now women led. They were coping but could do little more. The pressures of life overmatched their abilities. They needed a return to normalcy and refreshed paths of cooperation.

I returned to Kigali with a number of thoughts: Women appeared to be in the majority; men needed women; women were already carrying a heavy burden; they were less likely to have been murderers; they were desperate to support their families; and they seemed to have taken on the children of deceased relatives. Instead of focusing on Rwanda's traditional division of Hutu and Tutsi, why not lift up the women of the country as the way forward? Hutus and Tutsis did not need to get along, but men and women must.

Women would need economic and political strengthening, so we looked to see if a woman-centered program might cut across a number of the challenges. The core idea was to identify women's groups all over the country and stabilize their economic positions so that they could expand their political reach. In a society that had collapsed, we could encourage a new dialectic—women and men, together, versus the failed and poisonous Hutu and Tutsi model, with its centralized, colonial past. We also sought to increase the influence of women as leaders, nurture trust, and address the immediate reality of thousands of vulnerable women, many of whom were heads of households.

Our official partner was the lone woman in the new cabinet, Aloisea Inyumba, Minister for Gender and Family Promotion. Inyumba, a dynamic force who had been the chief fundraiser for the winning rebel side, the Rwandan Patriotic Front (RPF), was resourceful and trusted. Despite that, she led a weak ministry and had few resources. In the course of the next two years, the Women in Transition Initiative (WIT) became the lynchpin of her ministry and set about elevating women to a new status in Rwanda. It provided staff to Inyumba's ministry and seed funding to reach out.

The explicit desire to increase the political influence of women's groups all over Rwanda made this program unique. Improbably, two American men, Greg Beck and Buddy Shanks, already working in Rwanda, served as the founding leaders, partnering with a dozen Rwandan women. From inside of Inyumba's ministry, their teams would visit villages every day, identify women's groups or eager prospects, and offer start-up funds and terms.

Known as the Projet du Mamas, WIT quickly reached 1,800 women's associations in nearly two-thirds of the country's communes. Through independent decision-making by the women and micro-grants to thousands, WIT energized small businesses and allowed 150,000 people to become self-sufficient. This model inspired them and allowed them to expand their influence.

In later recollections, Buddy Shanks, the WIT director from West Texas, wrote about a visit to a town on the Congo border:

> One young woman quietly talked of her past and the horrible and miserable ordeal of being on the run with the interahamwe, the youth groups that killed so many. She recalled how her mother became exhausted due to the constant movement and how she had stated her intention to return to her home commune in Gisenyi. The interahamwe shot and killed her mother. The daughter decided to keep quiet and eventually escaped.
>
> The WIT team revisited and monitored the women's groups in that area on several occasions. With each trip, we observed an increase in the women's spirits, better clothes, improved health, and even some evidence of visits to the local *salon du coiffure*. Equally visible was an increase of land in agricultural production and a decrease in military patrols. An association member in Kayove stated, "Not only do the families of the 15 WIT-funded women's associations have Irish potatoes to eat, but ALL families in Kayove can now afford to buy potatoes and feed their families." [12]

Buddy went on,

> I wasn't sure about ALL, but potato prices throughout Rwanda dropped more than 50 percent within a year, and in some communes more. In Mutura, the fourth commune WIT funded, the burgomaster told us his commune is the top producer of Irish potatoes in Rwanda, "grâce à WIT." Whatever part WIT played in increasing the potato production in the four volatile communes, we did act quickly to provide money directly to the 68 women associations, which gave them the means to purchase quality-planting seeds. [13]

My colleague reported about his last monitoring visit and the letter a woman offered as he prepared to leave. "It was the same woman who had earlier told us about losing her mom," he said. "By this letter, we want to thank WIT for the sincere love that you have shown to our women. Mamas of Rwerere were close to death when you first arrived. Now women, widows and their orphans sing a song to praise WIT. This letter is a small nothing, but it means a lot because it comes from the depths of our hearts."[14]

WIT was not the only organization working in Gisenyi communes, but perhaps the only one providing funds directly to the women associations that allowed them to make their own determinations. The Préfet commended WIT's method of channeling funds directly to the beneficiaries and not passing them through intermediaries.

"For many of the women, it was the first time they had set foot in a bank, much less opened a bank account. Many of the women, especially heads of households, now have the wherewithal to make their own financial decisions and are not dependent on handouts or food distributions."[15]

Tiny amounts of well-directed funds, often less than $50, allowed more than 150,000 in 1,800 women's associations to return to life and increase their political influence. WIT sought to decentralize and give rural women the means to make decisions that affect their communities. With repayment rates between 85 and 90 percent, they took charge.[16]

U.S. taxpayers made this possible—and I believe we got our money's worth. Not just because it was a modest amount of money, but also because it helped to set one more country on earth in a peaceful direction—something that always benefits the United States, in its alliances, trade, and reduction of threats. Rwanda still faces plenty of challenges—but the United States helped the restart.

On a later visit to Rwanda, I stopped to see several WIT projects. One was a mushroom-growing enterprise, led by three women, who between them supported almost 50 family members. The United States helped them get started with support for a growing shed, and Kigali hotels and restaurants purchased their mushrooms. A little store was now part of their business and they had recently added a Coke machine as they became a neighborhood gathering spot. The move from subsistence to community influencers was underway.

9.

On a brilliant Sunday morning, I walked to a downtown Protestant church with Ambassador Dave Rawson and his wife. There was still no traffic and the natural beauty of Kigali, with its perfect climate and flowering trees, filled our senses. A half-full church was another sign of normalcy.

The ambassador was a religious person, having grown up in the region as the son of a Methodist missionary doctor. At every meal, we would start with grace and be joined by a number of visitors from all over Rwanda. With a native's mastery of Kinyarwanda, Rawson's life-long affection for the country and its people grew. Despite great local knowledge, the genocide came as a total surprise to Rawson and the lingering shock of loss and horror remained. He knew so many on both sides of the killings.

Perhaps he was too hopeful about the peace talks. Maybe he was a prisoner of his own great knowledge. Almost surely, he was part of a tiny universe of U.S. government experts, working in semi-isolation on a nonstrategic part of the world, who did not enjoy much support or leadership engagement.

Many of us missed the threat of the genocide. Too few reacted in an effective way. When we finally arrived, we did not heed local voices, as we should. Yet, in the entrails of one of history's worst slaughters, we did find ways forward.

Rwanda had two extreme realities to address: genocide and a return to normalcy. That need, which we captured well, produced a focused strategy on those two items, plus a fresh start. The human rights monitors, trials, new laws, and bringing them home to the populace were all innovations that showed our respect for dealing with the genocide—the number one thing on many minds, but also in their hearts and guts.

A return to normalcy was not easy, because you could not return to the prior state. A new normal was necessary. WIT saw that and the path it followed broke with the status quo ante, the failed past, and causes of the genocide.

Rwanda has made great strides. Peace continues and a strong national plan has gained the support of governments and donors from around the world. When Minister Inyumba died in December 2012, her obituary reported that "Rwanda had a higher percentage of women parliamentarians than anywhere else and women occupied more than half of senior government posts. One million people had been brought out of poverty, free education was available until the age of 14 and a national health insurance scheme was in place."[17]

Many challenges remain. Rwanda today still struggles with its political balance. A singular leader, Paul Kagame, has not found a successor and is torturing the constitutional process to stay on. Opposition figures and independent voices suffer.

Rwanda is at last capable of making the right decisions.

10. LESSONS APPLIED

These are among the early lessons I took from Rwanda: Make sure that you feel the pain of the people. It is not possible to move on unless you empathize; a genocide requires full recognition.

Second, make sure that policy and practice inform and support each other. Big ideas must be executable so beware of overpromising.

Third, when you have an almost impossible job, be aggressive in picking the right leader. There is no chance for success without a wise and uplifting guide, interpreter, and mentor.

Fourth, the United Nations works best when its members make real contributions. When we thrust our vital institutions into the middle of an unprecedented situation, we need to back them up with practical support. Our success depends on them—and they cannot do it without extraordinary assistance.

5

HAITI

From Exploitation to Participation

I.

After 200 years of strong-armed exploitation, Haiti was not ready for a smooth transition to democracy.

In the 18th century, Haiti was the crown jewel of France's colonial empire—so profitable that when France got the choice of holding on to Haiti or the vast expanse of the United States that became the Louisiana Purchase, Paris had little difficulty making the decision. The fields were so lush and the land so productive that the slave masters could afford to work their slaves to death—not worrying about the losses or the cost, unlike every other plantation state in the world.

Haiti shed its brutal French masters in 1803, but that did not make its people free. Former slaves took on the task of subjugating their neighbors, repeating the French patterns. The U.S. military occupation from 1915 to 1934 installed a series of puppet governments that crushed attempts at resistance, killing 15,000 during that time.[1] Under the repressive regimes of Francois "Papa Doc" Duvalier and his son, Jean-Claude, known as Baby Doc, Haiti was stable from 1957 into the 1980s, but the wealthy, connected few continued to despoil it. After Baby Doc fled in 1986, coups, armed attacks on voting stations, and rigged elections thwarted moves toward democracy. These ruinous foundations produced a country that has been the poorest in the West-

ern Hemisphere for decades, with low life expectancy, sky-high unemployment, and limited access to energy, clean water, and nutrition. A
RAND report from 2010 described Haiti's daunting challenges as
"acute problems layered on chronic ones."[2]

The state's failure to sustain a vision or create the self-sustaining
institutions that could make societal improvements is Haiti's dominant
story line.

Scores of well-meaning organizations have come into that void over
the past 50-plus years. For decades, American diplomats, development
professionals, humanitarians, soldiers, missionaries, anthropologists,
and others have made it a special project. Their good works have produced "a thousand points of light" all over the country, but the overall
trend lines have proven to be stubbornly negative. There is a solid
argument that civil society, either by itself or within a context of negative governance, will never be able to reverse them. To do that, there
must be a greater coming together.

2.

By 1990, Haiti's six million residents and a diaspora of two million had
grown impatient with their static homeland. Those who had left found
success in other parts of the world. Not so for most in Haiti. The
problem was not Haitians; it was their system.[3]

The December 1990 presidential election should have been a pivot
point toward a brighter future. The United States and international
donors helped set up an electoral system and provided a watchful eye.
Haitians were unafraid. The body politic felt that they might take a step
to reverse centuries of history.

On Election Day, turnout was heavy, ballot counting precise, and
the results clear. From a diverse field of a dozen candidates, the charismatic *Titid*, or "little priest," Bertrand Aristide, won in a landslide. Long
a champion of social change, the former Salesian father captured the
zeitgeist with his slyly disruptive campaign phrase, "from misery to poverty with dignity." His newly created party adopted the rooster as its
ballot identifier. When you asked Haitians whom they might vote for,
the joyful response was "Cock-a-doodle-do."

Over several months, I witnessed much of the election as a volunteer political party trainer and election observer. The Haitians' care and attention to detail impressed. In Gonaives, Haiti's "City of Independence," where dogs and chickens added to the election-day revelry, I saw poll workers place each ballot box on a central table, count the ballots, and cross-check the numbers with the voting rolls. Then, they held up each ballot, read the choice aloud, and placed it in a candidate's pile. At a postelection debriefing for former president Jimmy Carter, who led the monitoring mission, Atlanta mayor Andrew Young said, "I wish our elections were this well-run."

The next step was backward. Eight months after Aristide took office, the head of the Haitian Army, General Raoul Cedras, seized power on September 30, 1991. President George H. W. Bush "called for the restoration of democracy" and worked with other Western Hemisphere countries and the United Nations to impose sanctions on the military regime.[4] Cedras reached and breached agreements[5] that would allow Aristide's return. Aristide would spend three years in exile in Washington, DC.

The coup was uncharted territory for the post–Cold War United States: a military takeover right in our backyard, in a new age for democratization. President Bill Clinton and the international community were under increasing pressure to act—for altruistic reasons and because thousands of "boat people" began to arrive on the coast of Florida in 1994.

In July 1994, the U.N. Security Council authorized the use of force to restore Aristide. Under the U.N. mandate, the United States prepared for military invasion as part of a multinational force of Caribbean and allied nations. Opposition from the foreign policy establishment focused on prior U.S. failures in Haiti, doubts about Aristide, and a sense that nothing would matter in Haiti, yet President Clinton proceeded with the planning.

In uncharacteristic anticipation, a number of U.S. agencies began meeting in midsummer in Washington, preparing for a U.S.-led invasion. Thanks to USAID's deputy Carol Lancaster, I received a call from General Wes Clark, then the head of planning for the Joint Chiefs. He was concerned that there would be no organized follow-on to the U.S. military. Right away, we met at his Pentagon office and he recounted his dissatisfaction from Vietnam. Clark spoke of a three-legged stool of military, politics, and economics, and how there must be balance for the stool to work. I pointed out that the stool had one leg and two tooth-picks and that the presence of my office only changed that a bit. He accepted the imbalance and remained sensitive to it throughout.

Recognizing that Haiti could be the first real test for our new Office of Transition Initiatives (OTI), our small team of four began to meet with every expert, diplomat, and nongovernmental professional we could find. We built rosters of prospective Haitian, American, and international staff, and identified ways to move resources rapidly. One channel was through a multilateral and we sought out the International Organization for Migration (IOM), which had worked in Central America and Africa.[6]

We reached out to President Aristide's handful of closest advisors exiled in Washington. Led by two trusted technocrats, Leslie Voltaire and Leslie Delatour, the Haitians recognized the enormity of the task and encouraged America's assistance.

Traditional U.S. development programs looked at issues like agriculture and infrastructure, leaving a gap around politics that seemed especially wide in Haiti. The Haitians welcomed OTI's focus on a central political development question: How might we help the Haitian people move from a system of intimidation to one of participation? The "two Leslies" knew that it would be impossible to produce the necessary change from the center in the most rural country in the Americas. Haiti's political progress would require local-level engagement to overcome an obstructive and inefficient capital centric tradition. We also took on the idea of redirecting Haitian soldiers to civilian work.

In one memorable meeting at the State Department, days before the invasion, General Clark, my OTI co-founder Johanna Mendelson, an expert in civilian-military relations, and I sat down with the deposed prime minister (and later twice president) René Préval. We assumed the U.S. military operation would be successful and wanted to minimize the Haitian armed forces' mischief. How could we pay the Haitian soldiers in local currency right after the Americans landed?

We asked Préval, "How many soldiers are there in the FAHD?" He had no idea.

"How much do they get paid?" Clark followed up. Préval had no sense.

We continued, "Where might we get enough Haitian money (gourde) on short notice?" Again, Préval did not know.

Exasperated, Clark said to Préval, through a translator, "Mr. Prime Minister, I work for the U.S. Army. We are good at getting from one point to the other, especially if it is a straight line. To do that, we need some facts."

Préval was not embarrassed. These details were not common knowledge in Haiti and he had not been in office long enough to learn. Others estimated that there might be as many as 10,000 Haitian soldiers, but Johanna expected padded payrolls and no-shows would reduce that number.

As the U.S.-led invasion launched in mid-September, Cedras and a bipartisan U.S. team of Carter, Georgia Senator Sam Nunn, and former National Security Advisor Colin Powell sought a last-minute reprieve from a forced U.S. landing. As the troop-filled planes left the United States, Cedras capitulated, preventing bloodshed. Twenty thousand U.S. soldiers began to arrive on September 19 in an "immaculate invasion."[7] No lives were lost. The official name was Operation Uphold Democracy and it went from a combat plan to peacekeeping overnight.

I would land with an OTI team in Port au Prince one week later to begin our work.

3.

In the first days, the U.S. military delegated local law and order to the Haitian police. This did not work.

The police were part of a despised, oppressive triumvirate that included the Haitian Army (FAHD) and local paramilitary enforcers, the *Tonton Macoute*. They appeared to sanction some violent attacks against Aristide supporters, testing America's "soft landing."

An early test was a peaceful march to honor 3,500 victims of the military regime in downtown Port au Prince on Friday, September 30. The U.S. military cautioned us not to be in the area. U.S. forces would secure the periphery and leave the policing of the protest to the Haitians. Thinking that the warnings were excessive, I had driven through the U.S. checkpoints into a too-quiet city in the morning. The streets were clear.

I was working at the USAID mission near the march when we heard the pop pop pop of gunshots. Suddenly, a handful of U.S. soldiers and security people ran by my window, guns drawn. The few of us that were inside the walls of the former motor court ducked and waited.

Within minutes, we received the first reports. Disaster had struck. As the crowd of several thousand left a cathedral for the short walk to the main cemetery, the *macoute's* political party, the FRAPH, set upon them. Jumping out of alleys and from behind buildings with machetes and guns drawn, the thugs sent the crowd running in every direction, dispersing the human rights protestors in chaos as a large contingent of international press looked on. The Haitian police made no visible reaction.

Dozens of demonstrators, observers, and an ABC-TV cameraperson were shot. The press questioned the wisdom of leaving the Haitian police in charge—and the hands-off role of the U.S. military.[8] Later that afternoon at a hotel on the hills overlooking the city, I overheard a radio correspondent on the sole international phone line filing his report on the "failure" of the U.S. intervention. Something had to change.

On the drive downtown the next morning, there were U.S. soldiers everywhere—in Jeeps or well-armed foot patrols. There was no doubt that the U.S. military was now in charge, a reassuring presence all over the city. Street life bustled as the Haitian public returned.

As we turned toward the waterfront U.S. embassy, we saw a group of citizens administering a *dechoukaj*, or ransacking, to the FRAPH political headquarters. With their official protection gone, the *macoute* were now on their own. The impunity and special privileges of decades was over. The U.S. forces looked the other way.

After a firefight between the U.S. Marines and a resistant Haitian police outpost near Cap-Haïten, the message was clear: the United States will not stand by and watch the authorities prey on the people. U.S. Special Forces teams of 12 fanned out into each of Haiti's states and a political opening appeared.

The word about a new order spread quickly. All over the country, well-armed *macoute* started turning in their weapons. Where owning a gun had been part of terrorizing the populace, now the mass of people could feel that it was time to restore justice. The prior dominant minority gave up its violent tools as part of the new way.

Of the many conflicts that I have worked on, this was the only one where I could feel and see the liberation of the public in a matter of hours. Where official violence and bullying persists, as it had in Haiti for centuries, there is often a need for a breakthrough action or moment. Sometimes, such overwhelming shows of force can serve an important purpose. Without those early moves by the United States, the Haitian public would not have escaped daily intimidation—a first and necessary step to broader participation and ownership.

4.

Redefining the role of the Haitian military remained a central political development challenge. For years, the FAHD had been the ultimate enforcers for dictators and the elites. Without them, police reform would be possible and the *macoute* would have no standing. In recent years, the military had also taken greater control of the government and other institutions.

Our initial intent was to keep the rank and file busy, so that they would not pose a threat to the U.S. military. We began by designing a demobilization, disarmament, and reintegration program (DDR) for the Haitian Army. Because of the urgency and political sensitivity that the former soldiers required, OTI took the lead. A paucity of prior U.S. civilian experience had only provided seeds, tools, and transportation to former fighters.

While the literature on DDR was limited, a USAID study suggested that there were two key elements: separate the soldiers from their regular commands, barracks, and groups; and involve their spouses and families as much as possible from the outset. Those principles guided us throughout.

With the assistance of the International Organization for Migration, a handful of dynamic internationals with demobilization experience in Central America and Mozambique began to meet with soldiers and their dependents. A downtown office became the new clubhouse as we counseled them on future careers and lined up opportunities—a clear break from their pasts.

We took care not to create a privileged population, since the Haitian Army was widely disliked. Working with a collection of private and public vocational technical schools, we began to see some post-military choices. Each demobilized Haitian was able to select a multi-month job-training course from computers to plumbing or construction. Within weeks, the first several hundred were attending daylong classes in a city near their homes.

Something was required of all parties during the training. The Haitian government paid the modest monthly "stipend" that kept the soldiers and their families afloat. The United States subsidized the vocational schools so they could take a crowd of new students, paid the tuitions, and provided lunch money. Former soldiers had to commit to perfect attendance or sacrifice all payments. While some had to wait for vocational school openings, the program kept a potentially troublesome population off the streets—and began to shape their future.

Around Christmas of 1994, President Aristide dissolved the FAHD, a popular domestic move. With intentional irony, he turned over the army's headquarters, a constant reminder of governing interference facing the Presidential Palace, to a new department of women and children's affairs. Our mission broadened to include more than 5,000 non-officers who sought a new way of life.

At the halfway point, the *Christian Science Monitor* described the program:

> They are 3,368 former members of the Armed Forces of Haiti (FAHD) who have traded their guns for tools and enlisted in a U.S.-funded program designed to help them enter civilian life.
>
> So far, about two-thirds of them have completed intensive six-month courses in such fields as mechanics, carpentry, welding, plumbing, electricity, masonry, refrigeration, and computer science. "It was good when I was in the Army, because it was one of the only ways I could provide for my family and children," says former soldier Jean Joseph, who is now looking for work as an electrician. "But I think things will be better because now I actually have a profession."[9]

We adopted a "minimal return" standard. If the program came up short, what would we have gained? In this case, we knew that the initiative had reinvigorated the vocational technical schools by providing enough students to pay for curriculum and facilities updates.

In an informal economy like Haiti, where official unemployment hovered around 80 percent and yet everyone is busy because there is no safety net, it makes sense to increase the skills of a large group of capable men. While we were unclear whether these new trades would be the answer, the program did make them more self-sufficient, kept them off the streets while the United States was an occupying force, and sped the transformation away from a militarized government.

5.

Honeymoons are brief in places like Haiti—and we wanted to make the most of this one. Our second ambition was to expand opportunities for local governance with immediate signs of progress. "Local ownership" and "speed" became our mantras.

We worked on the wise assumption that Port au Prince would be overwhelmed. Lacking capacity to begin with, things would only get more complicated with the arrival of the U.S. government and its allies in their full glory.

For Haitians to feel as if they were part of a new day, it would be essential for any assistance to be at the local level, where most of them lived. To build up democratic practices, we would seek to work through any mayor's offices or similar local organizations that we could find.

We recognized that most of our ideas would require an on-the-ground reality check. We did not have a preconceived view that our assistance would fall into an existing category, such as medicine, education, or infrastructure, though it might. Local voices and Haitian volunteers would drive the choice. We designed our program to be direct, fast, and catalytic, responding to what motivated people enough that they would be willing to do most of the work and contribute what little they had. This generated concern from our Washington colleagues, who were used to designing, reviewing, and approving programs over months and years.

For two weeks in early October 1994, we deployed six three-person teams of Haitians and internationals throughout the country to observe and digest the post-invasion situation. In hundreds of meetings, the teams found a desperate craving among Haitians to move on, with a deep-seated desire for normalcy. Haitians wanted to see their children in school, their goods in the markets, and their homes repaired. Justice was on everyone's minds, from revenge to forgiveness. In the rural highland town of Hinche, our team saw a lynched *macoute* hanging from a tree. Another team sat around a fire and witnessed neighbors forgiving former tormenters if they apologized and asked for a fresh start.

From the teams' findings, we designed a local governance program.[10] Funding would go where citizens came together, without favoritism. Haitian responsibility would expand by addressing local priorities, chosen by the people of the area, through intense community participation. We saw the decentralized initiative as a way to test emerging local leaders, give them a chance to prove their worth, and involve large numbers of people in self-governance. Mayors and other locals would participate in a virtual political development institute—learning the fundamentals of democratic engagement while addressing pressing challenges. The real measure of progress would be local communities coming together to solve common problems.

To make sure that communities were participating in the selection of the projects, we applied the following criteria:

- The selection of the project had to include a group of motivated locals.
- Decision-making must be open and democratic.
- The group had to make a financial, labor, or in-kind contribution that would match or exceed the modest amount of U.S. funds.
- The programs would have transparent, real-time monitoring and visible public reporting to prevent waste or fraud.

To execute the plan, we set up more than a dozen offices all over Haiti, as close to U.S. Special Forces outposts as possible. Right away, two-person international teams hired Haitians and began to solicit local initiatives. Office hours in local municipal buildings and town squares invited participation. Teams reached out to informal groups in each area, from school parents to farmers. The muddy northern shore city of Port-de-Paix proved to be a center of civic engagement, with well-developed, community-spun plans for improvements showing up each month.

Our attitude was simple: if you are not willing to play by these rules we will work with the next town. We knew there was not enough money to "fix" Haiti, so we went where there was support for real local governance, which the Haitians accepted as common sense.

Within six months, the partnerships captured Haitian resourcefulness, with a governance purpose. On an evening drive in rural Miragoane, we drove by a pile of U.S.-donated cinder blocks, left that day at the bottom of a hill for a town's new school. By the next morning, the residents had hand carried them to the top, showing their ability to organize.

In the lower peninsula fishing town of Jeremie, running water reached only a few wealthier homes. For the first time, a town meeting allowed the villagers to debate and vote on a way to share and spread a precious asset. Our young staff helped to pull together the exchange and made sure that a respected local led the process. A raucous session ensued, pitting the traditional privileged few against a broader public. The result: a more equitable distribution that amazed most.

When a flood plain near Jacmel needed a bridge to shorten market trips by hours, we saw Haitians breaking up the stone by hand and women carrying it across fields to a U.N. bulldozer to get started. The women had elected a local man to lead the effort. As he proudly strutted the site in his New York Yankees hat, they teased him with a sarcastic song: "He is our leader, our great leader!" But they all reveled in the freedom of choice and the solving of a long-standing problem.

On one trip into the Artibonnite area of Haiti, near the famous Albert Schweitzer Hospital, the U.S. ambassador Bill Swing and I visited the dedication of a new community-built and painted school. Bill is one of the world's most affable diplomats, but the three-hour car ride tested his enthusiasm for a two-room schoolhouse. Yet, when we arrived, the Haitians' explosion of energy, sense of achievement, and pride of ownership was infectious. The entire town was there to celebrate the school raising that they shared. Hope was returning.

In Hinche, several towns came together to improve an impassable road, cutting travel time and wear on vehicles. None had been willing to move ahead on their own—what would be the point? With our seed funding that incentivized cooperation, the towns' leaders found a common solution.

In little more than two years, more than 600 groups built or improved school buildings, at an average U.S. subsidy of close to $3,000.
So that Haitians could see where the resources came from, we posted
budgets and funding at each site. The designs were always modest, and
in almost every case the project fit the community's ability to pay a
teacher, afford books, and establish a baseline operation. Many of the
schools the Haitians built would not pass U.S. inspections, but they
improved the students' situations.

The Haitians knew it was about their futures—and the little we had
done recognized that core fact. Too often the work that Americans do
in conflict zones reflects our own sense of purpose—a formula for long-
term responsibility and diminished local advancement. A peaceful future is only secure if the local people own it.

In every case, we asked something of all parties. The "process became the product," since the way people undertook the projects was
central to the goal of changing the politics of Haiti. [11] We were agnostic
about schools versus water versus a toll system to repair the local roads;
what we insisted upon was an open and pluralistic way of doing business. Though the Haitians completed more than 1,000 local projects,
our measure of success was the thousands of Haitians who had taken
ownership of a community need and engaged with fellow citizens to
address it.

6.

Considering the importance of policing, we almost never get it right. In
the late fall of 1994, we started with several advantages in Haiti.

Former New York City police commissioner Ray Kelly, an exemplary career officer, was leading a group of more than 400 international
police monitors, funded by the State Department, the first visible reassurance for a citizenry that had nowhere to go when a crime occurred.
It was clear that interim policing was necessary and the monitors provided that.

In one celebrated instance, Kelly was walking in Port au Prince's
downtown when a crowd chased a market thief into a building. The
gathered mob called upon Kelly to enforce the law. Wasting no time,
the commissioner rushed into the building, apprehended the bandit,

and brought him out in handcuffs to a cheering throng. The Haitians wanted justice, and the arrest suggested a new way.

At the same time, Kelly noted, "You can't police someone else's country. The Haitians have to do it themselves."[12] That would prove to be a daunting challenge. As the *Chicago Tribune* noted at the time, the Haitian police "viewed their role as keeping the lid on the nation's restive poor and illiterate masses. Through brute force and terrorism, they almost succeeded." The country had never had a police force under civilian leadership.[13]

Among Kelly's first steps was to change the visible identifiers of the existing police. All over Haiti, repainted mustard-yellow stations became a light blue. A major part of the rebranding included new uniforms, which the United States would contribute. Somewhere in the bowels of the U.S. government, the color of the uniforms became a contentious issue. Kelly had advocated for a dark blue, much like his beloved New York police. Time went by as Haiti waited. With a major event in the second city of Cap-Haitien only days away, what would the police force wear? Finally, during a meeting in the ambassador's conference room at the U.S. embassy, a colleague burst in and announced, "I come with the rarest of Washington commodities: a decision. Navy blue!"

Nevertheless, Washington had not thought of everything. Who would pay to have the pants hemmed in Cap-Haitien? The senior talent in the meeting made an executive decision: we would pass the hat among ourselves and spare the delay.

Other progress advanced. Prisons began to function and international monitors went on joint patrols with the Haitian police and undertook initial retraining.

Building trust in the new police force was harder than changing appearances. Citizens remembered individual cops and their prior abuses. They chased officers away, plundered police stations, and took up vigilante justice. A spontaneous public outcry directed at the seeming empowerment of the old police marked that first event in Cap-Haitien. New building and uniform colors could not cover the history.

Despite glitches, the police monitor program was a success because of Kelly, the reassuring presence of hundreds of professionals from many countries, and the pairing of existing Haitian police with international counterparts. The single, biggest contributor was the welcome of the Haitian people: they wanted a change and they saw the monitors as an important start.

Within months, the State Department began a much larger program that sought a comprehensive reinvention of the police. It was designed and then overworked in Washington, and had several resulting major weaknesses: a centralized national police force versus one that was more localized; a recruiting model that failed to reach more deeply into the existing populace; a single training site; an artificial ceiling of 5,000 police;[14] and insufficient funding to maintain equipment and retain recruits.

How might we have made more progress on this tough issue? Most countries have a national force, but policing is one of the best places to seek decentralized solutions. It is hard to build a central police force anywhere on earth. Better to start with smaller, dispersed experiments in a few cities. Each might have national standards, plus its own over-sight and requirements, but expanding local leadership and citizen in-volvement is vital. There will still be a bell curve of good, average, and bad forces, but improvement can come faster from local accountability and sharing what works across forces. An added benefit is that the national force will no longer be part of a political takeover.

7.

"All Haiti needs is a new military, political and economic class," a jaunty Salesian priest told us early on. He laughed at the thought and was amused that we imagined it possible.

Of course, time has been kinder to his view than to ours. Even before the 2010 earthquake that leveled so much of the country, Haiti was on a winding path. After Aristide returned to the presidency in 1994, he served only 14 months—less than half of his elected time. Aristide, the champion of the poor and oppressed, never seemed to find a governance agenda. The enormity of the challenges facing Haiti over-whelmed him and other leaders, who all lacked the tools to address them. Aristide never had the opportunity to learn how to govern before Haiti rushed back into an election campaign.

The country never recaptured the momentum of change from that first free and fair election of 1990. Aristide would return as president from 2001 until a tiny rebellion chased him from the country in 2004.

Haiti's government started to offer a vision and define strategies for growth and poverty reduction in 2007, reform in 2009, and national recovery and development after the earthquake in March 2010, but they neglected state-building.

Then, the earthquake destroyed much of Port au Prince. The quake, along with hurricanes and tropical storms in recent years, killed more than 300,000 people, injured an equal number, and displaced 1.3 million. A massive cholera epidemic struck in 2010, killing several thousand more and paralyzing the recovery. The earthquake beat down Rene Préval, who ended his second term as president in 2011 unable to make decisions and subject to the pettiest of provocations.

The United States was inconsistent and little help during this time. We allowed a small gang of rebels to truncate Aristide's second term, and then jumped in with a fulsome effort after the earthquake. Still, after the earthquake, the Associated Press reported "that only 20 of 1,583 U.S. contracts for recovery aid went to Haitian-run enterprises (worth $4.3 million out of $267 million)."[15] While Haitians are starting to matter in the politics of Florida and New York, there is no clear direction from the diaspora.

In the international community, Haiti is the "Republic of NGOs." More than 10,000 nongovernmental organizations have stepped into the governing void, but with gaps in coordination, no unified approach, and no central authority, progress remains spotty. Much like our efforts in the 1990s, good work in one place can vanish into quicksand.

Somehow, the mix of interventions, generous assistance, invasive diplomacy, and disregard does not come together to improve Haiti's prospects. Yes, it will always be a work in progress, but with the full engagement of Haiti's people, the promise is achievable—something that America can help to make possible.

It may be tempting to dismiss the entire country as irredeemable. However, there have been good works happening all along. Motivating a resourceful and resilient people is always better than a foreign transplant. There is promising work, even if broader events overwhelm it. The key is to find it, nurture it, and give it every chance to bloom.

8. THE LESSONS OF THE 1990S

The 1990s confirmed that war will find you. Even in the midst of American reluctance, denial, and delay, the conflicts of Bosnia, Rwanda, and Haiti became our business. For different reasons, those three countries came to dominate the national security community's attention—however belated the focus.

The shocking lack of preparation and the awkwardness of our responses highlighted political divisions and the weak state of existing institutions. At the same time, the burgeoning number of conflicts and the near vacuum of those eager to step forward allowed for a freer hand of peacebuilding experiments, innovations, and initiatives. Frustrations with conventional responses grew and there was a modest amount of funding available to test ideas and build models.

It became clear that there was a need for a new kind of assistance, focused on political issues and stability for the long term. The established fields of diplomacy, long-term development, and humanitarian response left a gap in violent, complex emergencies.

Critical building blocks appeared for application to today's conflicts. The following section will draw three major lessons, from the broadest level to the workings on the ground.

I. Start Early, Accelerate Your Learning, and Prepare the Political Will.

"Awful situations have a way of leading to violence." This should not be a shock. One of America's few public intellectuals in elected office, New York's U.S. senator Daniel Patrick Moynihan, pointed out that "there are today just eight states on earth which both existed in 1914 and have not had their form of government changed by violence since then."[16]

The earlier we recognize the volatility of a situation, the greater the choices to mitigate or redirect. Sober and timely preparation does not automatically lead to intervention—it should provide a range of alternatives.

Conflicts are consuming events and even a superpower cannot be effective as a dilettante. Immersion is required. There are many ways to do it, but a surplus of humility is desirable. To the many rules of engagement that policymakers have developed, we might consider the following: "If the U.S. does not know 100 people in a place, please do not send any soldiers." That simple dictum might have kept us out of some of the biggest disasters in America's history.

You would think it safe to assume that before the United States gets into a foreign engagement, it has a good understanding of the other country—its political dynamics, religious or ethnic fault lines, economic interests, alliances, culture, history, and myths. That was not the case in a series of U.S. failures where we lacked a modicum of local insights. True, Washington is crowded with experts on virtually every place on earth, but their on-the-ground understanding is often out of date, especially in complex, fast-moving conflicts. Worse, experts often shut out others from the non-policy world, stifling expansive thinking.

The cardinal sin of conflict problem-solving is a failure to know the place and its people. On several notable occasions, ignorance dominated U.S. action. What we find in those cases is a quagmire.

That need not be the way. Learning and engaging is not an exotic art. There are many time-honored ways to improve understanding, even in the most fragile environments. If we can take these methods to heart, our work will get better. If we do not, the odds of success are daunting.

James Surowiecki makes the case that combining dozens of individual, independent voices is more likely to produce a valuable insight or conclusion than any one person or even expert. He argues that diversity and a common desire or ambition produce better decisions. In many ways, these are the essentials of pluralism: free markets, open societies, and democracy—just the elements we seek to promote.[17]

When I received my regular intelligence briefings at the State Department, I would often ask the briefers, "How confident are you in these findings?" The best ones would reply, "Two to three on a scale of ten—with ten being high." This kind of modesty is welcome in a Washington where so many conversations start with, "The fact of the matter is . . ."

Our work in the 1990s set in motion several key principles.

Listen to learn. Whatever you think you know, it is not enough. This is not about perfect information; it is about constant learning. In fluid situations, change is a given, so be expansive and inclusive.

Call upon a wide range of people and sources, at length and in an iterative fashion. Build upon what the last person said. You must avoid jumping to conclusions and check your biases often. Wait for the wisdom to emerge and germinate. No one has a view of the whole, so the pieces will only come together with care.

The best way to do that is to get on the ground and to let it wash over you. Context is king and having a feeling for a place—its history, myths, humor, and favored narratives—is vital.

The premier conflict researchers of the era, Bob and Cindy Gersony, recognized the need to immerse in intense field analytical work. Deploying to war zones for three months or more, they would interview hundreds of local people to make breakthrough findings. Through iterative conversations, they created replicable insights that set American policy in constructive directions. It was never enough for them to describe a situation—they always offered affirmative steps that the United States should take.

Engaging with local citizens should animate our work, often suggesting possibilities, raising deep-seated reservations, or imagining a better way. Try to understand what is motivating those who will be most responsible for turning things around. Active listening and conversations that build on prior discussions, often one on one, many times with smaller groups, provide openings. Insights come from the most unexpected places, suggesting ways to make an impossible problem addressable.

Listen; seek out a collective wisdom and resist the consensus view. Beware the urge to rush to judgment or to be the first person with the answer. The only way to capture the wisdom of the crowds or the weight of the evidence is to expand the observation circle well beyond the usual players. Sometimes it is a telling detail—or the opening to a larger idea.

Be prepared for the experts to have it wrong. Even with an in-depth understanding of the community, it is hard to sort out a situation.

Once you are in an acquisitive frame of mind, the insights will accrue. In Rwanda, the accumulation of decades of victimization was undeniable. From Haiti, we saw that the only way to escape exploitation was to flee—even if it meant drowning on a perilous sail to Florida. In Bosnia, Rwanda, and elsewhere, we saw messianic leaders who accepted apocalyptic results as the natural extension of their egotistical histories.

In every conflict situation, America must reside in the acceptance of complexities and the building of relationships. Without those key attributes, we will not be a trusted partner. If we are not trusted, the burden becomes ours and the United States will not succeed.

However difficult the challenge, it is the hope of success that will capture the imagination of America's citizenry. This is not an abstract idea. Our public wants engaged political leaders, informed and forward looking. Political will is essential in a democracy—with the full involvement and shared sacrifices of many.

II. Capture the Political Essence and Acknowledge That Security Is the Precondition for Progress.

At the heart of every conflict is a political train wreck, dysfunction, or history of maltreatment. Victimization is prominent on most sides, so respect and trust are rare commodities.

A deep-seated curiosity about the politics of a situation is fundamental to making progress. This is politics writ large, the combination of economics, governance, sociology, anthropology, and more, brought together to better understand how things get done in a conflict place. There may well be an invisible hand, in the form of a handful of ruling families or a general, but for the United States to be helpful we must appreciate those undercurrents. Wars may disturb and shake up existing relationships but a never-ending search for additional insights is required to encourage solutions. Anyone working in a conflict country must appreciate the gestalt of the place.

In places like the Balkans, we must resist the temptation to move to a "favorite" model. As the oft-cited author of the *Black Lamb and Grey Falcon*, Dame Rebecca West, observed, outsiders—unable to contemplate that everyone was in some way cruel to everyone else—picked a pet group as the innocents and all others as guilty.

After absorbing the patterns, rhythms, and feeling of a place, the next challenge is to see how the people can increase their influence. War zones are not targets for a return to the "way things were." Welcome the disruption of familiar practices. The status quo stinks in a violence-wracked place. Change is required and the best opportunity is to increase the role of an often-excluded population. Invest in those who are comfortable with change. Challenge political conventions and experiment with small pilots until you find something that works.

Find ways to jump the obstacles and the players you appear to be stuck with. Mass media, including social media, is a powerful tool for reaching the public. Reliable information, often visual, is critical, so find ways to disseminate it. Remember that a little liquidity goes a long way, such as in the housing rehabilitation experiment in Bosnia.

Seek out new partners, often people who have not enjoyed political prominence but have proven themselves in other ways. Women, young people, and faith and business leaders are promising and have seldom caused the mess. Together they are also a majority. In most conflicts, there is a "silenced majority" of women, youth, and others who must be mobilized for change to stick.

In Haiti, the exclusion of the vast majority of citizens from the political process was the fundamental concern. Unleashing that potential was, and remains, central to that nation's progress.

Haiti confirms the belief that a reversal of fortune will take more than resourceful people, good intentions, and money. They will help, but local politics must reflect a range of players.

The experiences of the 1990s showed that the best way to expand the political influence of average citizens was to focus on the foundational freedoms of movement, speech, and assembly. Accepted documents such as the Universal Declaration of Human Rights provide a basis for those discussions that is not U.S.-centric. With these in place, elections and governmental reforms are possible. Too often, the technocratic exercises of holding an election or creating new programs or agencies of government preceded the securing of those most basic freedoms.

Our experience with the Women in Transition Initiative in Rwanda was a felicitous blend: it created a partnership between a neglected population and a new ministry with a perceptive and well-placed leader—in the service of a country that was adamant about change.

All of this assumes that people feel safe. Without that, none of us will move on to other parts of our lives. Individual progress is possible, but societal advancement will not happen.

Haiti began to open up when the army and police no longer enabled the *Tonton Macoutes'* intimidation of the populace. In Bosnia, the peace agreements would follow the ethnic hollowing out of the country, but the post-accord removal of violence depended on the presence of international police and soldiers.

The end of the 100-day genocide in Rwanda brought a degree of peace—though disturbances continued in border areas. Even as we funded 15 women's farmer associations in the Kanama commune of Rwanda, next to so many of the *genocidaires* in the Congo, it was clear that personal safety was paramount. As the president of one organization told us, "During the last two months, we have been able to sleep in our own houses and have not been awakened by gun shots during the night. Now that you have provided us the means to buy good planting seeds, we pray for peace so that we can plant, harvest and provide for our families."[18] The new government of Rwanda was able to deliver security in even the most remote regions—one reason that the country has moved ahead, though political problems remain.

The people that America sends to work in conflict settings must combine the lead skills of the different dominant professions. A desirable mix is the political acuity of a good diplomat, the longer-range vision of a development professional, and the action orientation of a humanitarian. If the civilians bring those skills, then the military can focus on its demanding job, making the place safe. We need the combination of interpretive wisdom and life-protecting guarantees that will allow conflict countries to reverse their ill fortune.

This lesson has gone unheeded in Iraq and Afghanistan and elsewhere, dooming massive efforts to rebuild countries in the midst of daily violence.

III. Accept the Uniqueness of Every Situation, Seek Out Local Opportunities, and Customize Your Response.

When you begin to understand the politics and the people better, you also see their capabilities. Conflict settings are trauma zones. Established relationships are gone and everyone lives through frightening, grotesque acts. Bullies and thugs have gained prominence. Violence and corruption dominate.

It is time to understand your limitations. You have seldom caused the conflict so this is no time to take charge of it. You can help, but the people of the place will need to be responsible and accountable going forward. Trust them to exceed expectations.

Be prepared to take a pass—the situation is not always ripe. If you jump in, find ways to catalyze the locals—with ideas, funding, and strong moral support. Try to avoid foreign ownership.

A case in point was Haiti's collapsed justice system. For a brief moment, a crusading minister of justice sought to make dramatic changes. Appointed by President Aristide in 1991 and continued in office after Cedras's coup, Guy Malary pursued reform: separating the army from the police, installing civilian control, and preparing for the return of the elected president. Malary's assassination outside of a church in the midday sun on October 14, 1993, with his driver and bodyguard, ended progress.

In many of these hot spots, there is not a deep bench of talent. People like Guy Malary are singular figures, almost irreplaceable. When we come across them, our hopes rise and we project our dreams for their country onto them. They become the center of our attention, in effect our "dear hearts." That is our wish and it often makes their jobs even harder and more dangerous.

When they are killed in cold blood, the change moment is altered for years: no one is standing by, ready to take over, and the ambition to do this work is wiped out.

That is what we found when we held a first meeting at Haiti's Justice Ministry in October 1994. Malary's successor was an aged judge with no agenda. When a sign-up sheet circulated, there was no way to make a copy in the ministry. One of the few staff present went up the street. A probate judge from New Jersey, in Haiti as an army reservist, became the senior advisor to the minister and did good work. However, the moment had passed with Malary's death.

Technocratic solutions blossomed from international capitals: a new law school, streamlined constitution, and the training of police in Puer-to Rico. All seemed so otherworldly.

How could we stay focused on making things better right away?

To imagine that these circumstances will produce a new system of government, a functioning political process, or other greater good is often overreaching. Yes, there is potential, and we must be sure that the help we offer fits the context and appreciates the beaten-down nature of the people. Just because the United States is there does not solve the core problems.

If the twisted wreckage of Bosnia, Haiti, and post-genocide Rwanda produce numerous possibilities, then there will be opportunities in the most desperate circumstances. The larger problem is to focus and make choices. Build locally through experiments and pilots—take what is present versus importing or overbuilding. In a place where everything is needed, find "the priority of priorities."

Seize upon them, test their efficacy, and be prepared to build out if they work or to cease and desist if they fail. Too often, those who want to help go in big. That large initial investment of funds and ego lead to a "too big to fail" culture that wastes resources and lives on ideas that once might have seemed worthy.

Failure is frequent. The best way to stay humble is to accept this likelihood, and to ensure that there is always a minimal return should the larger enterprise fail. Early, modest tests help to reduce the cost or waste of failure—and then to accept their results.

Be comfortable with risk and figure out ways to moderate it. After all, these are the scariest places on earth.

The 1990s provided bountiful lessons: be selective; engage and appreciate the context; focus on the central political issues; bring fast, early, and agile resources to bear; experiment with pilots and tests; decentralize decision-making; inspire a culture of ownership and responsibility; prepare to adjust direction; and trust the locals. We saw this in Bosnia, Rwanda, and Haiti.

The United States took a step forward with the creation of new offices and innovative practices. It did not "transform" Bosnia, Rwanda, or Haiti, but it catalyzed change and gave local citizens a chance to make it on their own. None became "shining cities on a hill," but all moved beyond the chaos of violence.

Somehow, we did not learn and the results in Afghanistan and Iraq would confirm that.

III

The Crucible of the New Century

I.

America entered the 21st century with a perspective on the growing violence and disorder, balanced between expectations and limitations. From the Gulf War through Bosnia, Rwanda, and Haiti, to NATO's war with Serbia, the United States captured valuable experience and exhibited "reserved behavior."[1]

Critics saw the 1990s as a loss, a time when America allowed dangerous forces to foment. They puzzled over why "American power was both unsurpassed and questioned"[2] and sought greater closure in places like Iraq, where the vanquished dictator, Saddam Hussein, remained entrenched in Baghdad after a war with the United States.

While a few remained obsessed with Iraq, David Halberstam described the Gulf War as "without real resonance" for most Americans. Four days of land combat by a professional army touched "few American homes." He described it as a "virtual war" that left "an aura of good feeling."[3]

Throughout the 1990s results lacked clarity. Difficult conflicts, with ambiguous beginnings and dissatisfying endings, marked the landscape. Americans wondered, "Why is this happening and why is so much left unclear?" Wars did not produce clear "winners and losers." Even when the United States engaged, the consequences remained distant.

One complication for both operators and the public is that we lacked post-conflict plans and ways to measure progress in the growing complexity. Did we agree on our ambitions? How would we know if the results are satisfactory? Could we adapt and change direction if we identified failings? Without definitions for success and failure, America was poised to stumble.

With the 2001 arrival of the George W. Bush administration in Washington, the United States was set to embark in a more robust direction. Harvard's Joseph Nye would worry about American "declinism" in 1990 and "triumphalism" in 2001.[4]

2.

When I started working at USAID in 1994, the difficulty of measuring progress was a popular discussion. Humanitarians saved many lives, but often the same ones for years. Development experts saw reductions in poverty indicators, but preferred to have their work reviewed over decades. Health programs surged as plentiful data confirmed direct impact. Democracy initiatives struggled as elections held and people trained did not translate into greater freedoms.

Worries about "results-based programming" did not produce much help; rather, an industry. Intrusive, expensive, and non-enlightening, the evaluations met resistance. Inspectors general blossomed but offered audit-like functions versus broader strategic critiques or directional changes for management.

Postmortems of disasters or of serious underperformance became the most telling international evaluations. Often led by respected figures, the reports that gained the most attention focused on well-known cases with independence, unsparing candor, and honesty. Driven by the desire never to repeat the same errors, they offered a cleansing effect. Two examples come to mind.

Following cataclysmic U.N. failures in the fall of Srebrenica and the 1994 Rwandan genocide, Secretary General of the United Nations Kofi Annan encouraged independent reviews of each. The reports set the highest standard of insight and disclosure, including Annan's own shortcomings.[5] They appeared in 1995 and 1999.

The Fall of Srebrenica is a brutal retelling of how Serb forces within the U.N.-protected zones exterminated 20,000 Muslim Bosnian civilians in mid-July 1995.[6]

While at UNHCR, I was involved in the second example. After Serbian threats and forces chased Kosovars from their homes in 1999, near-catastrophic conditions resulted at the Macedonia border and elsewhere. Individual nations, including the United States, responded well, but disappointment in the United Nations' refugee agency persisted. Several donor countries asked for, and U.N. High Commissioner for Refugees Sadako Ogata agreed to initiate, a full review of the agency's preparedness and response to the Kosovo crisis. Many inside of UNHCR did not welcome the intrusion.

The leader of that effort, Astri Suhrke, insisted on the independence and integrity of the process and succinctly stated to UNHCR's Executive Committee meeting, "In difficult circumstances, UNHCR did not do well." Faulted were UNHCR's anticipation, provision of emergency services, staff deployment, and more.

The candor of the report and the value of their recommendations extended to the team's view of international evaluation methods:

> Most of the current evaluations of the Kosovo emergency are single-agency or single-organization focused, and therefore may not generate a comparative perspective and may lose cross-cutting issues. The evaluators would encourage joint evaluation of responses to major emergencies, including comparison of multilateral versus bilateral approaches.[7]

Thorough and professional, the report was defining and yet the gaps continued.

While the reports disclosed the nature of the United Nations' problem and served as catalysts for change, the institutional incapacity to make dramatic progress remained. *A More Secure World: Our Shared Responsibility*, the Report of the Secretary General's High-level Panel on Threats, Challenges, and Change, resulted in 2004.[8] Its 16 distinguished world leaders emphasized the growing interdependence of a tumultuous world and the need to rethink the use of force, the structure of the Security Council, and the lack of tools for dealing with post-conflict peacebuilding—a gap between peacemaking, peacekeeping, and development. The secretary general wrote, "Our institutions must overcome their narrow preoccupations and learn to work across the whole range of issues, in a concerted fashion."9

Even when the studies are clear and thoughtful, their contribution to reforming our institutions is in doubt. They seldom help to prevent a catastrophe. Recognizing the difficulty of knowing a place and our impact on a conflict, I grew eager during the early days of the Afghanistan and Iraq Wars to build a holistic, people-first way to measure progress.

Both conflicts offered significant opportunities. From the outset, America's efforts in Afghanistan and Iraq set aside lessons from the prior decade while making new mistakes. Once again, America underestimated the enormity of the challenges, made a careless entrance, and failed to deliver joint, integrated approaches. Our efforts to transform entire regions and elevate societies into modernity bordered on utopian or even messianic ambitions.

America's two consuming wars of the 2000s cried out for course corrections, adjustments, and fresh strategies. In the case of Iraq, I began to draft a blueprint in the fall of 2002 for a postwar reconstruction—six months before the U.S. invasion. The belief that the sacrifices of war deserved the investments of peace anchored our work. We also worried that absent a post-conflict plan, the United States could be stuck.

6

IRAQ

The Enormity of the Task

I.

The drums of war began pounding in the Washington summer of 2002. Iraq's dictator, Saddam Hussein, had crossed the line of civilization and President Bush and Vice President Cheney were agitating to end his 23-year rule. The buildup to the war produced shocking disclosures of Saddam's reign of terror and news of America's preparations.

While unsure about the purpose of the war, I was certain that the United States would spend every effort preparing for a military triumph—without imagining the more difficult task of restarting post-conflict Iraq. A small team at CSIS began to draft a blueprint for rebuilding Iraq. The great advantage of the think-tank world is the ability to address, in a timely fashion, the gaping holes that Washington's big institutions always provide. My own experience presaged that there would be little preparation for the post-combat phase.

Not knowing when the fighting would begin, I believed that a practical, postwar plan should be in the marketplace by Thanksgiving. It was more complicated than expected and we began to share our plan, *A Wiser Peace: An Action Strategy for a Post-Conflict Iraq*, in January 2003. In an effort to gain widespread distribution fast, we sat down with two leading journalists, of the *Washington Post* and the *Wall Street Journal*. They recognized the value. Their editors responded much as the administration, saying it was too early since the war had not yet started. Soon it would be too late.

We proposed "a promising future for a prosperous Iraq at peace with itself and its neighbors."[1] The focus was on a nonintimidating environment, open participation, rule of law, and relief from the financial obligations of Saddam Hussein's regime, which we estimated at a crippling $360 billion. We argued that Iraq could not produce enough oil to service the debt and that a global restructuring would be necessary.

A Wiser Peace was an early prototype, more a Model T than a Tesla. Still, what distinguished it was the absence of a competing public plan. While the State Department had convened 17 Future of Iraq roundtables around multiple subjects, they gained no traction in the DOD-dominated run up to the war. Snubbed by Cheney and Rumsfeld, State's 2,500 pages of ideas fell by the wayside—not even becoming part of the debate.

At the last moment, the Pentagon started to prepare for the postwar period. Retired Lieutenant General Jay Garner, who distinguished himself in the earlier Gulf War in 1990 and in the aftermath in the Kurdish north, began to pull together an interim administration for Iraq. Visitors to his DOD office found few people and little structure. Within days, Garner would be in Kuwait, holding meetings and planning on the run. When he arrived in Iraq with 20 aides on April 21, violence and looting plagued cities and the United States was not providing public safety. A cadre of inexperienced political loyalists would show up to help Garner in Baghdad. Those with prior experience would be disheartened.

Operation Iraqi Freedom, fought between March 20 and May 1, would be a triumph of modern military warfare. The postwar difficulties became nigh impossible thanks to the near total absence of a plan.

Our plan began to attract public attention in April, after the war was two weeks underway. A *New York Times* column by Princeton economist Alan Krueger said the report "should be required reading" and drew special attention to the great burden of debt that hung over Iraq.

On May 1, 2003, President George W. Bush spoke to the nation from the deck of the USS *Abraham Lincoln* and declared "an end to major combat operations." While he stated, "Our mission continues" and "We have difficult work to do in Iraq," the presence of a "Mission Accomplished" banner led to some premature euphoria.

American and allied forces had swept through Iraq in less than two months between March and May of 2003 with 138 fatalities and 514 soldiers injured. Senior officials predicted a brief postwar experience, paid for by Iraq's oil revenues.

Reports of recurring violence began at the time of President Bush's televised address. As often happens, the news did not come from official sources—rather from soldiers, a few journalists who stayed on after the invasion, or from NGOs, the United Nations, or other independent visitors. While the short-lived war against Saddam Hussein had ceased, there now was a perplexing, decentralized series of events that created a broad feeling of insecurity. Oil pipelines exploded, roadside bombs disrupted travel, and assassinations killed people that the United States was counting on, including senior religious leaders.

There were additional troubling signs. Where had Saddam gone? What happened to the vaunted Republican guards? "Who is in charge?" replaced the euphoria of Saddam's removal.

In late May, a long-serving member of the House Appropriations Committee, Representative Frank Wolf, traveled to Iraq to see how things were progressing. The Pentagon was not yet encouraging official visitors so Wolf found his way into Iraq with an NGO. In a three-day visit, he was convinced that the situation on the ground was not positive. Upon his return to Washington, the Republican congressman from the Northern Virginia suburbs reported on his concerns to his constituents.

As part of a 27-member high-level commission on post-conflict reconstruction at CSIS, Wolf had immersed himself in the subject for the prior year. Not an alarmist, Wolf contacted his friend, Secretary of Defense Donald Rumsfeld, and suggested that the situation deserved "a second opinion." He cited concerns about security, "the linchpin to winning the peace in Iraq," and said the Iraqis "must be an equal partner in the process." Wolf also supported funding up to $500,000 for local U.S. commanders so that they could solve practical problems fast.[2]

In light of the bipartisan committee's report and our prior study, Wolf recommended that CSIS lead the review. CSIS's president, John Hamre, asked me as the leader of the Post-Conflict Reconstruction Project to pull together a team to visit Iraq within a few weeks. Once it was clear that Ambassador Jerry Bremer would welcome our group of five, arrangements moved quickly.

Ours would be an independent report that would not be subject to government review. Hamre insisted that it be constructive with actionable ideas.

2.

There was no feeling of normalcy when we landed in Iraq on June 25. After a brief military flight from Kuwait to Baghdad's airport, where there was no commercial travel, we boarded a minibus for a concerning ride into the Green Zone, a completely shut-off part of the city. Otis Redding was the Detroit bus driver's sound track, but "Sittin' on the Dock of the Bay" provided modest comfort along the exposed highway into the city. The U.S. military had already removed trees and bushes alongside the road that might hide attackers. The high-rise Al-Rasheed Hotel near Saddam's former Republican Palace, now the headquarters of the U.S. operation, was a bunkhouse for American soldiers and visitors with limited water and energy, though more than the rest of the city. We checked in, though it felt like a target.

Inside the palace, there was a frenetic level of activity, but no clear sense of direction. Combined with an absence of air-conditioning in most of the building and 110-degree days, the hundreds of Americans were stifled. Few had any knowledge of Iraq, the language, people, or society, which compounded their almost total inexperience in a complex conflict situation. Engaging figures showed up, like former New York City police commissioner Bernard Kerik, but they seemed out of place. Separated from events on the ground, America's top officials appeared to be "caged talent."[3]

As we traveled around Iraq, we saw how hard it was to get out of the U.S. government headquarters inside of Saddam's former Republican Palace. Surrounded by a mass of inexperienced people in a barricaded chunk of central Baghdad real estate, the most seasoned "often complained about the palace's debilitating isolation, probably the single most important factor in the occupation's short-term failure."[4]

One exception was retired ambassador Hume Horan, a "storied Arabist who had served as an ambassador to five countries and completed tours in Iraq, Jordan, Saudi Arabia, and Sudan."[5] Horan was one of our hosts as we drove in a five-car, gun-toting, zigzagging caravan to the

Shiite holy cities of Najaf and Karbala south of Baghdad. He was only in Iraq for six months this time and was "trying to unsnarl Shiite politics. It was a formidable job and, of the Americans here, probably only Horan could have tackled it,"[6] wrote the late great journalist Anthony Shadid. Like Shadid, we saw that Hume "knew what he was talking about." We also saw that he liked to hear Iraqis speak.

Horan developed a respect for the Shiite leaders around the most senior figure, Grand Ayatollah Ali Sistani, and encouraged them to deal with their own internal divisions as a "family problem." The United States sought the containment of the rabble-rousing Muqtada Sadr, but Horan made clear that we were not "making great conversions." He said, "When we reproach them for their passivity, we don't have five to ten thousand people at our doorstep."[7]

Life in the Green Zone had a surreal quality and it presented a daily annoyance to Iraqis. In a July 2003 focus group in Baghdad, locals complained to us of the shutting down of entire sections of the city by the United States, with bridges closed, roads barricaded, and traffic disrupted. "We could get closer to Saddam than we can the coalition. He shut down a quarter of the city. The Americans have doubled that."[8] Our taking over the despot's palaces also rankled, as did the long waits Iraqis endured to enter.

Car rides to other parts of the city were few and had a Dukes of Hazzard quality. Wherever we went during our two weeks in Iraq, the sense of imminent danger was constant. Unlike the dozen other conflict places I had worked in by then, Iraq in the early summer of 2003 felt like something awful could happen at any moment. I found myself saying "Vietnam" when I meant Iraq.

Our host, Ambassador Bremer, gave the team full access to his people, made sure that we were able to visit many of the key areas of the country,[9] and asked for a full brief before we left in July. Bremer arrived on May 11 as the administrator of the Coalition Provisional Authority and had outsized responsibilities in a country with no clear government and a large U.S. military presence. Some thought of his role as similar to MacArthur in Japan, referring to Bremer as the viceroy. There was little evidence that Bremer's distinguished career, much of it shaped as a trusted aide for two secretaries of state and in ambassadorial assignments to Europe, prepared him for this chaos-filled moment.

Still, Bremer appeared to relish the challenge. At our first late-evening meeting, the ambassador had just returned from the inaugural concert of the restored Baghdad Symphony, a festive celebration that brought out most of the post-Saddam wannabees. He clearly enjoyed the range of the job, the steep learning curve, and the opportunity to make a difference in the toughest challenge on earth. A disciplined and bright individual, Bremer gave it his all—and was overmatched.

Many of the vital, and fateful, decisions of those early days were under the watchful eye of President Bush and U.K. prime minister Tony Blair. Bremer had frequent video conferences with the two leaders. Combined with the forceful personalities of two determined ideologues, Vice President Cheney and Defense Secretary Rumsfeld, Bremer received plenty of guidance. It is hard to imagine Bremer deciding to abolish the Iraqi military and rid the government of all Baath Party members, two of the most controversial early decisions, without the approval of the others. Those decisions made a difficult job even tougher—and were among the choices that the United States had finessed in Japan and Germany.

These were bullish times and Bremer was on the cape. I have often thought of him as a cautionary figure: no matter how talented you might be, there are situations that exceed your prior exposure, grasp, and abilities. How do you not become a victim of circumstances?

At the end of our 11-day visit, we had visited half of Iraq's 18 provinces and spoken to more than 250 people. We reported to Bremer. It could have been a wake-up call. The situation was too fraught for us to be anything but direct. His staff expressed concern, worried how Bremer would react, and told us that we might only have 15 to 20 minutes. We spoke of a "campaign of sabotage and ongoing resistance" and said, "The next 12 months will be decisive; the next three months are crucial to turning around the security situation, which is volatile in key parts of the country. All players are watching closely to see how resolutely the coalition will handle this challenge."[10]

Of the seven key recommendations, we highlighted these: American soldiers would need Iraqi and international supplements right away in order "to address the need for increased street-level presence in key conflictive areas"; avoid overloading the just-formed Iraqi Governing Council "with too many controversial issues. The natural desire to draw anger away from the coalition by putting an Iraqi face on the most difficult decisions would need to be balanced with a realistic assessment of what the council can successfully manage." Near-term jobs and activity would be essential, even if they required massive public works projects and reviving inefficient industries. And the job was so big that only decentralization would work.[11]

He listened and asked questions. On a couple of our insights, it appeared that he might not agree or believed that the situation was better than we had observed. In one instance, we mentioned that the daily Iraqi newscasts that the United States established and financed needed to be more independent, aggressive in their coverage, and more practical in the information provided. The profound changes in culture that we unleashed needed guidance on how to do it. We had even heard that the United States might withdraw its funding because the news was not as favorable to our view as desired. The stifling of a basic freedom that undergirded the U.S. intervention would be disastrous. Recognizing the peril of being misunderstood, I doubled back to reinforce our findings with clearer language. Bremer had too much going on and it was not clear that our message resounded. We left after nearly an hour with a pit in our stomachs.

America was in a tough situation, trying to do too much too fast, without good base knowledge. As the first independent review of the postwar period, the report received full global attention, including a Pentagon-hosted press conference. The review was oft quoted, but not followed.

3.

Circumstances continued to worsen in Iraq. On a September 2003 visit to Baghdad's Central Morgue, Neil MacFarquhar of the *New York Times* described the "grim statistics" of "a terrifyingly lawless twilight zone: 462 people dead under suspicious circumstances . . . in May, some 70 percent from gunshot wounds; 626 in June; 751 in July; 872 in August. By comparison, last year there were 237 deaths in July, one of the highest months, with just 21 from gunfire."[12]

An international poll of Iraq in December 2003 showed that of 11 institutions tested, public confidence was lowest for the U.S. and U.K. occupation forces, with just 21 percent support. At the same time, 54 percent expressed confidence in local community leaders and 70 percent in Iraq's religious leaders.[13]

In April 2004, almost as many Americans died in that month, 137, as had in the prior year. Those injured grew to 514. Iraqi deaths began to soar. While the U.S. government denied the label, Iraq was in a civil war.

Rumors began to circulate that Ambassador Bremer would be leaving and I grew concerned that his departure might bring forth another "mission accomplished" moment to shape President Bush's reelection narrative in 2004. In light of the devastating events in Iraq, I did not think it fair to say that all was well.

The moment was remindful of a speech given by Vermont's independent-minded Republican senator, George Aiken, early in the Vietnam War. He ruefully suggested that the United States get out of Vietnam and dedicate a fraction of its war spending to a global public relations campaign that declared victory. On October 19, 1966, he said, "The United States could well declare unilaterally that this stage of the Vietnam war is over—that we have 'won' in the sense that our Armed Forces are in control of most of the field and no potential enemy is in a position to establish its authority. . . . Declare victory and get out."[14] While it may well have been the wiser course in Vietnam and in Iraq, the United States did not choose that path.

Anticipating Bremer's and the Coalition Provisional Authority's transfer of sovereignty to an interim Iraqi government on June 30, colleagues and I set out to see if we could measure progress in Iraq from the perspective of the people of the country. I had seen poor polling by the United States in Bosnia and felt that our research needed to be more textured and insightful. A rich blend of quantitative and qualitative data would make that possible.

In developing the model, we determined that the ambition of any intervening international party should be to reach the tipping point: in other words, *to be a positive catalyst for local improvements, enough so that the people of the place have a fighting chance to make it on their own.* We sought to avoid the hubris of external responsibility for the end state.

The initial measurement model for Iraq started with simple goals:

- Could we show the impact on people's lives?

- What information would make a result credible?
- How could we make a rich mix of data digestible for busy and perhaps under-informed decision makers at the highest levels of government?

While we recognized that there was no baseline to build on, we felt that a rich mix of sources could tell us how Iraqis felt in each of the four key pillars of the CSIS Commission's framework: security and public safety, governance and participation, justice and reconciliation, and economic and social well-being. In order to make the model more dynamic and multidisciplinary, we created a tipping point definition for each:

- Security: I feel secure in my home and in my daily activities.
- Governance and Participation: I have a say in how Iraq is run.
- Economic Opportunity: I have a means of income.
- Services: I have access to basic services, such as power, water, and sanitation.
- Social Well-Being: My family and I have access to health care and education.

Within each pillar, a five-tiered hierarchy of human needs allowed our field interviewers to translate what they heard onto a simple x and y grid.

In June, seven trained Iraqi researchers conducted 400 iterative "structured conversations" with more than 700 Iraqis in 15 cities. Combined with six months of data from 60 media outlets, 17 public and official sources, and 16 polls, the information enriched our sense of "achievable goals." With flexible and abundant data, we sorted it in multiple ways to see if relationships existed between issues or regions.

The findings in *Progress or Peril? Measuring Iraq's Reconstruction* presaged troubles ahead. "In every sector we looked at, we saw backward movement in recent months. The goals we articulate are not utopian but rather set out an achievable Iraqi state, with a clear sense of direction, as seen from the perspective of the Iraqi citizen."[15]

Even at that early date, there was troubling evidence of the insecurity felt by Iraqis—and of its huge influence on the other sectors. Initial progress on health and education had reversed by the end of the study, due to people feeling unsafe. A 35-year-old male mechanic in Fallujah said, "Terrorism will never end in Iraq. . . . It is difficult to uproot, since the groups find the political and social climate favorable and a solid base of people believe in their ideals."[16]

Capturing Iraqi Voices reported "modest expectations" and "skeptical optimism." Based on the trends, the report stated, "the optimism appears unrealistic and could dissipate rapidly."[17] With a great deal of information crunched, Iraq was not yet a success. Most of all, Iraqis needed to feel safer.

With the United States bogged down in so many places, from regional disagreements to massive power plant generator projects, a recurring focus of effort became the training of the new Iraqi military. At a CSIS panel, a passing mention was made that the United States was understaffing that mission, our stated top priority. If we could only get half the complement of 400 U.S. trainers to do the most important job in Iraq, what did that say about the rest of our effort?

As the session ended, Eric Schmidt of the *New York Times* pulled me aside. Based at the Pentagon, he had not heard about the shortfall and recognized its import. A few days later, he called back with the official explanation: these were normal rotations, temporary people filled in from the United States, and the problem was overblown. It was not. Shocked by the stock response, I said, "Oh come on, Eric. This isn't the kind of work that can be done by substitutes." To his credit, Eric pursued the facts and showed in a front-page article that in a vital and finite way, the United States was not delivering on a core promise.

With the baseline documentation in place, we followed up with additional reports on Iraq.

4.

"The biggest mistake of the occupation was the occupation itself,"[18] Iraqis often repeated. The United States made no plan, was unprepared to pull off whatever it came up with, stayed much longer than it wanted to, and kept making up ways of measuring progress.

As the war ran on, I heard of a briefing that a top general for the war effort had provided to President George W. Bush in the Oval Office days before the U.S. invasion in March 2003. It was a disturbing memory for the former aide who recounted it. The senior officer had described how U.S. forces planned a swift and decisive march across Iraq, culminating in the seizure of Baghdad. "Shock and awe" bombing followed by a rolling thunder. The president then asked a simple and logical question: "Who will be left behind in each of the villages to run them as we move through?"

The general's response made sense: "Marine lieutenant colonels and a few soldiers." The briefing continued. What shocked the president's staffer was that the general had made up the answer—there was no such plan. At a critical moment on an important question, the president did not get the truth. [19]

Somehow, that became the plan. As we met with U.S. officials in the Shiite holy cities of Hillah, Najaf, and Karbala in the summer of 2003, it was clear that young Marine officers provided whatever authority existed inside of those cities. In many places, there was a Coalition Provisional Authority (CPA) regional outpost, but the soldiers provided the on-the-ground insights and enforcement. As we spoke to one impressive lieutenant colonel, he described a major concern among a bucket of challenges: how to allow, monitor, police, and perhaps control massive public demonstrations in the post-Saddam era. This was an existential question for the small group of Marines, camped in the center of the city, right alongside the area where thousands of Iraqi Shiites gathered. Quantico does not feature a "crowd licensing procedure," yet that adaptation resulted.

Similar experiences took place all over Iraq. A West Point graduate told me of his two Iraq tours as a young officer, starting in the first year. He spoke about being responsible for a town in the northwest of the country, one hour from Mosul, in an area that ISIS would overrun a decade later. After he was there for a few days, his superior officer came for a visit and asked, "Have you stood up a government here yet?"

The young officer did not know this was his responsibility. After a brief moment he asked, "What kind of government should I set up?" Reflecting on his academy and high school courses and memories of Wisconsin, he inquired, "Should it be a strong mayor, town council, or part of a county system?" His boss did not have a clue and left him to go ahead with whatever worked. There would be no further guidance or central model.

Within six weeks of his arrival in a remote part of Iraq, the freshly minted American military officer identified a dozen tribes in his village and asked each of them to send a single representative to a new governing council. Once convened, they decided on the popular election of a new mayor. That all took place and an Iraqi mayor took office—under the watchful eye and care of the U.S. military. The young officer voiced a concern: "I am not sure that he would survive without our presence."

The American's resourcefulness and sense of achievement dominated. He had made the most of the challenge. He also questioned the greater wisdom. If self-governance was going to be important, why had America done so little planning? Did we think we could impose a new system in a strange place in a matter of weeks? Would young military officers be the right people to do this work? As we talked, we both came to the same question: "Could you ever do something like this in the U.S., say in Sheboygan?"[20] We doubted it.

The hubris of America struck us both. It did not get better with time. As the occupation continued, the presence of the U.S. forces became the central concern of many Iraqis. People wanted less violence, they had hoped that the U.S. military could provide a peaceful environment, and when that did not materialize, they lost enthusiasm.

Should America stay or go? How could we measure Iraqi's will? In a January 2005 *New York Times* op-ed, Sheba Crocker, Craig Cohen, and I said there should be a referendum vote in Iraq on just that issue. "The two questions uppermost in the minds of most Iraqis right now are these: how can we be safe? And when are the foreigners going to leave? A referendum gives Iraqis the power to decide these questions themselves in a more straightforward way than sorting through a ballot of 7,000 candidates or waiting for a new constitution to be written and ratified. . . . [A] referendum would show our commitment to empowering the Iraqis. We're not saying we're leaving; we're saying that it's up to the Iraqi people to decide what's best for themselves."[21]

I believe in engaging people in the large questions, especially when defined in clear, understandable terms. The debate on a question of such import would have forced Iraqis to consider critical questions of public safety and governance. An up or down vote in Iraq would have advanced national ownership at just the right moment.

Popular votes are a useful tool for measuring public satisfaction. The outpouring of Iraqi voters on January 30, 2005, for first round legislative elections showed that the desire to determine their own futures ran deep. It had been half a century since Iraqis expressed themselves at the polls, and that day served as an inspiration for all.

As America promoted a series of legislative and constitutional elections throughout 2005, we pursued a technocratic path and missed the opportunity to capture the imagination of a ready people.

When a democracy like the United States stays in another country for more than a few years, it weakens both nations.

5.

Even as we overstay in a conflict zone, America often lacks the most basic skills to succeed.

With a reduction of violence in 2008, America's ambassador to Baghdad, Ryan Crocker, visited a main shopping street to mix it up with the merchants and returning shoppers. Progress was vital to the restoration that the U.S. and Iraqi leadership sought and the public presence of our ambassador was a confidence measure. It was also important to get his direct perspective.

The United States was fortunate to have Crocker there, a thoughtful regional expert, fluent in the language, and with prior service in Iraq. His Haifa Street tour was a success, but I found one element of the news reports troubling. Of several thousand Americans in Iraq, Crocker was among a handful that could operate on their own in the entire country.

Earlier, in the spring of 2007, I had tested the importance of American capabilities as a member of CSIS's Smart Power Commission. As part of my work, I toured four states that would figure prominently in the 2008 elections: Iowa, New Hampshire, South Carolina, and Minnesota. Over two weeks, I asked and listened to 235 people in 35 meetings—from individuals to town hall gatherings to radio talk shows—talk about "smart power." What did they think it should mean and look like and how would it work? We sought out the range of political opinions, from liberals in St. Paul to conservatives at Bob Jones University in Greenville, South Carolina; from students and police chiefs to labor union and business leaders everywhere. Almost all worried that the United States had become arrogant.

When there were more than a few people gathered, I would ask, "If we could spend $500 million to build a large new embassy in Baghdad or the same amount on training 500 Americans to know the language, understand the history, and work in Iraq, which would you choose?" The overwhelming response from every quarter was "prepare 500 Americans to have the street smarts to operate on the ground in a place like Iraq."[22]

The bad news: As I asked the question, the United States was already building one of the largest embassies in the world in Baghdad. Priced at $500 million, it would cost closer to $700 million—and never be staffed with people who could mix it up. Most of those on the compound would provide security. All would be there for a year or less. Few would have the skill sets to operate with the proficiency of Ambassador Crocker.

6.

The Iraq war continues to be troubling. It is the strongest recent argument for a new approach to the way America intervenes in failing states.

For almost seven years, America made huge sacrifices and investments with scant progress. By December 2009, 4,424 American fighters had died in Iraq and another 31,952 had suffered injuries.[23] More than 1,000 civilian employees of the United States and between 100,000 and 500,000 Iraqis lost their lives, with many thousands injured.[24] Four million Iraqis fled their homes. The United States accumulated direct and related costs totaling $3 trillion[25] without any special funding or taxes levied. Our actions weakened the international order, as we interpreted global standards and practices to our own short-term benefit. America's arrogance diminished our global standing. After a formal U.S. military withdrawal on December 18, 2011, America began to claw its way back. It was to be a brief moment.

"Iraq was a war of choice versus a war of reaction," General Stan McChrystal said. "We had from 1990 on to prepare," yet focused on the invasion. We discovered more complexity, worked on "flawed assumptions" about building anew, and thought of ourselves as liberators even as we became occupiers. Once that occurred, "all of the political and economic frustrations came to the forefront and were pasted on us. We just were not prepared for that. . . . [W]e certainly should have thought through the unanticipated consequences of our actions."[26]

The American public despaired at our leaders' inability to solve complex problems. The 17-year war in Afghanistan, our longest in history, would compound the loss of confidence.

7

AFGHANISTAN

Measuring Progress

I.

On October 7, 2001, the United States attacked Afghanistan in response to al-Qaeda's 9/11 jetliner terrorism. It was an initial success.

The Taliban were defeated, a new government installed, constitutions drafted, and *loya jirgas* held. A broad international coalition, including NATO's farthest geographic reach, established a peaceful presence. Tens of thousands of refugees returned from the neighboring countries and humanitarian assistance provided life's essentials to a populace coming out of shock. The World Bank–U.N. Development Program–Asian Development Bank completed a joint preliminary needs assessment that estimated reconstruction costs of Afghanistan for the coming two and a half years would be from $2 billion to $3 billion. Great skill was involved even as we reached back to the traditional military and humanitarian practices.

"The original plan for a post-Taliban Afghanistan called for rapid, transformational nation building."[1] A tougher way forward was inevitable.

From the beginning, we had two competing goals: to fight terrorism and build a lasting democracy. Deals with warlords in pursuit of counterterrorism threatened the idea of a free and open state. Authoritarian behaviors and human rights abuses by friends of the coalition undermined the rule of law. General Dostum, now the vice president of Afghanistan, became a poster child for this inherent contradiction—one that as of 2018 is in its 17th year.

Opposing ambitions showed up in more quotidian ways. On one occasion, the president of Afghanistan's new central bank spoke about the great progress of a new currency, computerized systems, and other state-of-the-art practices. A returning Afghan refugee, who had been teaching accounting at Providence College in Rhode Island for 15 years, he described the promise of the new technocratic model. For an hour, the Washington audience marveled at the progress. As he reached the end of his presentation, we asked a favorite question: "What worries you most?"

His answer told so much about the operating challenges of Afghanistan: "That a warlord will walk into one of my banks on any day and make a withdrawal even though he has never made a deposit."[2] Armed people with advantageous positions could undermine the entire system in a wink.

The central bank example also highlighted the difficulty of measuring progress. By all accounts, there were more trained officials, better systems, clearer accounting, and a path to a modern, international financial institution. The outputs were admirable.

The outcomes were in greater doubt because the broader context of the country remained a captive of the competing forces of the prior two decades. Whether it was the warlords or the Taliban, those who used violence to advance their ways retained excessive influence.

As the United States spent billions of dollars in Afghanistan, my colleagues and I at CSIS expanded our Iraq measure of progress experiment. It was not enough to do good things; we wanted to know what mattered most to people and whether the full-on engagement of America and the international community was making lives better.

In a process that would cost $250,000 per study, my colleagues and I at CSIS engaged dozens of people and thousands of points of information in the design of a new model. Our work would start with an immersion into Afghanistan's daily life. What would we see and how might we measure progress?

2.

High in the snow-covered hills two hours outside of Kabul, the road ended in a tranquil community of 30 or so houses. Our SUV had somehow made it over the nearly impassable final two-mile climb and there in the brilliant morning sun lay a quiet, riverside village. We were there to visit a micro hydro project that was providing the first electricity to the area.

No one was visible, but as we disembarked, a man popped out of the jagged rocks. As we walked to the sluiceways and dams, another appeared and before long, a group had gathered. Our translator, a young Afghan engineering student, quickly engaged them in a lively, jocular exchange and there was little doubt that the arrival of a light or two, some refrigeration, and, inevitably, a television was going to transform this placid place.

Everyone we saw spoke of the wonder of the newly arrived electricity and we enjoyed tea on the patio of a nearby home. Despite the winter cold, the protection of the valley and the warming sun combined with an ornate silver-like tea set to make for a comfortable conversation with our Afghan hosts.

They were pleased with the newfound power and the project seemed to work in almost every way: it was a simple design, easy to maintain, the appropriate scale, great local ownership and oversight, and affordable. It would not require much ongoing outside support and it was making an immediate difference.[3]

We asked about their sense of safety, the local police, any military presence, and recent incidents. They expressed confidence in the local police, complained about the state of the roads, and were upbeat about their own situation. They expressed nervousness about national trends, political leaders, and events in Kabul. Similar thoughts arose throughout the day.

As we left the village, car-size holes in the dirt road slowed our passage and we stopped at a police checkpoint and outpost. Another chance to listen to a group of Afghans. Once again, our talented translator made a near-instant connection with a handful of local police. Their jobs required them to deal with all local violence, show real judgment, and usually resolve disputes without further legal intervention. While family disputes were especially difficult, the police seemed to like their role in the community.

After a few minutes of observing our conversation with his officers, the chief came out of his simple cinder block building. He too described the value of their work but also highlighted the low pay and missed paydays—and compared them to the generous compensation, income, housing, uniforms, and materials of the new Afghan Army. All were vastly superior to those belonging to him, a 25-year veteran of the Afghan police. To illustrate the preferred treatment, he gave us a copy of a high-end local paper, produced by the American base in nearby Bagram, for the newly privileged military.

Our next stop was closer to a village, where the United States had built a new women's center. Like most Afghan buildings, a high wall offered protection. As the gate opened, we drove into the inner courtyard, where a dynamic flow of local women worked without the ubiquitous burqas of the neighboring streets.

The woman who ran the center was one of the most impressive Afghans we met during our hundreds of interviews and she described a range of positive initiatives, from maternal and child health to education, family counseling, and employment. A handful of energetic and articulate young colleagues surrounded her and all described the favorable changes in their rural center. There were also warnings: the leader described the late monthly budget support from the ministry in Kabul and said that it was now three months behind. Limited government funds did not reach this American priority.

They also spoke of the slow acceptance of their work among local people and of personal risk in the town. Before we headed out on the road, our small group sat on the steps of the women's center for a quick picnic lunch. As we enjoyed the setting and the now-afternoon sun, one of the most outspoken young women that we had just met with approached the gate to leave. With great care, she adjusted her light blue burqa over her Western clothing, made sure that none appeared, and somehow shrunk before she stepped out onto the street. The contrast of her confident inside-the-wall person and her apprehensive preparation to return to the world beyond was concerning.

We made a day of talking to anyone we saw along the way, enjoying a warm reception. A curious disconnect appeared on that day in Parwan and Panjshir Provinces. Many good things seemed to be happening. Why did they not come together?

As we traveled throughout Afghanistan, this became a repeating phenomenon. At another women's center in Ghazni, a returned refugee teacher told us how she had saved the life of a young woman who fell in love with a non-family-approved man—and then lamented that her own husband could not find a paying job and might return to Pakistan. Brilliant budget documents detailed how Afghanistan would be self-supporting within ten years—but the cost of the new military, after the U.S. subsidies ended, looked like it would consume most of the paltry tax revenues for a long time. An independent radio station was providing reliable and popular information to an entire region—but there were no advertisers in the local market stalls and other businesses of the area. There was a shining new courthouse on the hill—but there were no judges, and if there had been, there would have been no place for the guilty in nonexistent prisons. New Kabul restaurants were thriving with their international patrons—but there was a requirement that the entries be a set distance from the streets to protect against car bombs.

When we asked, "How is your program going?" people offered good reports: schools built, new courthouses, women's programs, the reopening of a major two-lane periphery highway, elections, a functioning health ministry, and the professionalization of the Afghan military. There was much to cheer.

When we asked how the greater Afghan post-conflict world was proceeding, the responses were more negative. The insights undermined our confidence. "If only the U.S. training of the Afghan military was going better." "If the Italians hadn't messed up justice reform." "If the Germans would provide more soldiers to stabilize their region of the country." "If the Afghans weren't so corrupt; if we dealt with this place like it was a narco-state," and more.

A mathematical equation came to mind. How could one hundred individual successes add up to one gigantic failure? It did not seem possible.

All of these statements of fact hinted at larger problems, but the response of the U.S. government was to keep moving ahead on all fronts. Was there any way to capture the value of individual work while making sure that the larger enterprise, the strategic advancement of Afghanistan, was front and center?

If coherence and effectiveness are critical to success, how could we find timely measures of progress that would help the Afghans and the United States to improve their performance right away versus having to wait for congressional hearings and special inspector generals to detail the shortcomings?

These experiences and studies provided the basis for our fuller Afghanistan measurement model. In the winter of 2005, there was positive news all over Afghanistan. Somehow, it did not come together in a winning form.

3.

In developing the Afghanistan measure of progress model in 2004–2005, we retained the ambition from our Iraq study to give Afghans a fighting chance to make it on their own. We saw this as realistic. This also allowed customization versus a universal standard. While Iraq was an oil-rich, middle-class society, Afghanistan was poor even before 30 years of destruction. As Secretary of Defense Robert Gates would later say, Afghanistan will not be "a Central Asian Valhalla."[4]

The initial study commented on many efforts as being "mostly quantitative in nature" and questioned the reliability of data in conflict settings. For example, Afghanistan had no census in 30 years and the last one was inadequate at the time. If you do not know the population, it is hard to have much confidence in other numbers.

The Afghanistan report sought to bridge the gap between the quantitative and the qualitative by "bringing together information from five sources, weighing them all equally to balance out potential biases."[5]

The five sources included more than 40 government and public organizations, nearly 50 daily news reports, 16 public opinion polls by 11 different groups, 112 interviews or meetings by CSIS staff with 662 Afghans and internationals, and more than 1,000 structured conversations with 1,609 Afghans by twelve trained local staff in 20 of the 34 provinces. These produced more than 7,000 pieces of information (statistics, anecdotes, and events) that we turned into data points—most of which described outcomes. Inputs, such as the amount of money spent or the stated priorities of a program, or outputs, the number of schools built for example, only became outcomes when the education levels of girls, number of trucks traveling on a road, number of elected officials serving in safety were unavailable.

While the early post-conflict moments can offer a productive use of inputs and outputs—detailing the number of refugees returned, people fed, or soldiers in a town—that data becomes stale. What begins to matter most is the sense of conditions improving and the enterprise succeeding. The resident public needs to feel that life is getting better. Hope and confidence fuel progress—and build trust.

We made several improvements from the original Iraq model. The justice pillar became explicit and we merged infrastructure, health, and education into a social well-being pillar. Under each of five pillars, new indicators provided more precise cross-tabulations of data. We could now process the results from around the country by region, gender, issue intensity, and other ways.

Most importantly, a simple graphic showed societal capacity (Are things getting better for all?) and the status of individual Afghans (Is my life improving?). This allowed for a subtler analysis. For example, if an individual felt safe because of a local warlord, their personal security was good but not necessarily that of others. We began to capture the ambiguity of a conflict setting through iterative exchanges.

A typical conversation might follow a simple pattern. Our interviewer would start broadly, "How are you doing?"

"Not bad. Things feel better around here, though we are not sending our daughter to school," the Afghan father would respond.

"Why?" we would ask.

"We fear that she will be attacked," the concerned dad would say.

From that exchange, our interviewer collected information on the schools, young women and education, and public safety.

While there was an immense amount of data, the report intended to produce an impressionistic sense of developments in the nation. We sought to provide a solid baseline measurement to give policymakers a clearer reading on the overall direction of Afghanistan's progress.

A follow-on study in 2006 did just that.[6] Troubling trends appeared in all five pillars, exposing weakness in the reconstruction strategy, in the leadership model, and in the initiatives of the Afghan government, the United States, NATO, and its allies. Afghans reported that security, governance and participation, justice and accountability, and social services and infrastructure were worse than the year before. Economic conditions were better. The lives of individual women improved, but not their societal position.

Once again, the conclusions foretold developments in Afghanistan:

- "Afghans are losing trust in their government because of an escalation of violence;
- Public expectations are neither being met nor managed;
- Conditions in Afghanistan have deteriorated in all key areas targeted for development, except for the economy and women's rights."[7]

Funded by USAID, the independent study produced official discomfort. *Breaking Point: Measuring Progress in Afghanistan* suggested that the U.S. government stood on a precipice.[8] USAID worried that it would offend its partners and conducted a hurried review of the methodology and results. This surprised us. Whereas America's Iraq effort was a closed shop, difficult to access, and resistant to outside ideas, the Afghanistan team remained open, solicitous, and eager for input. After a frenetic exchange that included calls to Kabul, there was broad acceptance of the report as a valid representation of the situation in Afghanistan. The findings were replicable.

The model provided a macro view of events and thousands of micro examples of successes and shortcomings. It also highlighted the overly complex design and nonintegrated nature of the international effort, with dozens of priorities, the franchising of certain tasks to individual nations, and the presence of multiple leaders, in addition to the Afghan government.

To concentrate the coalition's thinking in a strategic direction, *Breaking Point* emphasized two specific areas for improvement: restoring public confidence in the plan for safety and mobilizing communities to contribute to the recovery. Detailed suggestions on how to achieve these results included:

- For security and public safety: "focus on Kandahar and Helmand provinces; treat the threat as an insurgency; concentrate on ways to counter the Taliban's tribal and charismatic appeal and tactics of intimidation; and restore confidence in the U.S. and international commitment." Specific suggestions included a consistent Afghan-led security presence in half of the 26 districts of the two southern provinces supported by a "rapid response protective umbrella" that would include an increase of U.S. helicopters from 35 to 70 or 100. Investing in cross-border human intelligence to improve the understanding of disenfranchised Pashtuns in Pakistan and Afghanistan was also critical, along with a shift in the antidrug effort.

- For the expansion of community engagement: "Move away from overreliance on Kabul and centralized systems; diminish the role of middle men and corruption; and enhance local participation." Ideas included the expansion of the National Solidarity Program, direct payments to Afghans, the incorporation of the informal justice sector, and a shifting of 50 percent of the development budget to the provincial level.

Following the release of the report in early 2007,[9] one dominant response materialized: "We agree with the findings and we like the boldness of the recommendations. Now, regarding our work in Afghanistan: that is going quite well and we do not see a need to make the changes you suggest. If only the others (Karzai, the U.S., the Germans, the Italians, etc.) would do what you suggest, we could turn this enterprise around."[10]

At a breakfast with the thoughtful U.S. commander, General Karl Eikenberry, I asked him about the need for more helicopters. His response was discouraging. They would be good to have but maintenance in the dusty conditions of that part of Afghanistan was difficult, it was unclear we could get the number, and other reasons. It felt like an excuse for inaction. We saw the helicopters as a sincerity test: if the United States wanted to win, it would have to find a way to protect the Afghan security forces in their early days in a timely fashion. When attacked in a remote area, the Afghans could not hold out for more than 30 to 45 minutes. Help that arrived after that would be useless.

We knew that our recommendations were not timeless. They applied to the moment. If adopted later, they might not fit. With the Pentagon worn down by two exhausting wars, the likelihood of action in the affirmative was slight.

The results of the Iraq and Afghan studies made clear that the single greatest obstacle to being able to measure progress is not the methodology or the commitment, but the inability to apply the results.

4.

The missed opportunities were everywhere. Carter Malkasian and four civilians would discover a growing rural insurgency in the Garmser District of Helmand from 2009 to 2011 as he joined 1,000 U.S. Marines in this remote southern Afghanistan outpost. Four years after our first reports, they were there to reverse a negative trend and "to mobilize the people to stand up against the Taliban."[11]

The lost opportunity had been from 2001 to 2006, when tribal politics, America's inability to establish the new Afghan military, corruption, and other problems led to the Taliban's takeover of the district's center. Carter wrote, "Seven hundred Afghan soldiers positioned in Garmser in 2005 might well have prevented the Taliban from ever returning, at a fraction of the cost of the 1,000 U.S. troops that would eventually deploy to the district."[12]

Immersed in the local culture, Carter studied Pashto, befriended tribal chiefs and became familiar with the modern history. While others saw the Garmser District of Helmand Province as ungovernable, Carter recognized that the Taliban, "with their set hierarchy," had proven otherwise from 1994 to 2001.[13]

By the time the Marines and Carter arrived, the Taliban had grown from a few hundred to thousands. "Opportunity had slipped away."[14]

Starting in 2008, the U.S. presence would restore some hope and Carter set about understanding the workings of the place to see if a new beginning might take hold. He dove deep into the history and saw that "old feuds . . . power-hungry khans" and an inability to defend themselves from the Taliban when divided[15] drove the tragedy. He measured what worked.

A tribal militia system had succeeded in the past with each community fielding "roughly thirty fighters, who functioned essentially as police. There were 300 in all. Twenty-five checkpoints dotted the district."[16] The district governor at the time described "a proven system" wherein a diverse group "were given charge of their own force . . . to pay for food, wages, and ammunition, wheat and poppy were once again taxed . . . with the blessing of the tribal leaders":

> The best men from every tribe joined the arbekai (tribal militias). These men tried to help the people. They came from good families

and would not steal from their own people. The people admired them and were willing to donate money for their salaries.[17]

For three years, the militia kept the Taliban away. The provision of basic justice and services, plus a council from 36 areas of the district "matched what the Taliban had offered."[18] While that has always seemed like a low standard, in Garmser it meant something.

The seeds of division were deep. Religious leaders, who had thrived during the Taliban, were disadvantaged. Immigrants were landless. Poppy expanded. Revenge was everywhere with some taking "a pound of flesh" and others threatening to throw the poor squatters "into the river."[19]

> The upshot of these rifts in society was that the Taliban never lost their base of support among the religious community and the immigrants, not to mention the support of the villages of their major leaders. . . . [Yet] as long as the tribal militia, border police, and tribal unity stood, the Taliban could not return to Garmser. Only when politics and power broke down these instruments of order did Garmser fall apart.[20]

By the time the internationals (British, Dutch, Australians, and Canadians) arrived in 2006, "their governments and military leaders did not realize how badly the situation had deteriorated."[21]

Carter gathered the information and built promising relations. *Washington Post* reporter Rajiv Chandrasekaran ascribed the "adoration" of the Afghans for Carter to a handful of key qualities: "his unfailing politeness . . . willingness to take risks . . . command of Pashto . . . . bucking the State Department's rules,"[22] and a respectful activist role that engaged fully with the elders.

"Malkasian was not like most of the others selected by State and USAID. He asked to work in the field . . . lived in a trailer on a dusty forward operating base. . . . What really set him apart was his desire to live in a remote district for two consecutive years . . . and his tendency to flout the regional security officer's rules." Most importantly, Carter felt that "the only way the Afghans will trust you is if you show that you trust them."[23]

Carter had a challenging mission, but he started by measuring what worked. With a familiarization to the people and their past successes, he could imagine a way forward.

5.

As he assumed office in 2009, President Barack Obama began a full-scale review of America's policy and progress in Afghanistan. "You have an obligation," he told Bob Woodward, "to work over, again and again, your goals, your mission, your progress. Are we staying focused? Are we preventing mission creep? Are we clear about the endgame?" The policymakers had to have extraordinary discipline during wartime, he added. "It entails so much of the country's resources, so much of our blood and treasure, and unleashes so many passions." Obama worried about "the ease with which something [war] gets momentum."[24]

In June 2009, General Stanley McChrystal became the commander in Afghanistan, and he set out "to conduct an accurate diagnosis and offer effective fixes."[25] He gathered a dream team of thinkers and sent them all over Afghanistan to assess the situation. This would feed into the president's review.

After seven years of war, force protection had become job one and our soldiers "had actually sealed themselves off from the Afghan population." One group of elders said, "The government robs us, the Taliban beat us, and ISAF bombs us. We do not support any side."[26] McChrystal concluded that addressing a prevalent fear and restoring Afghan confidence about the future was paramount. He recognized that villagers "would not commit to any side until convinced it was safe to do so."[27] While appreciative of the intricacies of the Afghan world, he concluded that their "culture was rooted in practicality and compromise."[28]

As he shaped a larger plan, McChrystal chose to focus a renewed counterterrorism effort on Helmand, the area that Malkasian worked in. After four prior summers of the United States and allies' clearing parts of the province only to see the Taliban seep back in, McChrystal made a practical decision. He reasoned: we had troops there already; time mattered in the run-up to the August elections; the Marines wanted a contiguous area to their current assignment; it was in danger of falling; and a demonstrated success in a Taliban stronghold would rebuild local support. McChrystal knew that the Afghans "owned the car" and that his coalition must be "the mechanics."

By late August, McChrystal's strategic assessment team had prepared their report. As he presented it to the secretary of defense and the chairman of the Joint Staff, he emphasized the need for a dramatic change in strategy and operations. "Protecting the people means shielding them from *all* threats." Predation, corruption, insurgent and collateral violence—all included.[29] He tried to separate out the discussions about money and people, recognizing that would absorb all the attention.

The strategy "identified 80 of Afghanistan's 364 key districts" that were essential for stability and survival. The focus would be on roads, urban and agricultural areas, and historic and cultural locations.[30] Called an "ink spot" strategy, it was like an earlier Soviet effort in Afghanistan. The upcoming elections were another critical component. Could they be free, fair, and safe?

The commander's request for 40,000 more troops drew much attention, but his own emphasis was on building an organization that was "now focused and moving in the right direction with the right culture . . . that could be successful."[31] That was a startling recognition of our shortcomings, almost eight years into the Afghan war.

While admiring of the thoroughness and conclusions of the McChrystal team's review, I felt that the timing was off. My fear in Afghanistan was that we had missed another set of opportunities and were now setting out to pursue what should have been yesterday's plan.

The president's plan, dictated by him in late 2009, was five single-spaced pages of taking responsibility.[32] It started,

> United States' goal in Afghanistan is to deny safe haven to al-Qaeda and to deny the Taliban the ability to overthrow the Afghan government.
>
> The strategic concept for the United States, along with our international partners and the Afghans, is to degrade the Taliban insurgency while building sufficient Afghan capacity to secure and govern their country, creating conditions for the United States to begin reducing its forces by July 2011.

The total cost for this option in Afghanistan is about $113 billion per year for those years in which we sustain nearly 100,000 troops in Afghanistan.

Major annual cost factors include: $100 billion for military operations and maintenance; up to $8 billion for the ANSF, depending on annual targets and allied contributions; $5.2 billion for civilian operations and assistance.[33]

Many of the findings of McChrystal's team and their strategy paralleled our earlier reports. That was not comforting. Places like Afghanistan evolve and change with such speed that a good idea is outdated within weeks. Options narrow and fewer choices remain. The Zeitgeist matters and solid measures of progress provide the tuning to fit the times.

6.

After spending more than a trillion dollars in a 16-year war, the United States is doing "just enough to lose slowly."[34] Following McChrystal's recommendation, the Obama administration surged 30,000 soldiers in 2009–2010 into areas like Helmand Province. From a peak of 100,000 U.S. forces, there were fewer than 10,000 by 2017. Torn "between assistance and dependence," the Americans are now advising, leading air strikes, and providing emergency protection. "We're like a Band-Aid on a bullet wound," lamented one American.[35] Public safety is missing in large chunks of Afghanistan. A new Secretary of Defense, James Mattis, is now in charge, and additional forces from the United States and a small number of allies are back in Afghanistan. The State Department's coordination office no longer exists and we await a clear plan.[36]

The Special Inspector General for Afghanistan Reconstruction (SIGAR) has tracked $117 billion of nonwar expenses. In 2001, Afghanistan had 50 miles of paved roads. Now, the United States has funded 10,000 miles, though 95 percent of those inspected are "damaged or destroyed" and 85 percent are not maintained.[37]

In February 2017, SIGAR reported that the government did not control half the country, thousands were leaving their homes, and opium production was at an all-time high. More than 1,000 schools closed for security reasons and three million students missed classes.

Afghanistan is now the largest reconstruction program in America's history and it covers everything from building a new army to local health programs. The last U.S. pledge is for $5 billion per year of non-military support to Afghanistan until 2020.

Much like McChrystal's review of the prior decade and ours from 2006 to 2007, SIGAR highlighted two concerns that put Afghanistan's future at risk: the effectiveness of the military and police, and corruption.[38] Sarah Chayes wrote in *Thieves of State*, "Development resources passed through a corrupt system not only reinforced that system by helping to fund it but also inflamed the feelings of injustice that were driving people toward the insurgency."[39]

Most chilling, it was hard to imagine Afghans wanting to fight for those leading their government in Kabul. More than 15,000 Afghan security forces have died in a war with no end, but the will is flagging.[40] When outnumbered Taliban fighters defeated a "demoralized government force" in Kunduz in September 2015, a lack of confidence in the central government was determinative.[41]

In his farewell speech in 2014, President Karzai called "America's mission in Afghanistan a betrayal."[42] With our constant shuffling of personnel and redesigning of strategies, many described the longest U.S. war as a series of "one-year wars." Institutions did their thing. "We triggered massive corruption through our profligacy; convinced a substantial number of Afghans that we were, in fact, occupiers; and facilitated the resurgence of the Taliban,"[43] wrote former CIA station Chief Robert Grenier. He went on to describe America as blundering and guilty of a "colossal overreach, from 2005 onwards."[44]

Our first report had described the difficulty in moving from the early effort to fight a war, feed and shelter civilians, and return refugees to their home country, to the establishment of a new government and modern society. We cautioned that it would be tough.

In a 2012 piece, "Afghanistan's Need for Reform: We Have Seen the Enemy, and It Is Our Anecdotes," Frances Z. Brown argued that Afghanistan's governance should be measured "against one central criterion: whether Afghan government institutions are prepared to 'hold' the country after the U.S. drawdown. . . . Shifting the narrative from one where a thousand vivid success stories bloom to one of objective assessment of reform won't be pleasant: it represents a move from the colorful to the colorless."[45]

7. LESSONS FROM AFGHANISTAN AND IRAQ

In Afghanistan and Iraq, soaring American ambitions encountered enormous challenges—and quagmires resulted. Thousands of U.S. soldiers, civilians, and local people died as initial war successes encountered complications and abbreviated plans did not prepare for the immediate aftermath of formal fighting. America carpet-bombed both countries with money[46] and the resulting reports and news stories shocked U.S. taxpayers, Afghans, and Iraqis.

Over nine years, the Special Inspector General for Iraq Reconstruction (SIGIR) conducted 220 audits and 170 inspections of more than $60 billion in U.S. spending. He pointed out that "ad hoc structures" produced interagency "discontinuities and disconnects." The SIGIR review of the Iraqi-funded and U.S.-led Development Fund for Iraq estimated a waste of "at least $8 billion" (out of $23 billion) from its inception in May 2003 until late June 2004.[47]

Over six years, the U.S. military spent $2 billion on 16,000 civilian projects through its Commander's Emergency Response Program (CERP). "Multiple reports by the Government Accountability Office have noted a lack of monitoring by the Pentagon," the *Washington Post* reported in 2011. Seen by General David Petraeus, then the top U.S. commander in Afghanistan, as "the most responsive and effective means to address a local community's needs," the CERP databases "did not record the villages or districts where projects were undertaken."[48] No measurements followed.

In 2016, the *New York Times* reported that the Pentagon had lost track of hundreds of thousands of guns that it handed out to Iraqi and Afghan security forces. Many ended up in enemy hands, and the true number of guns lost is unknown. Sensible questions still seek answers. How can an operation as large and sophisticated as the U.S. military fail to have a system in place for tracking deadly weapons? And why is it that this only comes to light long after the fact?

Clear plans and regular measures of progress would have helped. Difficult and sometimes "impossible" circumstances are more addressable with a sense of direction and timely reviews. Here then are the three major lessons from this chapter:

I. Clarify the Original Intent and Goals Before You Immerse the United States.

Is failure an option or a guarantee? It depends on our vision and sense of balance. Rory Stewart and Gerald Knaus describe the contortions and corrosion of intervention: "'The international community' ends by oscillating between exaggerated fears and an inflated sense of its own power, between paranoia and megalomania, reflecting in its lurches its half-conscious insecurity about its lack of power, knowledge, certainty, and legitimacy." The "absurdity of heroic international plans and leadership" leads to a damming misinterpretation of the entire situation.[49]

I like the balanced view that the former head of the U.N.'s peacekeeping operations, Jean-Marie Guéhenno, offers in his memoir, *The Fog of Peace*. Guéhenno argues for a "prudent interventionism" and recognizes that failure is possible. He says, "An enterprise becomes moral not because it is a fight against evil, but because it has to consider conflicting goods, and lesser evils, and make choices."[50] We did not do that in the two big wars of America's 21st century.

If we stop overselling the ambitions of the effort, it is possible to manage expectations. Assert modest claims in the designs of programs, in the reporting of results, and in appearances before regulators; that will reinforce the enormity of the challenge and the erratic nature of progress. Even the phrase "state building" is grandiose. A more realistic description would be "jump starting"—helping a people, society, and government to get going.

In 2017, General McChrystal would reflect back on Afghanistan in a sober way. He recounted our rush to respond to 9/11 and described our failure to "go to school" in a range of ways. That produced "a policy that on a superficial level seemed very logical," which in turn "ran into pressures, forces, interests, and equities of people that are, I won't say immovable, but very difficult to move." He summarized our collective surprise: "Afghanistan in particular was a case of finding a problem of much greater complexity, much deeper roots, and much more difficult issues than we appreciated."[51]

When asked what we had learned, McChrystal responded,

> In the case of Afghanistan, immediately after 9/11, in terms of military action we should have done nothing initially. I now believe we should have taken the first year after 9/11 and sent 10,000 young

Americans—military, civilians, diplomats—to language school; Pashtu, Dari, Arabic. We should have started to build up the capacity we didn't have. I would have spent that year with diplomats traveling the world as the aggrieved party. We had just been struck by al-Qaeda. I would have made our case around the world that this is a global problem and that the whole world has to deal with it. I would have spent the full year in preparation. I would not have been worried about striking al-Qaeda that year; they weren't going anywhere. We could have organized, we could have built the right coalitions, we could have done things with a much greater level of understanding than we did in our spasmodic response. Politically, doing what I described would have been very difficult. But I believe that kind of preparation was needed.[52]

We saw one country in the coalition prepare for Afghanistan in a thorough way. Prior to committing troops in Afghanistan, the Dutch parliament engaged in a full-scale review of the Netherlands' potential engagement. That debate produced one of the more fulsome discussions held in any of the NATO countries. The result: a more balanced approach with required and scheduled public updates. Such programmed oversight is more common after the fact.

As America headed to war in Iraq and Afghanistan, we should have heeded history. Milt Bearden, a 30-year veteran of the CIA, warned, "No nation that launched a war against another sovereign nation ever won. And every nationalist-based insurgency against a foreign occupation ultimately succeeded."[53]

II. Commit to Real-Time Measurements of Progress.

It is inconceivable to think that massive multibillion-dollar engagements lack these simple ingredients—yet that is the case in most international interventions.

Believe in measurement and commit to its independence. Build it into your plan, set money aside, and keep it agile so that it does not entangle the already complicated situation you are tackling. Start with a baseline measurement, a clear sense of direction, and early, regular, and public reviews of progress. Without a starting point and a destination, effort and motion become the measures. That is not enlightening.

Trustworthy and credible information is collectible, in a transparent fashion, in the middle of a war. While there are certainly outstanding issues and further refinements, a "weight of the evidence" approach can produce objective and depoliticized data—along with political insights.

Random information is often useful. In Iraq, the levels of violence became a constant source of debate. Thus, when Neil MacFarquhar reported on the dramatic increase in corpses at the Baghdad mortuary, there was confirmation of a negative trend. It also highlighted the intimidating effect throughout Iraqi society. If thousands were brought to a central facility, how many more were being shot or road-bombed that were not reported? How many just injured? What of the thousands who witnessed the events or felt lucky to have avoided a bullet? It was not hard for us to imagine a city that was terrified, where the citizenry was hiding inside their homes or fleeing elsewhere. Life could not possibly return to normal.

Similar help came from a corps of talented journalists. With extensive experience and contacts and greater ease of movement, their superior understanding of the context is a natural complement to the work of seasoned diplomats and the intelligence community. Multiple source stories allow for a deeper level of reporting than we often see in channels that are more formal. Their natural iconoclasm also challenges the hierarchical ways of the U.S. government. At a Princeton public meeting, I heard a sage CIA retiree explain why he knew more today than he had as a spy: "I have complete access to open source material."[54]

An unquenchable thirst for information prevents entrapment by conventional wisdom. The arrival of big data, with "datafication" (the ability to take information and convert it into numbers), and the ability to then interpret it with expanding computer software capacity and algorithms is making this work ever more valuable.[55] How we measured progress in Iraq and Afghanistan provided an early example of the "profound changes" needed: collect a mass of data; accept messiness; and use correlations. As Kenneth Cukier and Viktor Mayer-Schoenberger explain, "Big data is different: it marks a transformation in how society processes information. In time, big data might change our way of thinking about the world. As we tap ever more data to understand events and make foreign affairs decisions, we are likely to discover that many aspects of life are probabilistic, rather than certain."[56] This is true in conflict places.

It is possible to measure progress in the toughest places on earth—and it all starts with the humility of curiosity and a comfort with introspection.

III. Follow Through in Tangible Ways and Make Sure to Address Larger, Systemic Changes.

Even when reviews are digestible and there is high-level interest, it is still difficult to make course corrections and improvements. Large bureaucracies have their own rhythm and figuring out how to work around numerous obstacles requires a fascination with intricate puzzles.

"At the Pentagon, " John Hamre, my boss at CSIS and former Deputy Secretary of Defense, would say, "You have to be ready to ask for something three times. The first time, they are intrigued; the second, they wonder if you mean it; and the third, it is time to take action." My own experience at the State Department required even more persistence. I would advise my team at CSO to "know what you want, and then be prepared to ask for it seven times. If anyone ever gives you the answer you want, take it, carry it out right away and never relitigate any of the prior negative responses."

A colleague at the State Department, who had spent a first career in the Navy, said this: "State takes so long trying to refine a plan to 95 percent certainty, that it often misses the opportunity. In the military, we get started on implementation at around 70 percent, fully recognizing that any plan often falls apart once the shooting begins."[57] We see these differences often in conflict places.

Timelines are useful. Too often, USAID and now the military believe that "more time and money" will determine the outcome of great challenges. I believe in a catalytic approach and therefore find that target dates for completion spur action. Deadlines are tough to meet in conflict places, but the initiation of corrective measures often inspires progress.

Real time adjustments build confidence—they show that leaders know what is going on and are willing to do something about it. Look for "sincerity tests," like the helicopters in Afghanistan or the training of the Iraqi military, to see if the United States is making the necessary sacrifices to succeed. If there are essential tasks that we must do well, confirm their completion. Much like Beyoncé's hit song to a reluctant partner, "Put a Ring on It," the United States should be ready to act if we mean it.

A positive example was Canada's review of their nation's role in Afghanistan. Parliament had approved a civilian and military commitment until February 2009 and Canada's 2,500 soldiers, based in volatile Kandahar, had suffered the highest proportional losses of any international force. As public opposition to the war in Afghanistan grew in Canada during 2007, the prime minister appointed an independent, bipartisan commission to recommend changes.

Headed by an opposition figure, former Liberal Party cabinet member John Manley, the distinguished panel sought out opinions well outside of official Canadian circles. Their 2008 report[58] is a model for engaging the tough issues and bringing them to the public's attention with constructive steps. "The Panel could find no operational logic for choosing February 2009 as the end date for Canada's military mission in Kandahar—and nothing to establish February 2009 as the date by which the mission would be completed," they stated.[59]

While the report turned out to be candid and balanced, it was also more optimistic than events would confirm. The expected growth of Afghanistan's security sector and self-governance were overrated. Still, Canada made important internal management changes. It also addressed NATO's deployment of allied fighting forces.

In every one of these conflict situations, the enormity of the challenge will guarantee few successes and many frustrations. Staying focused on the larger enterprise and whether dozens of individual initiatives are combining to produce a greater good is vital. While there was real progress in Afghanistan and Iraq in multiple areas, the U.S. interventions never came together to capture the imagination of local people. America was stuck in two wars without end.

IV

Current and Future Challenges

At first blush, America embraced Syria's peaceful rebellion in March 2011. Even after the regime began bombing in April, our ambassador, Robert Ford, courageously appeared alongside demonstrators in Hama in July, putting the United States on the side of liberalization.

In August, President Obama said for the first time that Assad must leave office. We had not started the revolt, yet we supported the freedom of expression that was blossoming in the heart of the Arab world. The rebels and their allies, including us, thought the revolt would end in success in a matter of weeks. America's early sentiments did not hold up when tested by a protracted, complex struggle.

Committing to a strategy of total destruction, the Assad regime launched unrelenting aerial attacks on liberated cities and towns. Missiles, shelling, and barrel bombs chased half of Syria's 25 million people from their homes. A million clamored for refuge in Europe, widening fissures and contributing to the United Kingdom's vote to leave the European Union. In July 2012, more than a year after the initial street protests, the International Committee of the Red Cross declared Syria a "civil war."

Powerful countries lined up on both sides of the conflict. Russia and Iran sought to protect Assad, while many Western and Sunni Arab nations backed the rebels. The Saudis, Gulf States, and Turkey supported different rebel groups. Some of our allies did not share our concerns about empowering extremists and assisted groups like the Nusra Front, a branch of al-Qaeda. Such support also abetted Assad's argument that all opponents were "terrorists." That provided a convenient excuse for Russia and Iran to expand the fight on the regime side— and slowed the United States.

For its part, the opposition bought into the "myth of the quick revolution" but were unprepared to envision "how Bashar leaves power and how the transition will occur."[1] The Free Syrian Army took shape, much from regime defectors, but it failed to cohere even as covert aid arrived.

In Washington, there were plenty of naysayers and distractions. Next to no one wanted another Iraq- or Afghanistan-style military engagement. The U.S. military remained stressed and overstretched from those conflicts. Opinion polls showed strong opposition to a larger U.S. role, and a skeptical public never heard a compelling argument in favor. (A few hawks called for the full-scale arming of the opposition military or even greater U.S. involvement.) America's economy was in a slow recovery and a do-nothing Congress threatened government shutdowns.

Friends ask, "Why Syria? Why then?" Faced with a full agenda and skeptical of a Washington-led drift to war, President Obama expressed resistance to taking on the Syria crisis with a full-blown effort. While the "ripeness" that we sought was weak, the "inevitability" of the Syria challenge provided an offsetting principle. Would the likelihood of a death spiral alter America's approach? Would we be drawn into an even uglier mess if we waited? Could we mitigate a ten-year war if we exercised force and restraint? Assad was a known quantity that was getting worse with time. His neighbors, our best friends in the region, all wanted his departure. As Assad exceeded our worst expectations, the likelihood of U.S. action grew—though only in response to the Islamic State threat.

I believe that the United States could have helped the Syrian opposition win their struggle against Assad. This would not be a time-worn effort to take out a dictator—something that is always harder than it looks. Rather, it would give the opposition a fighting chance to make it on their own. When the American government offered familiar, ineffective options, leaving President Obama unwilling to increase his commitment, we should have sought new ideas. As the military struggle and diplomatic efforts dragged on, we did not seize other opportunities.

We failed to address the top concern of every Syrian I met: A leader who wantonly bombed his own people. We failed to ensure that humanitarian aid reached those in most need, regardless of which side of the conflict they were on. We did not give meaningful support to the local efforts that showed promise in stabilizing parts of the country, allowing a new system to take root. In the process, we overlooked the knowledge we had accumulated in the wars of the 1990s and the quagmires of Afghanistan and Iraq.

It did not need to be so.

8

SYRIA

What Matters Most?

I.

Every conversation with a Syrian started with one topic: Assad's aerial bombing. The rebels and citizens in liberated areas were defenseless against the bombs, which destroyed lives, schools, hospitals, infrastructure, and morale. It had stopped the rebels' momentum and confused their ranks. It had to stop before serious progress could resume.

Discussions from the Pentagon to the White House to the op-ed pages offered an uninspired set of options: providing antiaircraft weapons to the opposition, creating and enforcing no-fly zones, and defining and protecting safe zones.

Antiaircraft weapons had a long and problematic history. Some of the arms that America provided to Afghan warlords to fight the Russians during the Cold War turned their barrels on us later. Losing such weapons to terrorists in Syria would repeat that debacle. The risk was high; at any moment, moderates made partnerships of convenience, survival, or tactical necessity with groups we considered terrorists. Broader efforts to train moderate armed groups were slow, ineffective, and eventually abandoned in late 2015.[1]

While a no-fly zone had been effective in parts of Iraq for 11 years after the Gulf War in 1991, it was a high-intensity effort that culminated in a full-scale bombardment at the start of the second Iraq war in 2003.

The Pentagon described the disabling of Syria's air force and ground defense systems as a greater challenge. The presence of Russian fighter jets further complicated matters.

As for safe zones, they would require reliable ground troops. The Syrian opposition forces did not appear to be strong enough. On top of widespread public opposition to sending U.S. troops, the failure of U.N. peacekeepers to head off massacres in Bosnia and Rwanda had shown the need for a robust commitment. Operating such a force inside a hostile country would also provoke numerous legal and logistical problems.

Given the limited options that exhausted government agencies presented, President Obama pursued a policy of restraint. At a meeting for a dozen administration appointees in the Roosevelt Room of the West Wing in early 2013, I asked President Obama about the bombing. "The Syrian opposition are among the most serious and dedicated people I have ever met in over 40 conflicts. When we started to help them there was a near certainty that they would be in Damascus within weeks," I said. "At that time 12,000 had died and they sought help to stop the bombing. What can we do, now that 200,000 have been killed?"

The president's response was thoughtful, informative, and reflective—but he did not lean in. He was caught in the conundrum. What would happen if we did more? Who would win on the ground? Would the sacrifice be worth it, since the results were so unknown? His questions led to further questions, not action. I believe that he deserved more choices and could have been more demanding of our creativity.

This was not a post-conflict situation. Rather, it required a timely, targeted action that would even the battlefield. Limited aerial attacks on military targets by the United States and NATO in Bosnia proved the value of such an effort, though late in arriving. Syria was an "in-conflict situation . . . fraught with difficulty" and requiring "an enormous commitment and integration of all parts of the national security apparatus."[2] That was not forthcoming.

Assad's loss of substantial territory and the defection of so many from his military suggested that a neutralizing of his civilian bombing could equalize the war. That in turn would give the opposition time to come together. Obama was still not ready.

2.

What else might have been possible given the reluctance of our president and generals? Two ideas come to mind. Both place Assad at the center of Syrian decisions and thus the target of any action. They accept that Bashar is a rational, cold-blooded, and calculating survivor who understands direct responses to his sadism.

The first was for limited, retributive missile strikes whenever Assad bombed civilians. If the regime attacked, the United States and its allies would target fighter jet bases and Bashar's personal property. America would make clear that Bashar's killing of thousands of innocent people would result in immediate consequences and give Assad pause before acting again.

Strategic retaliation would have defined our intolerance of the shredding of decency and international standards. It would have emboldened the Syrian Free Army and created a more level contest. Assad would determine the frequency by his own actions. It would test the balance between sovereignty and the responsibility to protect civilians, making clear that flattening your own country in order to stay in power is not a 21st-century option.

Could the United States execute a limited series of strikes versus falling into a prolonged war? Do we have the self-discipline to carry out targeted missions and not escalate a conflict? With care, it is possible.

Had we done this before the regime lined up backers and attacked widely and with impunity, we might have stopped the bombing and pushed Assad toward serious negotiation. Instead, increased international involvement from the Russians and massive human flight and destruction reduced the effectiveness of this option. We missed the moment.

A second way to disrupt the bombing required an assertive humanitarian approach.

Throughout most of the war, 80 percent of the relief went through government-controlled centers. Often, the Assad regime violated accepted international standards for secure and free distribution. All U.N. goods went into Damascus, where the government handpicked its distribution targets, helping only groups supporting the regime. The regime would lay siege to entire cities then only provide relief when the opposition withdrew. Airstrikes and militias attacked and intimidated U.N. convoys.

On February 22, 2014, a unanimous vote of the United Nations Security Council supported the free and open provision of humanitarian assistance.[3] This aid became one of the few areas of agreement between the Russians and the United States, at least on paper. Was there a way to build off this fragile consensus to interrupt the bombing? Historic airlifts in Berlin, Sarajevo, and Kosovo suggested promise.

As 2.5 million Germans dug out of Berlin's post–World War II rubble, disagreements among the victors led the Russians to close off land-based supplies to West Berlin. A U.S.-led alliance responded with an airlift. On June 26, 1948, the United States initiated "Operation Vittles." Two days later the British joined with "Operation Plainfare." A core calculation was that any effort to block an unarmed humanitarian flight would be an unprovoked act of aggression by the Soviets.[4]

At its busiest, planes landed in West Berlin every 45 seconds. When threatened with a stoppage, 300,000 Berliners gathered to protest the possibility of a Soviet takeover. Less than a year later, the Soviets relented and ground supply routes reopened on May 11, 1949. Two weeks later, West Germany became a nation.

The Sarajevo airlift was also instructive. U.N. ground deliveries sometimes had to negotiate 90 roadblocks to get relief goods the 400 kilometers from Zagreb to Sarajevo.[5] In order to break the jam, the United States and Turkey organized airlift missions in April 1992. UNHCR started regular flights on July 3, with 11 on the first day.

While it was hardly the answer to the crisis, the people of Sarajevo welcomed the supplies—and the symbolic support. All sides of the conflict tried to obstruct or divert aid from civilians. Still, this imperfect, short-term solution would go on for three and a half years, providing far more help than harm.

In addition, the Sarajevo airlift created opportunities to build political space by forcing changes in obdurate behaviors. When Bosnian leaders halted the distribution of goods at Sarajevo's airport as a protest against the treatment of Muslims in eastern enclaves, the United Nations suspended the land convoys and the airlift. The move was controversial but effective, drawing attention to the abuses of all parties. Within five days, distribution began again after all suffered the embarrassment of international attention.

In the middle of the Kosovo war of 1998–1999, Serbs lay siege to Kosovar fighters in a mountain range. The most senior USAID humanitarian official, Hugh Parmer, commissioned Ukrainian planes to airdrop packets of food and emergency supplies. Kosovars hailed this microairlift as their lifeline.

When assessing the risks and fallout from these decisions, we sometimes forget that humanitarian work is defined by its core mission: to save and protect lives. Sometimes these risks are worth taking, even required, to get beyond the immediate hurdles and keep that mission alive.

Humanitarian purists would argue that they need to preserve their neutrality in conflict at all costs in order to be effective. But a case like Syria, where not taking sides amounted to endorsing the regime's illegal and reprehensible practices, shows that it's not always possible. Berlin, Sarajevo, and Kosovo are examples of stepping outside normal conventions for the larger purpose.

In Syria, as we searched for ways to mitigate the violence and break the political gridlock, I sent a note to Ambassador Ford and other U.S. partners suggesting that the United States back an airlift into Aleppo. With much of Syria's largest business city liberated, why not call out the government's intransigence by proposing and planning international aid, daring the regime to block it? If successful, it could provide a starting point for building progress. Opening the airport to regular flights would create the need for an on-the-ground distribution system, breaking down the siege-like conditions in Syria's once largest commercial center.

This would be in the greatest humanitarian tradition and might produce a political breakthrough. Like other missed opportunities, the airlift idea did not gain traction as the United States muddled down the road. Principals focused on rounds of fruitless negotiations and I did not pursue the proposal with the kind of relentless energy that is required in a large bureaucracy. Ideas such as this require commitment and the administration had its eyes on a negotiated breakthrough.

Instead of taking a gamble on an alternative course, our efforts in Syria became a humanitarian fig leaf—saving a life only so that it might be lost another day. America largely stuck to traditional options, some of which might have been necessary to resolve the conflict. None, however, were sufficient without a halt in the bombing. The result was that when Syria came knocking, the United States answered with ambiguity of purpose and reluctant assistance.

3.

At the same time that these choices played out on international stages, there were meaningful efforts at peaceful change on the ground. Though the opposition lacked cohesion and knowledge of issues like governance and communications, there were innovations that we sought to support. Recognizing that President Obama would not move on the bombing, we sought other ways forward.

The opposition's underdeveloped state was no accident. For more than 40 years, the father-son rulers, Hafez and Bashar Assad, had suppressed and massacred dissent with cold-blooded efficiency. In our first conversations, Syrians spoke about 40,000 political prisoners, held in a series of Assad horror chambers. They did not expect to see those people ever again. The Assads' thoroughness compared to the cold-blooded organization that I saw in Rwanda's genocide—with more modern methods.

Political talent had long since fled, leaving untrained citizens, disconnected from and suspicious of each other, to lead when the time came. They were also unknown to outsiders, like us, who sought to help them.

Given the nature of the suppression, it is not surprising that the movement that arose in 2011 was local, not national; doubtful of outsiders; and lacked experience in governing and organizing. United in their opposition to Assad, the organizers and prospective leaders remained disconnected from each other.

With the closing of our Damascus embassy in February 2012, our primary source of information and engagement ended. We also lost the organizing focus of a country team and a resident leader, the ambassador.

At the State Department, a lone desk officer made daily Skype calls to the opposition in Syria. When asked whether 100 more like him would help, he answered, "A thousand!" Such a simple operation, a mainstay of political campaigns or new product roll-outs, is unheard of in our national security community, despite the ease and value.

To address these weaknesses, the United States began a cross-border operation, based in neighboring countries in early 2012. My CSO team was the initial overt player. The greatest promise was in multiple regional centers. Local leaders emerged, took on governance responsibilities, and began to build followers. We spoke about "developing a farm system"—a way to grow future talent.

Courage marked those still around. In dozens of meetings with close to 200 Syrians, seldom did I run into an activist who had not spent time in a jail, suffered physical abuse, or lost a close friend or relative at the hands of the regime.

As a small part of the U.S. effort, CSO began to train and equip the nonviolent Syrian opposition that could make it out of Syria and into Turkey. Hosting regular groups of activists for training sessions that focused on political mobilization and governance transitions, the United States expanded its reach to hundreds of opposition figures. In the weeklong courses, the United States developed relationships with emerging local officials. We started to hear their needs and to see their potential.

From this vantage, the United States could help to incubate Syrian ideas and to produce frameworks for others to build upon. The Syrians valued the assurance of working alongside the United States and our allies welcomed the structures and connections we opened up.

As we delivered nonlethal assistance such as medical supplies, computers, and the tools of daily public administration, the United States gained influence on an emerging generation of political chiefs, local governors, and councils. Throughout, we monitored their movements to and from our training centers in southern Turkey, to make sure of their personal safety. At every single meeting, the Syrians spoke of their gratitude and wanted to expand the relationship.[6]

Still, before long, cracks started to show. One of America's most prominent civil disobedience experts, Maria Stephan, worked for CSO with the opposition from Turkey throughout 2012. After six months she wrote to me, "I can attest to the challenges of supporting an opposition whose courage far exceeds its ability to organize and mobilize. It's been painful to watch a popular uprising quickly escalate into a civil war, and even more difficult to watch terrorism overshadow a popular struggle." She went on to say that they could not "inspire confidence domestically or internationally" and that bolstering "opposition coherence remains a huge challenge."[7] Assad continued to sow disorganization with computer hacking, arrests, and the bombing.

America's diplomatic effort hinged on creating an effective national opposition coalition. We should have known, from reports like these, that it was a long shot. It might happen over time, but it would require patience. We propped up one central group after another, only to see the structure collapse. CSO supported an office of Syrians to coordinate international assistance from Istanbul but found that they could never generate support from within Syria. We cut off our aid within a year.

Repeated attempts at diplomacy collapsed, not least because the fractured opposition lacked organization. Talks in Geneva and elsewhere took place, with disappointing results. It is possible to weaken one side and strengthen the other, but our investments did not match the opportunity.

Yet the opposition's vision for a more open and just society and commitment to change was the deepest and most genuine I have seen. We saw their steadfast commitment in the hourly risks they took to traverse a perilous Syria to cross the border for sessions in Turkey. Once there, the activists' dedication was sincere and affirmative, focused on an open and trustworthy Syria.

A meeting with a group of Lebanese bankers was instructive. Syria had been an important market for them before the war, with more than $1.5 billion of deposits and $800 million of loans. They spoke with respect for the way that Syrians honored their agreements and took a long view.

One said, "When the fighting began, a Syrian car dealer took his cars and sold them throughout the region, never missing a loan payment." He contrasted that behavior with Egyptian customers. "When Mubarak sneezed in Egypt, the loan payments stopped immediately."[8]

Morale atrophied. Discouragement set in. At one meeting of local councils, a Syrian stood up and told my team, "Before we start talking about anything, I quit." He went on, "No more generators, trucks and materials. They're not helping so get lost." Others joined in and the venting continued. Finally, there was a ten-minute "smoke break."[9]

When they came back a consensus view had set in. "We are all broken people. Our lives will never be the same. Syria will not be a country."[10] Exhaustion would become the third major opponent for the original revolutionaries—right alongside Assad and the extremists.

Nevertheless, the daily work with the opposition provided real-time insights and information plus political impact—all elements that enhanced the broader diplomatic effort. Whereas the United States had destroyed the political infrastructure by intent in Iraq, in Syria we sought to sustain local institutions. Judges and other officials, recent defectors, became key figures in our network.

The promise is still unfulfilled.

4.

As the State Department neared spending $1 billion in Syria at the end of 2012, I spoke with Ambassador Ford and the head of State's office of foreign assistance, Rob Goldberg, about reviewing our practices and expenditures. With funds distributed in three-month tranches, it was difficult to build a long-term strategy or test new ideas.

All parts of State involved in Syria agreed to meet on the next round of spending. We invited the Defense Department and the intelligence community. Due to the travel of key people, it took three months to convene, which gives some idea of the difficulty of coordinating among these offices on a fast-moving situation like Syria.

Remarkably, with a billion dollars out the door, this was the first meeting of this kind. The meeting opened with an overview of where the billion had gone. Some were surprised to learn that close to 90 percent of the money went to humanitarian and refugee programs. This important work is expensive to run, but generally addresses only the aftermath of conflict, not its causes. Everyone there knew that stopping refugee flows and suffering required a political solution. Yet we saw that only 10 percent of the funding went toward that goal. Would other choices reduce the suffering and flow of people?

We asked "How are things going in Syria?" There was an immediate consensus that it was not going well.

We then asked, "If we all do our jobs as well as is humanly possible, how will that change the direction in Syria?" Again, there was a rapid agreement: not at all.

At that point, the discussion had to expand. What might we do differently? What do the Syrians most need? How do we become strategic, agile, and operational?

Despite the right questions, the resulting exchange proved infertile. Why? Was the reality of the bombing so overwhelming that nothing else mattered? Did our bureaucratic structures restrict creativity? Are people so stuck in their assigned roles that getting "outside of their lanes" is impossible? We all felt the frustration.

After conceding that the White House was not ready to stop the bombing, we focused on other forms of personal safety and local governance—the two most promising areas for catalytic investment and often cited needs. Ambassador Ford offered encouragement.

To win, the moderate opposition would have to prove its value to the Syrian public. We recognized that the bombing would continue and that cohesion would take time. Yet, opportunities existed. We knew that personal and public safety was the primary concern of people all over Syria. If the opposition could deliver a modicum of protection, it was their best chance of convincing people of their ability to govern. We also saw that the opposition was capturing the imagination of the Syrian citizenry, from the outset. Could we help them expand their reach?

5.

Perhaps the most successful public safety program the United States helped seed was the White Helmets. It was a local idea that we tried to improve, providing supplies, training, and funding. Firefighters, paramedics, and nurses are always among the most trusted public officials in global surveys. In Syria, they addressed dramatic needs in bombed areas and showed that liberated leaders cared for those who remained. Towns created their own teams, recruiting from local communities. This kind of a successful model is a powerful building block in the midst of death and destruction.

A parallel success was the police in liberated Aleppo.

Besides bombing, the primary daily concern inside "liberated Syria" was safe streets. When not being shelled, Syrians wanted to get on with their lives in peace. In Aleppo, we saw a path to assist.

During the war, thousands of Syrian police defected from the government. Many remained in their home cities, seeking to continue as first responders. Communities accepted the police for risking their lives by leaving the regime and remaining in their neighborhoods. They were credible.

With the country at war and limited revenues for the newly independent municipalities, most of these remaining police were not paid. Through our regular contacts with the local opposition, CSO got to know the respected chief of police in Aleppo, General Adib Shallaf, and discovered that he had a professional force of 1,200 police still on duty. Their presence reassured people in the liberated part of the city and served as a firewall against extremists, who also sought to recruit from their ranks.

It was clear to the United States and our allies that maintaining that police force in Aleppo was a good idea—one we hoped to expand. CSO's approach was to provide security now, build from the bottom up and prepare to merge at the national level—when ready. Because of the logistical challenges and communication difficulties, programs like this were unusual for the U.S. government. The competing proposals were more standard options, such as training a new group of Syrian police in Jordan. That idea, eventually rejected, would have cost more, taken longer, and removed scarce capable people from their homes for months. Similar programs launched by intelligence agencies and the Defense Department became major financial and performance embarrassments.[11]

How could we help the Aleppo police to stay on the job, in their homes, and from joining the extremists who threatened them? In talking to the chief and the city's interim leaders, it became clear that a monthly stipend of about $200 for officers and $135 for the rank and file would allow them to keep working. Radios and vehicles would improve their efficiency.

The equipment and the stipends had to travel from southern Turkey into Syria. Any cross-border operation into a war zone is complicated— this one especially so. Some days, the Turks would interfere—closing the crossing, taxing a piece of equipment, or just objecting. As the war progressed, the Turks would support their own Syrian police—a continuation of Turkey's overriding concern with the Kurds, a large part of the Syrian opposition.

At other times, the routing inside of Syria would run into combat. Tracking the funds and trusting the delivery people was also tough. We tried to confirm transactions with photos and videos. To reduce the cost and exposure, we worked with our British and Danish allies, who shared our belief that the return was worth the risk. With the monthly stipend, initial professional law enforcement was possible.

Inside the U.S. government, even this kind of pragmatic step can be fraught with complications. After we'd been delivering the assistance, less than $180,000 per month, for a few months, State's lawyers asked whether any police might be linked to terrorists. They had no evidence, but if the media or Congress found a connection, it would be an embarrassment to State and ruinous to the program.

We vetted the chief and his top 35 officers. Nothing suspicious turned up. Still, the lawyers would not sign off on the next tranche until we had looked at the entire group.

The United States has a long-standing policy of vetting foreign military forces for human rights violations before providing aid. Expanded to include links to terrorism, the Leahy vetting process[12] helps to prevent U.S. funds from reaching those who commit heinous crimes.

Of course, it was possible in the chaos of Syria that some of these officers had ties to terrorists. However, we also knew our databases in Washington would be unlikely to identify them. We hadn't had access to or interest in these forces before the uprising. We did know that vetting the force would be slow and laborious because of the involvement of multiple parts of our own government. To me, the risk that a handful of the $135 monthly payments would fall into terrorist hands seemed well worth the tradeoff of 1,200 trained police on the streets. Our allies, the Danes and Brits, agreed, but once our process began they became more timid. But the inside U.S. government objectors declined to consider this cost/benefit analysis; one terrorist was too many.

At a long evening meeting with Chief Shallaf in Istanbul, we discussed ways to vet his Aleppo police corps for possible terrorist connections. The chief was adamant that a review of his entire force would be unnecessary and invasive. Already exposed to life-threatening retribution, his police did not want to give additional personal information to the U.S. government. WikiLeaks' recent publication of thousands of classified cables was fresh in his mind. He did not see us as a safe guarantor of the police profiles.

To counter his argument, I said, "At my hotel check-in, I just provided most of what we need for vetting: name, date of birth, home address, e-mail, and cell phone. If we run the security checks by building the profiles ourselves, it will take weeks to complete the task. Please share that information with us—to avoid delays."

Shallaf would not back down. "My computers are hacked by Assad. I cannot put those names online. If I send someone with a list, they might get killed." He sought our trust.

Already injured in assassination attempts, Shallaf was a leader who knew what was possible. One of our most enlightened partners, skillfully balancing the United States and his core constituency of nervous police, he had the courage to walk away from our financial backing. The chief wanted to take something home to his long-suffering people, but knew this was a compromise too far.

Disappointed, I concluded, "A delay of three or more months in payments should be expected. I fear that will put your entire force at risk."

Back in Washington, I sought to find a simpler solution than vetting 1,200 street police. I offered to face any blowback on the Hill or in the media, but we ended up laboring through the vetting for three months—despite raising my concerns directly to Secretary Kerry. He voiced his agreement and said that the entire mission would be at risk if we delayed, but for weeks, the inertia of excessive caution plowed on as we awaited a decision.

We assigned extra people to review databases and cross-check those names we had, with few returns. Each step would take hours and days. About 5 percent of the police showed up on some list of concern, but the information often proved incorrect upon further investigation. Even the 1 percent or so that remained after cross-checking raised questions about the validity of our systems. Still we labored on in a Star Chamber of our own making.

With the help of the assistant secretary of state for the region Anne Patterson, multiple appeals, meetings, and memos shook loose a decision from the National Security Council, and the stipends resumed. We halted our extreme vetting. Did the delay and involvement of senior officials improve the decision-making or disperse the risk? Perhaps, but I believe that it further damaged our relationship with Syrians whose service and trust was a great benefit. In the meantime, the police went unpaid for a dozen weeks, during which time our two enemies, Assad

and the jihadists, advanced. Similar initiatives in other regime-free cities, like Idlib, slowed. A good idea was nearly crippled.

These wars are not overpopulated with "good guys," so when we
increase the risk that our friends must take, we are shooting ourselves in
the foot. We knew that if the United States and our allies did not back
the police, undesirable parties would. In Aleppo, we left a vacuum
surrounded by extremists.

For a moment, the new government proved that it could deliver
public services, even in a war. With our allies, we built upon that start
by further professionalizing the police with uniforms, handcuffs, vehicles, motor bikes, office centers, and skill training. Policing, grounded
in a community, matters.

Our inability to take a wise risk further weakened our vulnerable
allies. Faced with an opportunity to prevent death and destruction,
America did not know how to seize it. This weakness was not a product
of our adversaries, but built into our own system. Even as the United
States made important contributions to governing and public safety, we
failed to make the most of it.

6.

Communications was a second critical element of developing a new
order in Syria. After decades of state-controlled news and information,
the emergence of cell phones, computers, and satellite television
opened up the Syrian market. Essential to the onset of the opposition's
demonstrations, social media took on a central role in offering the Syrian public competing voices and ideas.

Right from the beginning of the protests, the Syrian opposition produced pointed, charming, humorous, and effective cartoons, videos,
essays, and podcasts. With 20 percent of households on the Internet
and 80 percent receiving satellite television programming,[13] Syria was
primed. Tens of thousands had Facebook, and LinkedIn and Skype
were common.

In earlier work in Indonesia and Bosnia, USAID's OTI had been
able to expand the reach of moderating forces with modest media efforts. In Indonesia in 1999, in the midst of an Asian economic crisis,
attacks on the Chinese population, and the collapse of a long-term

dictatorship, a U.S.-supported national television campaign addressed the need to expand public debate and solve problems without violence. Designed by Indonesians and executed by a premier documentary film-maker, Garin Nugroho, the brief commercials captured the public imagination. Farmers, fishermen, students, dads, and daughters expressed their views that peaceful disagreement was desirable and possible as the country moved from an authoritarian leader to more open political debate.

Syrians were already undermining Assad's authority with a combination of devastating artwork, photos of torture, reports of attacks, and ridicule. In one series of cartoons, Assad was a rubber ducky, with his distinctive long neck and a crown askew on his head. It came from an intercepted message from Assad's wife, calling him "Ducky." Stickers of a yellow Assad duck showed up all over Syria. How could we build upon the diminution of a bully through humor?

We first supported a multimedia production shop of Syrians, all based in Istanbul. BasmaSyria became an advertising agency for the opposition, a center for posters, stickers, websites, and independent production of news videos. Able to collect film from all over Syria, BasmaSyria was an important distributor of the latest film clips, with footage running on the BBC, Al Jazeera, and other global outlets. While CSO was an initial funder, as BasmaSyria morphed into a series of new entities, independent financial support arrived. Many of the media centers that are now all over Syria came from BasmaSyria.

Activists wanted antiaircraft weapons and missiles, but they valued the ability to share their vision through rich content of a nonsectarian Syria with a broad-based civil society. In an article that questioned whether this kind of U.S. assistance is relevant during a war, one activist said, "'We want a civil state. It is important to train activists about this. . . . So these people can rebuild Syria tomorrow,' she said. 'It's very important now—not tomorrow, now. We had nothing, in 40 years, not one word, just clapping for the president. We have no idea about freedom.'"[14]

We also tried to use existing media in surrounding countries to expand the audiences for opposition sites inside of Syria. If more people would become consumers of opposition websites, the movement would grow faster. Data suggested that the most popular regional programming was soap operas. We tested some spot advertising on a few satellite stations to see if it might increase the number of visitors to opposition websites. The response was too modest to be cost effective.

Then we met a Syrian-American doctor[15] who had started a pirate FM radio station, Halab Today, in Aleppo, to provide up-to-date information on roadblocks, bombings, and personal safety. People wanted to know where they could travel safely. As violence increased, his audience grew. He mentioned that there would soon be a television station in the liberated part of the city—starting with a simple crawl that alerted citizens to dangerous places. He told us that technology upgrades, from collecting and reporting technology to stronger signal transmission, would reach more people. We backed his efforts, and surveys confirmed growing audiences.

Inspired by that model, we searched for other partners throughout Syria. Around Damascus, a Syrian oppositionist taunted the authorities by doing live FM radio broadcasts from close to the presidential palace. His guerrilla-style, 30-minute reports from a portable transmitter generated a broad listenership. Most of the other major cities had broadcast entrepreneurs sending out weak signals. So we sought to increase their reach. We backed a dozen transmitters and microtowers, which were mobile to stave off bombing, sniper attacks, or seizure.

We sought to open the country to independent local media for the first time in 40 years. At a modest cost of a few million dollars, CSO provided improved and secure equipment, along with professional training and coaching. Within months, there were a dozen or so radio and TV stations in every part of Syria, covering 80 percent of the population.[16] Normally these initiatives cost tens of millions.

As part of the commitment to maintain the independence and credibility of the Syrian voices, the United States did not address editorial content. Professional training and mentors, often respected journalists with experience in the region, guided the Syrians. We knew the Syrians could better gauge their audience's needs and tastes.

In January 2014, the United Nations' peace envoy, Lakhdar Brahimi, worked with the United States and Russia to convene a second round of peace talks called Geneva II. An earlier meeting produced important guiding principles, but low expectations accompanied this round of talks. Nevertheless, it was the only chance offered. With the heroic assistance of a Swiss diplomat, CSO helped a handful of Syria's new, independent journalists secure visas so they could join the world's coverage.

For the first time, Western journalists saw independent Syrian news people challenge their government's minister of information and ambassador to the United Nations. In front of the world, the Syrian reporters asked direct questions of those who bombed them. The rest of the press was awestruck and filed stories on the Syrians. It was one of the few breakthroughs of Geneva II.

One day they chased the minister into a breakfast meeting, filming the entire event. On camera, they stated, "You say that you cannot find ISIS—that they are hard to locate. Well, here is a map which shows you where they are." The video went viral.

Reliable information began to meet the Syrians' pent-up demand. Radio complemented the resourcefulness of the opposition: "Syrians could pick up a pencil and a microphone and fight the war with truth and information. American assistance and the Syrians aligned well on this."[17]

To this day, the opposition outflanks the Assad regime in most every communication category because of the wider range of sources and independent reporting standards. From on-site reporting and videos of the latest atrocity, to films about the White Helmets, the Free Syria story dominates the local and global narrative, despite the natural advantages of the Assad regime. The opposition is seen as more credible. Media centers have proliferated all over Syria, the radio stations continue in the region, and it is one of the few advantages that those who started the revolution enjoy. In Syria, access to information is of great value, though not yet determinative of change.

7. LESSONS APPLIED FROM SYRIA

In Syria, we forgot valuable lessons from prior experience in conflicts. We did not know the opposition we sought to support; we lacked a government-wide, integrated strategy; and we did not move quickly or early enough. We may have avoided land combat and delivered aid, but we missed many opportunities to promote catalytic, potentially game-changing ideas. By December 2017, the United States had 2,000 soldiers on the ground in Syria and conducted regular bombing. Here then are three lessons from Syria:

I. State Your Purpose and Remove Ambiguity.

Our mission in Syria should have stated, *"We will do everything possible for the opposition to win without committing U.S. ground troops."* That was within our capacity and would have put a different, more creative range of options on the table. Instead, we are stuck between "keeping the lights on" by providing minimal support to the opposition and "keeping the Syrians alive in a dark room"[18] with humanitarian aid.

Clarity breeds commitment. The failure to articulate a core argument for why Syria matters contributed mightily to more than seven years of brutal suffering.

The American public needed to hear that the original Syrian opposition was a genuine revolutionary movement—grassroots and peaceful in its founding, supportive of an open and just society, and eager for freedom. It also needed to know that Assad has the deaths of 400,000 at his feet, threatens his neighbors and our regional allies (Israel, Jordan, and Turkey), serves Iran's menacing interests, and provides a focal point for all manner of regional destabilization.

A clear and simple mission would have unleashed two focused U.S. goals: (1) build up the opposition to make them more able to win and be able to lead when they took over; and (2) stop the bombing.

Instead, we had a mosh pit of ideas from "managed transition" to "contain and mitigate" to "refrain from jumping in with both feet" to negotiated ceasefires—all somehow elevating and restoring Assad's standing in a future Syria.[19] Agreements with Russia for de-escalation zones kept being violated—or provided a chance for the regime to focus its attacks and then double back.[20]

Where the United States made a first-rate effort, in the removal of chemical weapons, humanitarian relief, and support for resourceful local initiatives, we made a real contribution to peace. Where we feigned interest—in military assistance, to halt the bombing, and to align our allies—we misled our Syrian friends. When we treated Assad as a rational actor, the United States made progress.

After Assad used chemical weapons on his own people in 2013, crossing President Obama's red line, we appeared headed for war. Obama then detoured, saying he would ask Congress for approval before attacking. As a result, almost 80 members of Congress cut short their weekends for a Sunday White House briefing. Public interest in Syria tripled, from 15 percent before Obama's speech to 45 percent in the days after. In other words, when asked to confront the situation, their investment increased. This is the type of informed debate we should have had all along; it may have changed the public's view.

The red line episode yielded one unexpected benefit: removal of 1,300 tons of chemical weapons from Syria, thanks to the Russians' picking up on an off-the-cuff remark from Secretary Kerry. It showed that success in negotiation was possible, but the United States did not push to broaden the discussions to an aerial ceasefire or real guarantees of humanitarian access. It was another missed chance.

America's Syrian friends expected a full-bodied commitment, but that expectation ran into a bureaucratic grinder. Almost every part of the U.S. government could have picked up its game. Instead we featured institutional resistance. Many hid behind the White House's reluctance and carried on as if Syria was not their problem. "Without a policy, what can we do?" became a common excuse.

Rather than building off the lessons of Afghanistan and Iraq, Washington bought into the argument that Syria would be one more quagmire. Of course, that potential existed. But not if we left a comfort zone that was failing us. The military should have offered high value military targets in retribution for Assad's savage bombing. Diplomats should have let go of the central leader and organizational model and worked with emerging local prospects. The humanitarians should have contributed to political solutions, like an Aleppo airlift. The intelligence community should have been able to identify local talent and produce better insights into Assad's vulnerabilities, the government's likely post-Assad capacity, and the terror threat.

Instead, we stood by like tourists and watched the inevitable consequences of inaction. Endless rounds of suffering, followed by a growing and predictable U.S. response that looks like more of the same: bomb and flatten, negotiate with the usual suspects, and hope for the best.

Instead of clarity, we were stuck with wishful thinking. "Our assistance sent a message of support but did not provide enough of any kind of help to make a dent on the regime or its allies. We led people on and may have even put the Syrians in greater danger" was the conclusion of my team in Syria. [21]

A clear and attainable mission is central to success. We did not identify one, much less explain it or live by it.

II. Address the Number One Concern of Those You Seek to Help.

Bombing was foremost in the minds of our Syrian allies and it needed to be in ours. Aerial attacks became Assad's defining advantage and we did nothing to neutralize them.

Legendary diplomat George Kennan's words are appropriate. "You have no idea how much it contributes to the general politeness and pleasantness of diplomacy when you have a little quiet force in the background."[22] Limited, targeted, and retributive actions could force Assad to change course—and nothing much else worked. We diddled as Assad bombed, and the results are painful to behold.

America's firing of 59 Tomahawk missiles on the Syrian airbase of Al Shayrat in April 2017 wiped away several myths, including the impenetrability of Assad's air defense. By striking fighter jets, hardened aircraft shelters, radar equipment, ammunition bunkers, sites for storing fuel, and air defense systems, in retaliation for chemical bombing by the regime,[23] we showed that America could neutralize Assad's single most destructive advantage. No clear policy was forthcoming, but the warning emboldened the opposition for a brief moment. Trump was hailed as "Abu Ivanka, the American."

The Syrians needed a consistent U.S. policy that sought every way to halt the bombing, from humanitarian airlifts to direct military punishment for attacks on civilians. We needed to say, "If you bomb, you will be bombed."

III. Capitalize on the Courage and Ingenuity of the Locals.

The Syrian uprising was sincere and dedicated, a nationwide movement for change led by locals—large, decentralized, and unknown. Many in the U.S. government did not know how to engage these groups. Some saw these local movements as a weakness, as they lacked a national leader. Our capabilities, and our bias, favor supporting single, united groups; it's easier to deal with one partner than a dozen. We did not adapt to this situation or take advantage of their strengths—to our detriment and theirs.

Assad's suppression of opposition made a cohesive core a long shot. Indeed, the centralized opposition was a construct that collapsed at its first test. We ostensibly wanted to help, but not enough to change paradigms to a grassroots-first approach. That would have been the best bet in Syria.

The foreign-based leaders we sought out, politically minded but living in exile, never gained traction in their erstwhile homeland. As my team put it, "The plumbers, pipefitters and auto mechanics who were leading the struggle inside did not know or respect [the diaspora] . . . and did not see them making the same sacrifices."[24]

The U.S. government also feared that aid would land in the hands of extremists. That soon became a self-fulfilling prophecy, as moderates, lacking our assistance, couldn't match the extremists' firepower. Some joined the extremists as a matter of survival.

At an Istanbul meeting with two of America's leaders on Syria and Iraq, retired general John Allen and Ambassador Brett McGurk, opposition figure Rami Jarrah warned the U.S. leaders against withdrawing aid because of the presence of ISIS. "Local councils are contesting extremists because of U.S. support such as medicine, food, media and governing tools," he said. "Take that away and you hasten the control of what you most fear. It is the worst thing you can do."[25]

Makes sense, the Americans responded. But the machine was already clearing out U.S. aid, fearing that it would touch terrorists.[26]

America's habitual ignorance of remote areas of unstable and fragile countries also bred an aversion to teaming up with the unknown. Beyond the capitals and a few major population centers, our blindness continues.

8.

Syria got worse. In mid-2014, the Islamic State of Iraq and Syria (ISIS) launched a campaign to establish a militant, ultraconservative caliphate, surprising the world by overrunning large portions of Syria and Iraq with relative ease. This explicit terrorist threat drew a quick response from the United States and Arab world, which launched airstrikes in September 2014. While ISIS was the stated target, al-Nusra, an off-shoot of al-Qaeda, was hit. Since they had provided some effective fighting for the opposition, the U.S. attack further confused our friends. Why not start with ISIS, which was universally hated?

In September 2015, the Russians began direct airstrikes within Syria. Despite their insistence that the strikes targeted terrorists, most hit moderate opposition strongholds. Unreliable behavior characterized most of our dealings with Russia in Syria.

By the end of 2016, America was deep into the bombing of ISIS-controlled areas in the east of Syria and Iraq. Concentrated in Iraq, the U.S. strikes began to diminish ISIS's grip on territory. Within weeks of its inception, the military action dwarfed the humanitarian and political assistance—in dollars spent and public attention. We prosecuted the ISIS atrocities, overlooking those of the regime. By this point, 400,000 lives had been lost, and 11 million had left their homes, including almost five million who traveled outside Syria's borders.[27]

In late December 2016, thousands of residents and opposition fighters evacuated "one of the world's great ancient cities," Aleppo, driven out by the bombing of the regime and its allies. "Some families burned heirlooms. . . . Ahmed al-Mashadi, an engineer, said his wife had cried as she watched the flames creep through her wedding dress. 'She couldn't carry it, but she couldn't leave it behind,' he said."[28] Pro-regime militias were looting all they overran. The United Nations called the nightmare "a complete meltdown of humanity."[29]

Despite more than $10 billion of humanitarian and military spending, the United States is not making enough of a difference in Syria. David Ignatius wrote in the *Washington Post*, "The U.S. decision to pursue a dual-track, halfway approach made the mayhem worse. . . . The effort began late . . . was a hodgepodge . . . and Kerry had the impossible job of trying to manage a policy that was going in two directions at once. . . . [H]e got crushed in the rubble of a confused policy."[30]

Syria is a tragedy that was not of America's making. Unable to work inside of Syria, the United States did not control many variables. But we could have mitigated, shortened, and, perhaps, helped end it. It took more than our traditional way. An openness to new practices and creative ideas was necessary—but that is a weakness of our national security community.

In a case like Syria, the United States must take advantage of what is present; instead, we pursued the familiar. We tried what we had ready, and when it did not work, we did it again. In Syria, there was a true and devoted majoritarian insurgency, though fractured. After so many years of oppression, they needed to be cultivated. Perhaps we held out too long for unity. Perhaps we thought the conflict would be over quickly. But we provided little to help them.

Those of us who worked there feel the sadness of missed opportunities. Our best minds and ideas failed Syria's revolution. Opportunities abound in these catastrophic places—if you are open to them. Local police forces maintained order; social media, radio, and TV stations blossomed; artists and authors expressed their resistance; young people demonstrated; thousands sacrificed their lives; many more sought to govern their municipalities and schools; courageous leaders emerged; extremism was opposed; and the search for a just peace continued. It goes on.

Now, Syrians face grim prospects. America's original allies, the moderate opposition, are a shadow of their promising start, squeezed into ever-smaller terrain. Islamic extremists remain a threat, though their territorial ambitions are dwindling. The conflict has destabilized Syria's neighbors, like Turkey, Lebanon, and Jordan. Refugee flows threaten allied governments throughout the region and Europe. Russia is in full proxy war mode, while the United States is asserting itself more on the margins.

"The Syrian state is a mere shadow of itself," a U.S. official stated in December 2017. They described "a severely weakened Syrian state, grappling with challenges including loss of oil revenue; severe infrastructure damage; increasing reliance on outside powers for cash, food and fighters; and a military barely able to keep multiple armed groups at bay."[31] Somehow, Bashar Assad is emerging as the near-term survivor—a leader who will never enjoy the support of Syria's people. He has succeeded in making Syria ungovernable by anybody.

Syria cracked the broader American conscience twice. Despite the gruesome suffering and hundreds of thousands of deaths, Google tracking showed that the public engaged in large numbers only during the "red line" crisis and again when a three-year-old Syrian refugee, Alan Kurdi, washed up on the shores of Turkey as he sought safe passage to

Greece in September 2015. The photo of his lifeless body cradled in the arms of a local policeman shocked Americans.

As violence dominated, there was little drive or purpose to America's Syria policy. President Obama recognized the widespread resistance within the United States to another war and he faced a string of daunting domestic challenges. An already distractible Washington hardly needed another preoccupation.

Our failure to find a new path kept us from helping the Syrian opposition win. Those who felt the exultance of free speech and governing responsibility were already exhausted when I last visited them in 2014. The president of the Free Aleppo Provincial Council told me at that time that the thrill was gone—replaced by the fatigue of not being able to provide for the thousands that he now led. "At first, I reveled in the ability to say what I believed and to speak critically of the regime. The new freedoms were intoxicating," Yahya Nanaa said. "Now, I have the responsibility for taking care of my people and almost no way to do it." [32]

9

WHAT MIGHT WE SEE IN THE YEARS AHEAD?

What emerging patterns of violence and wars do we see?

With the defeat of ISIS in Mosul in the summer of 2017, there was one more confirmation that taking and holding territory invited the wrath of conventional firepower. The ISIS dream of building a new caliphate lay in the rubble of numerous cities where U.S. and allied bombing destroyed their geographic bases and economic expansionism.

This experience paralleled the territorial pretensions of others in every part of the world. Even those whose only footprint might be a cell phone could now be spotted most anywhere on earth and targeted. Nomadic terrorists in Somalia or al-Qaeda chiefs in Pakistan are now subject to a drone strike or a Special Forces mission.

The more difficult threats now have adapted, evolving to fit into the landscape or growing out of existing structures. While overall global violence is dropping, the appearance of unpredictable attacks or bombings almost anywhere at any time is changing the sense of security for people everywhere. Those events that were happening in distant places with "strange" names now occur in London or Paris, or on a military base in Texas.

Combined with the miniaturization of weaponry and the connectivity of communications, we are more likely to see individual violence, informal networks, and disturbing actions than the taking and holding of territory. There will be exceptions, such as Russia's seizing of Crimea, and there are enough unsettled border disputes between states to fuel a few more decades of militarized confrontations.

Still, the flow is to regularize the violence into the normal course of life. In this chapter, we will see how that was attempted in four countries and how the United States sought creative ways to increase our beneficial role. These all come from my time at the State Department's Bureau of Conflict and Stabilization Operations (CSO), where we tried to catalyze peaceful local initiatives: in every case they are first steps, with most of the responsibility in local hands.

In Kenya, the violence is an extension of traditional political activities; in Nigeria, violence is a central part of the national narrative; in Burma/Myanmar, violence continues in proscribed, ethnic areas; and in the Northern Triangle of Central America, it is part of a plague of gangs, narco-traffickers and organized crime destruction.

Emerging threats will be clothed in familiar garb. It is incumbent upon those who seek to expand peace to find new and creative ways to empower local communities to ward off the violence.

There is a great deal of room for improvement, and these stories offer promise.

I. KENYA'S ELECTION VIOLENCE

The Kenyan elections of 2007 had been disastrous. A new volatility appeared as traditional political elites inflamed tribal divisions and youth groups rampaged. "Vernacular radio," a series of 40 or so idiomatic stations, became platforms for the mobilization of violent activities and incitement. When the vote counting turned problematic, chaos ensued. More than a thousand people died in several weeks of violence, 2,500 reported sexual assaults, and more than 300,000 left their homes. Local authorities did not deal with the mayhem and in some places inflamed it. The national army responded and international negotiators, including Kofi Annan, the retired secretary general of the United Nations, sought to help. Economic growth dropped by half.

Kenya, a center of African stability and the hub for international progress in eastern Africa, reeled.

In the post-disaster response, Kenya instituted a number of reforms, including a new constitution, police, and justice structure. Among the forbidden political acts was hate speech and the singling out of groups for attack. A massive structural change of government led to the devolution of authority with provinces broken down into counties and elections of governors and assemblies. A promising chief justice, with authorities to resolve election-related disputes, took office. Many parts of Kenyan civil society became more active, creating a supportive infrastructure for the expected 2012 election. Business and religious leaders recognized a need for greater responsibility. Social media entrepreneurs developed new ways to identify emerging threats.

Despite the formal steps taken in Kenya, a sense of foreboding about election-related violence remained. Conversations with Kenyans still centered on "tribal interests" and "voting your tribe," and a presidential rerun of tired leaders did not augur well. Disputes remained about potential candidates implicated in the 2007 violence, including possible trials before the International Criminal Court in The Hague. With no new national police chief, the first line of response was in disarray. The press mattered, but suffered from self-censorship and doubts about its 2007 coverage. A growing youth population appeared vulnerable to exploitation and a nervous public waited with its fingers crossed.

In many ways, Kenya looked like a classic conflict prevention opportunity. Could the United States be helpful?

2.

To work anywhere in the world at the State Department, you must have the support of the traditional power centers, the geographic bureaus, and their embassies. Bilateral relationships dominate and turf protection is constant. As CSO took shape in late 2011, I met with each of the regional assistant secretaries of state to identify priority countries.

With decades of exemplary service in Nigeria, Uganda, and Kenya, Assistant Secretary for Africa and Ambassador Johnnie Carson garnered widespread respect. He spoke of the many election challenges facing the continent and finished with Kenya. "If there is a repeat of 2007, it will be awful!" he said. We spoke about the special challenges of Kenya and agreed to a three-way call with Ambassador Scott Gration, embattled as an outsider within State and at the embassy in Nairobi, yet trusted at the White House as one of the few retired generals to support Barack Obama's early presidential candidacy.

Together we threaded a number of bureaucratic needles and sent a small team to the embassy to help integrate a range of U.S. government election-related efforts. With our colleagues from USAID and State, the initial field analysis suggested that two areas of Kenya warranted special attention: Rift Valley, where violence peaked in 2007, and the Coast, where long-standing land disputes and divisions threatened. As a result, CSO sent small teams to both areas to provide greater insights and to identify and build new partnerships.

On a visit to the village of Burnt Forest, our police-escorted mini-caravan pulled over to look at some of the destruction from 2007. By the time we got out of our cars, a group of 30 to 40 "youths" (in Kenya this means from 18 to 40 years of age) surrounded us. We decided to hold a series of impromptu, roadside focus groups, with the members of our party each asking a series of questions of five to ten young Kenyans.

The results spoke volumes. Here in a deep rural area, prone to violence, a group of underemployed "youths" seemed conversant with critical elements of the Kenyan election run-up. The prior day's arrest of a parliamentarian for "hate speech" and the constitutional clause that addressed it received approval, by name and section. They spoke about leading candidates and their jeopardy before the "ICC (International Criminal Court) and The Hague" (its home location). Their sophistication confirmed the high level of attention and anxiety that Kenyans at every level of society had for the election. We continued to reach out and learn more.

With the oft-delayed election scheduled for March 4, 2013, CSO recognized shortcomings in our efforts to help the Kenyans. Initial mobilization of concerned groups was progressing but we did not feel as if there was critical mass or that the connection to the police was adequate. We also wanted to expand our target beyond the Rift Valley, since a top of the ticket coalition altered tribal pressures.

Thanks to a USAID colleague, we lucked into a fall 2012 meeting of the dozen major recipients of U.S. assistance in the inflamed Rift Valley area. Often, these events turn into dog and pony shows, with each program detailing the wonders of their work. With limited time, we engaged in a rapid-fire exchange.

"Irrespective of your personal or organizational work, what do you think is the most important challenge facing Kenya?" I asked.

"The upcoming election and related violence" was the immediate consensus of the attendees.

"Are you doing everything you would like to address that challenge?" I continued.

"No," they answered.

"What might you do?" I pursued.

A surprising set of possibilities appeared. The director of a horticultural program responded first. "We only have 500 farmers in our initiative, would they be of any value?" he asked.

My response was intuitive. "If you started with 500 farmers in the U.S., you could probably get elected governor of almost any state except for Texas." The Kenyans instinctively understood the potential.

Next to speak was the head of an AIDS project. "We visit over 200,000 households a week." Others chimed in, including a university group of over 5,000 students. The potential of a large, diverse network excited them.

If they organized themselves to promote a peaceful election and served as a check on those who employed violence, their numbers would serve as a powerful early warning system for the police and might outflank incendiary elements. Furthermore, their active presence would require the justice system to play its official role, particularly in terms of a rapid response to disturbances.

What did they need to come together and play their parts? Pressed, they all said that the immediate addition of a staffer or two for a six-month period around the election would allow them to mobilize their networks to prevent the spread of violence.

Within six weeks, the United States provided a modest amount of funding that empowered the Kenyans to engage in the most troublesome issue facing their country. The $650,000 or so that was spent on more than 100 Kenyans working inside of local organizations to deal with their own futures would have paid for fewer than five Americans for the same period. U.S. assistance helped to mobilize greater forces with new energy and fresh messages of nonviolence.

The groups and other elements of civil society came together as Champions of Peace, the Kenya Election Violence Prevention and Response (KEVP) initiative. The Kisumu chapter would report, "The creation of an 'Early Warning Early Response Call Centre' . . . enhances public-police cooperation, which for a long time had been characterized by suspicion and hostility."[1]

It was not perfect. Some felt that the election continued a Kenyan tradition of "negotiated democracy," which formalized existing divisions; others, that the United States traded "stability over accountability" to produce "the worst of all nonviolent outcomes." Still, the United States helped Kenyans to diffuse destructive political energy.[2]

While the election results did not produce a leadership change, the restoration of a peaceful political process was a vital first step.

3. NIGERIA'S DAMAGING NATIONAL NARRATIVE

As violence spread in Nigeria in 2012, I heard from the secretary of state's office. An expansion of Boko Haram attacks threatened entire states in the north and spawned regional terrorism. They took over large swaths of countryside and the kidnapping of dozens of girls from a regional school shocked the country and the world. Instability in the petrochemical-producing south put the government's revenues at risk. Even the multinational oil companies, often able to operate in their own safe zones, hedged their investments.[3] In the capital of Abuja, a bombing destroyed the U.N. headquarters. Meanwhile, the super-city of Lagos, with more than 20 million people jammed into a too-small urban mess, had a concerning edginess.[4]

Nigeria mattered to the United States. With Africa's largest population and economy, Nigeria provided significant energy exports and served as an anchor in a turbulent part of the world.

A dynamic society of 150 million with rapid economic growth, Nigeria faced a range of modernization pressures. After a series of disappointing governments, and now led by an "accidental president," Goodluck Jonathan,[5] Nigeria seemed incapable of dealing with the emerging violence. Unpopular military regimes compromised the armed forces. Corruption charges discredited public officials throughout the country. Urban and rural divides grew.

Most troubling, a national narrative that violence pays in Nigeria emerged. That became our central challenge.

As our teams sought insights and partnerships, they noticed openings. We saw that failures in the central government created opportunities for governors and met several capable technocrats. We heard that an explosion of radio, television, and social media, with hundreds of thousands connected by Facebook and LinkedIn, provided a new check on officialdom. Large populations of Catholics, Anglicans, Muslims, and Evangelicals spoke to the diversity of the population and a visit to a super-church, outside of Lagos, with its 9,000-seat sanctuary and television production, hinted at rapid societal transformation. "Occupy Lagos" and other movements kept coming up in conversations. An entrepreneurial instinct flourished.

How might we help the Nigerians to bring together their native dynamism with some of the opportunities we saw everywhere? To challenge "violence pays," an initiative would need to reach directly to the populace, minimize the role of the central government in Abuja, use the sophistication of all media, and appeal to the abundant native pride in identifying local solutions.

Addressing a problem like the spread of violence in a sprawling/brawling place like Nigeria is difficult. Doing it in short order and with a limited amount of money (we imagined $5 million) compounds the challenge. Your only chance of success is to go with the energy of local people who harbor similar dreams and know how to appeal to a broader public.[6]

Often, I have heard people say, "What we need is a national dialogue." Seldom have I witnessed such a desired event. What we began to imagine in Nigeria was a compelling exchange built upon the ability of Nigerians to replicate their own peaceful local solutions in an amped-up environment.

Physical danger in the north limited our work there. The embassy in Abuja directed us to the violence in the Delta region and with the assistance of the Lagos-based consul general, we focused on that oil-rich area. We believed that a success there would reach into other parts of Nigeria.

The Delta was fraught with challenges, including kidnappings, hostage takings, assassinations, pipeline tapping and illegal refining fires, official corruption, and intimidation. Though there was an amnesty program in place to compensate thousands of "youths" involved in the violence, it would end soon. An anxious calm prevailed.

We flew into Port Harcourt to meet with potential partners.

4.

Sometimes you just get lucky. Over coffee in a Port Harcourt hotel, we spoke with Ken Henshaw, the thoughtful young author of several reports on the breakdown of society in the Delta. After congratulating him on the quality of his work, we asked, "How many people do you think read this?"

Half-joking, Ken said, "About seven." That led us to a conversation about increasing the impact of his work, something that had been on our minds since visiting a range of progressive programs in different parts of the country.

As we spoke about the possibility of popularizing through the media the peaceful advances of Nigerians, Ken expressed himself in his English-educated best, "Brilliant!"

We then asked, "How do we make a connection to the world of Nigerian entertainment and news?"

Then there was a moment of divine-like intervention. He said, "I am the middle son of three. If my youngest brother were here right now, we could not walk down the street with him, because of his celebrity. He is the host of a wildly popular television show, and everyone knows him. You need to meet with him when you return to Lagos."

And so we came to meet the host of "Nigeria's Got Talent," Andre Blaze Henshaw, and in turn "Superstar Director Jeta Amata" (that is the way that he is greeted and spoken to by most people), Nigeria's preeminent film director. Working with them and a wonderful steering committee of business, religious, social, and political figures, the Niger Delta Legacy Engagement started and a plan developed.

At its heart was a series of locally produced Nollywood films, made by local "youths," that would present real-life problems and offer nonviolent, Nigerian-made solutions. Nollywood is Africa's largest cinema industry, with films made in days for less than $50,000 and distributed throughout the continent and into Asia. Most are soap opera–like morality plays, watched in gatherings throughout Nigeria.

In order to reach a national television audience, Jeta Amata would film the selection of the towns, the recruiting of the young moviemakers, the production of the works, the grand openings, and the local dialogues, and turn that into a 13-week reality television series called *Dawn in the Creeks*. The entire country would see the television show plus the daily advertising and promotional spots.

Local talk radio, blogs, Facebook, Twitter, and posts cross-promoted the series, which appeared on every major Nigerian network. The excellent studies, reports, and local initiatives that the Nigerians identified blended into the popular messages.

It exceeded our expectations. Jeta Amata's amazing work with *Dawn in the Creeks* humanized the new narrative. The films and the young Delta teams that produced them met national audiences at a Lagos red-carpet event and on *Today*-like interview programs everywhere, and a second season took shape.

Local town meetings complemented the national dialogue. On a visit to the riverine kingdom of Nembe, we saw a city of 150,000 caught up in filmmaking and the issue of violence. As one of the first three towns that Jeta had selected, Nembe went through a couple of months of team development, filmmaking, and public meetings. Locals were stars in the movies and a wide swath of the population engaged. A creative spark touched their lives where it most mattered and we witnessed the start of a community-wide discussion on violence.

The American ambassador's arrival and the attendant celebration was one more reaffirmation that Nembe and Nigeria could bring the talent of their people together to redirect the destructive forces of violence into more constructive channels.

As one of the young filmmakers, Regina Joseph, said, "I want to change the story on Nembe. People think we're militants. The story is 'Fight, fight, fight. This war, that war.' But we're more than just that." In polling following the series, 83 percent of those watching said they were inspired, 67 percent felt connected to the shows, and 88 percent said that *Dawn in the Creeks* would inspire change.[7]

Throughout the country, the core message that Nigerians could peacefully resolve difficult issues dominated the airwaves.[8] Taking on a dominant story line is one way to reverse a tradition of violence. It is only a step in a longer journey, but an effective start.

5. BURMA—BREAKING CYCLES OF VIOLENCE

Amid the euphoria of the opening of Myanmar's political system in 2011, there was a real concern that the Burmese ruling class would try to finesse the ethnic conflicts that threatened stability in large parts of the country. Ongoing fighting and more than a million people displaced in the prior decade, with hundreds of thousands in refugee camps in Thailand, made denial difficult. Yet, that would be the natural course of business. As long as the violence was in remote areas and the responsibility of the military, the dominant Burmese ethnic group could go about the business of joining the rest of the world and disregard the violence.

After extensive discussions within the U.S. government, it was clear that America's policy would have three central elements: open up the military-dominated political system to more democratic civilians; deal with the ethnic wars all over Myanmar; and do business with this promising market of 60 million people. It was the feeling at CSO that the first and third elements would get plenty of attention—and that the ethnic minorities' struggle would be the forgotten determinant of long-range success.

It was not easy to see how to engage. Wherever we searched for an opening, there seemed to be a mysterious or invisible military hand dominating. The post-2011 reform package had created civilian positions but a visit to the sprawling new ministry buildings in the recently created capital of Naypyidaw left us with two confusing insights: that the real authority was elsewhere and that these promising officials were raw—just learning their jobs.

Thanks to the creative work of CSO's deputy assistant secretary of state, Jerry White, and his team, we began to find a way forward. Jerry had been the co-founder of the Land Mine Survivors Network and he saw the unifying potential of approaching both sides of the conflict through the land mine issue. We would use the mutual abhorrence of land mines and the many lives they had cost or ruined on both sides to begin a dialogue that focused on awareness and mapping. If we could help bring together people who hated the same thing, perhaps a broader discussion would follow. Of additional benefit was the presence in the country of Norwegian and U.N. land mine efforts. Initially, it could not include land mine removal, since earlier efforts led the fighters on both sides to access new territory. The trust deficit was still too great.

Kayah was the right place to start. In the middle of Myanmar's stretched-out eastern border, Kayah is the smallest of the long-embattled ethnic states. A mountainous outpost of fewer than 300,000, less than twice the size of Delaware, Kayah and its Karenni people have featured six decades of fighting, truces, broken cease-fires, massive dislocations and relocations of people, and human rights violations.

In the past few years, while more peaceful than other areas, Kayah's experience mirrors the post-1948 independence struggle between the national government and its 17 major ethnic rebel groups. Initially excluded from the new central government, the Karenni have embraced the idea of autonomy under a federal system. That has been painfully slow in coming.

Its size and a relatively successful cease-fire were promising. We also thought that its remoteness from Yangon, the nerve center of Myanmar, could provide some space and time to initiate a new model for engagement of all parties. A national peace process was underway, with a trusted senior confidante of the military ruler in place, but the multicentric nature of the nearly 70-year civil war was testing his modest operation.

6.

Through mist-covered hills on an early fall morning in 2012, an American delegation flew from Yangon into the sleepy capital of Kayah, Loikaw. Embassy personnel, led by Ambassador Derek Mitchell, an expert in Myanmar, filled all twelve seats of a small Burmese airliner. The presence of the first U.S. ambassador to visit this provincial center confirmed that the United States was deeply committed to promoting the peace between the government and the ethnic minorities.

We were catalyzing something that might otherwise be set aside—either on purpose, or because it was too tough, or less important if other matters came up. The United States could play this role.

As we drove around the mostly dirt roads of Loikaw we began to see the potential. The governor, a military officer and appointee of the regime, offered a warm welcome and expressed enthusiasm for a series of community meetings about land mines. A small prosthetics organization and workshop introduced us to the community of survivors that Jerry saw as bridging the gap between sides.

In the middle of the town, we stopped at the headquarters of the rebel movement. It was a fully established office protected by a few of their own armed guards, with meeting rooms for the fighters and members. What did that level of out-front presence mean? We saw few national military or police, yet all felt that the regional commander was likely to be the most influential figure. He was out of town.

A longstanding Catholic mission hosted a simple but gracious luncheon and we had a chance to meet a range of people from all over Kayah. Again, they voiced their enthusiasm for a fuller discussion with all parties. At the state university, we observed how Kayah had suffered. Not only did the campus seem to have limited financial support from the national government, there was also a suggestion that faculty members who had irritated the authorities elsewhere ended up in Loikaw for extended cooling-off periods.

In a meeting with a group of 15 students, I saw how remote this university was from the rest of Asia. Not one of the students had cell phones and the only computer was in a nearby café. Much of that was due to exorbitant charges for SIM cards, imposed by the central government throughout the country to limit exposure to new ideas. With prices dropping from $1,000 to $50, and soon $5, in Yangon, I felt that on subsequent visits to Kayah there would be an explosion of cellular technology. That would be an irreversible change.

All were ready to expand their cooperation over the land mine issue. What mattered most was not the progress on land mines, which had an inherent value, but rather, the coming together of parties who had found scant opportunities to cooperate in decades.

Complications came from everywhere. The ham-handed Burmese way with ethnic minorities would continue and a long-expected national ceasefire suffered delays. Local breaks in the fighting allowed all sides to rearm and reinforce themselves and initiate fresh incursions. The Chinese inserted themselves into the Kachin group negotiations—and the Burmese rebuffed them. The dealings of the military and civilian leaders with the stateless Rohingya in Rakhine state led to ethnic cleansing, with hundreds of thousands wallowing in temporary camps in both Myanmar and Bangladesh.

Yet, there was something promising happening in Kayah—perhaps a model to build upon.

7. GANGS AND MORE IN NORTH CENTRAL AMERICA

The problem was disastrous. El Salvador, Guatemala, and Honduras faced a combination of drug lords, organized crime, and gangs—and the world's highest homicide rates.[9] Drugs transited through all three countries and entire neighborhoods were emptying.[10] To survive, young people were taking huge risks to reach the United States, seeking "asylum from the drug gangs' violence."[11]

Secretary of State Hillary Clinton was frustrated. Counterparts in the northern triangle of Central America kept beseeching her for more effective U.S. help to reverse a cascade of violence. When she asked within the U.S. government what we might do, the answers kept coming back as "more of the same." Skewed to fighting drug trafficking, the U.S. portfolio featured flight monitoring, police equipment, training and vetting, and some initial work on target communities.

The secretary's insistent pleas and mounting evidence that our approach was not working stirred Assistant Secretary of State for the Americas Roberta Jacobson to convene a small emergency meeting in early 2012. The five of us who gathered recognized that the present course was untenable.

With characteristic directness, former ambassador to Colombia and then assistant secretary of state for International Narcotics and Law Enforcement (INL, more commonly referred to as "Drugs and Thugs") Bill Brownfield said, "Let's assume that 50% of the problem is that people don't know what we are doing and that the other 50% is we need to do something different."[12] That cleared the air and we began to imagine alternatives.

We needed new approaches, including a shared focus on key towns and neighborhoods. Within weeks, small teams visited the region and I had a chance to follow and look at the challenges. In each of the three countries, there were intriguing local initiatives that appeared promising—and in need of catalytic assistance.

8.

In El Salvador, there was an experimental truce between the two largest gangs. With a senior advisor, Chuck Call, we met with the negotiators, charismatic monsignor Fabio Colindres and the formerly hard-line ex-general David Mungia Payes, now minister of public security. "Mano duro" or hard hand policies dominated El Salvador's history, to little avail. With 10,000 gang members in jail, executions and extortion did not diminish.

It was a sober discussion. The priest and the minister described the sophistication of the gangs' operations, much of it learned in Los Angeles when Salvadorans fled the earlier civil war. The minister told us, "We are in a state of war, with 15–20 murders a day, so I had to bring the warring parties to the table." The gang truce had started just weeks before and already the homicide rate was fewer than five per day. [13]

With most of the senior leaders imprisoned, the monsignor coaxed the two gangs, Mara Salvatrucha (MS 13) and the 18th Street Gang (M-18), to come together at a dinner. When he invited just the leaders, they objected. Trust was absent, so he included their entourages. A wary gathering of about 30 followed, each keeping to their side of the room. With chicken from the country's favorite chain, Pollo Campero, the parties warmed. Cigars concluded the evening. There had been no business conducted, but the secret talks were underway. The agreement to stop the killings came later.

Skeptics abounded in the capital of San Salvador. We heard: the truce will not last; the gangs are being coddled and their leaders now have large screen TVs in their jail cells as a payoff; the minister wants to be president and this is a political calculation; the gangs are doubling down on their other activities; and more. Much of this was true, but for the first time in years, the homicide rate was dropping dramatically.

We sensed that Minister Mungia Payes understood the delicate balance between producing meaningful change without appearing to favor or privilege the gangs. He had been the military's negotiator with the leftist rebels during El Salvador's 12-year civil war, ended in 1992. The discussion focused on how best to communicate this inherent riddle to a doubtful and exhausted public. Should those who caused the problems get all of the attention? What special treatment might reach the victims of the gangs' violence?

We thought that the United States could help address the thorny knot of special treatment for the perpetrators and victims' rights—and that our support would matter to the El Salvadoran public. We also offered encouragement for expanding the initial agreement on homicides into other gang rackets. The risks scared our U.S. government and international partners.

It was not to be. Within the U.S. embassy, there was considerable opposition, especially from those who worked in law enforcement. They believed in the hard line and saw the truce as a gift to undeserving bad guys. Lacking a consensus, it would take the full commitment of the U.S. ambassador or an order from Washington to gamble on the truce. I reached out to Ambassador Mari Carmen Aponte, one of my favorite colleagues and a classmate at State's school for emissaries. Having just overcome a long-term Senate hold on her nomination plus a one-year term appointment, which had expired,[14] Aponte was not ready to focus her efforts on this high-risk initiative. I saw it as a chance for great creativity and the best way to change a catastrophic status quo. It became clear that we did not convince key supporters of the need to invest in the truce.

After 18 months, the truce collapsed and homicides spiked again. The "iron fist" returned, armed confrontations grew, extra-judicial killings became commonplace, and gangs expanded cross border operations and were labeled "terrorists" in El Salvador. The flight of local people to the north resumed.

Organized crime dominated in Guatemala. Violence prospered but the issues of corruption, official impunity, and professional criminals were central. In the course of our visit, it was clear that our embassy was not open to a change or additional efforts. At a charming luncheon hosted by the ambassador on his lovely backyard patio, we heard, "We don't need any more of Washington's alphabet soup here—we have enough already." The existing portfolio was sufficient.

When we arrived in Honduras, Ambassador Lisa Kubiske was calm, ready, and accepting. She recognized the enormity of the violence problem, saw how defining it was for the entire country, had thought a great deal about what to do, and welcomed any help that might be forthcoming.

Lisa saw a political opening and directed us to several incipient opportunities. She also accompanied us to many of the meetings and left little doubt that dealing with the proliferating violence was her top priority. Others at the embassy and in Tegucigalpa took notice.

Honduras was metastasizing: "Well-funded transnational criminal organizations combined with local gangs are destabilizing the country's democratic institutions and making it one of the most dangerous countries in the world in terms of violent crime."[15] The death spiral included the world's highest homicide rates,[16] almost no successful prosecutions, bloody accounts in local newspapers and television, and a minimal response from political leaders. Internal battles for leadership positions consumed the ruling class, while the lack of public safety was clearly job one.

The ambassador and her team identified some promising openings that would benefit from U.S. support. The recently created Alliance for Justice and Peace (AJP or Alianza) brought together nearly 150 civil society groups to push for change in the police and justice systems. Its chair was the Rector of the Autonomous University, Julieta Castellanos, who lost a son the previous October (2011) when police kidnapped and killed him and a friend. Alianza would anchor a series of efforts to purge the police of human rights violators and corruption, remove the attorney general, and maintain a spotlight on violence as a national scourge. American support for an independent Central American experts' review of the attorney general was the sort of targeted assistance that the Alianza sought and received. Later, during the presidential campaign, the Alianza ran a series of television commercials on the importance of turning the violent tide.

With the support of the business community, the Honduran Congress had passed a first-ever tax on businesses to expand the fight against crime. Most doubted the government's ability to collect the expected $50 million and appropriate or spend it in a helpful way. Again, we offered U.S. support in the form of technical assistance. The ruling party wanted visible crime-fighting equipment on the streets right away and grew impatient with the combined business/government/civil society commission that was in charge. That led to some impetuous spending, especially on hardware—and at the last accounting only 6 percent of the Honduran revenue was going to prevention programs.[17]

The United States also worked with a Tegucigalpa NGO that had begun to transform a crime-riddled neighborhood by building trust relations between witnesses and the police and prosecutors. Founded by a committed American who lived with his family in one of the roughest areas of the capital, the program reached 85 percent convictions in homicide prosecutions—an unprecedented rate in a country where murder cases went away. They also saw the national potential in their model. The Christian-based Association for a More Just Society (AJS) supported families in high crime cities like San Pedro Sula, and found that "it takes four to 15 visits to persuade a witness to testify."[18]

Calling upon a mix of experts from Colombia, Costa Rica, Mexico, Dallas, Seattle, and Philadelphia, the United States engaged with the Honduran vice president to increase her public role on preventing violence and advance the prosecutions of a handful of high-profile cases.

The murder of 570 children in 2015 helped to explain the prior summer's arrival of "18,000 unaccompanied Honduran children . . . on the United States border."[19] By working in Honduras, the United States was solving a problem that it helped to create. Investing in local solutions is the wise and most economical way forward. If we are willing to spend billions to build a wall to protect ourselves from the onslaught of terrified children, perhaps we could spend a fraction of that to help make their own country more habitable.

9. LESSONS APPLIED

I. Prepare High Level Support

Unconventional situations require creative approaches. Large bureaucracies do not comfortably accommodate these. While soldiers have a great deal of leeway in combat situations, civilians need faster-than-usual decisions from above. Considering the obstacles that always appear, it is wise to arrive in a country with as much Washington backing as possible. Preview the work in a range of places and try to bring people together at meetings or on conference calls from the start.

It is vital to have the support of the ambassador and to minimize the turbulence from the country team. Alignment with their Washington bosses and the desk operations that back them up is critical.

As I have worked in global hot spots, I have noticed a phenomenon in the ambassadorial ranks that bears attention. All will report that there is a hell of a problem. Of those, about half will spend their two-to-three-year assignment saying that it is under control, with the hope or sincere belief that it can be contained while they are in the country. Minimizing trouble is a career enhancer in a risk-averse bureaucracy.

The other half recognize the severity of the situation, resist denial, and are open to assistance. Seldom does Washington bring a solution, but the recognition of reality is the first step.

I have found those who welcome outside help to be among our best ambassadors. Embassies are not crises oriented or prepared. Often when events get complicated, there are emergency evacuations or extended home leaves and shortages of people. Few regular staff have the special experience needed. On occasion, upon arrival in a country, I have seen the contorted face of an ambassador, almost like *The Scream*, Edvard Munch's famous Expressionist painting. That can be healthy.

II. Embrace the Unorthodox

War is often the result of a failure of the usual. While there are cases where the status quo ante is desirable, in most of the future cases we will seek dramatic change. By definition, that puts us into uncharted behaviors and programming.

The thought that the U.S. government would support and promote a reality television series as a way of encouraging a new, nonviolent national dialogue in Nigeria was a stretch. Investing our prestige in a gang truce proved too much. Both were outside the norms.

III. Beware the Camouflage

Many of tomorrow's problems will arrive looking like yesterday's. There is an excellent chance that disguises are the best way for them to gain access. Once the crises unfold, it is wise to expect the unexpected, especially when invisible networks, internet guidance, and other breakout tools and technologies accompany them. Like mutant diseases, they will be in active evolution.

We have already seen the jujitsu of American cyberwar tools used against us. The same will happen with drones and advanced weaponry. Social media is a mixed bag for good and evil. If we think the challenge is a familiar problem, we are likely to underestimate it.

Political violence should be containable—until the "youths" no longer take instructions. Ethnic-based warfare seems to have a clear definition until "us" and "them" blend in so many ways.

It will take great restraint to customize our responses to the myriad threats the coming decades will bring. If we approach these as individualized crises instead of trying to categorize them broadly, we will be more successful.

V

A Better Tomorrow

Is the United States prepared to deal with monthly international crises?[1] Not even close. Our present strategies, structure, and culture almost guarantee that we will be playing catch-up all the time. What can we do to maximize our impact and value?

Nonstop calls for improvement come from every quarter, fueled by a powerful belief in the ability to renew the State Department and the civilian elements of U.S. foreign policy.

Private groups are active in the debate and produce invaluable research. The Carnegie Corporation of New York took the lead in foundation funding, making clear that "profound stresses" and "the recent rash of 'internal' wars and genocides" required a dramatic rethinking of our approaches and institutions.[2] The early work of the Post-Conflict Reconstruction Project at CSIS offered a constructive, four-pillar framework in 2002 and drew attention to the inadequacy of our responses.[3] In 2008, former secretary of state Madeleine Albright and Secretary of Defense William Cohen co-chaired a task force that issued a report titled *Preventing Genocide: A Blueprint for U.S. Policymakers*, which emphasized practical steps to prevent mass killings.

Hundreds of thousands of Americans gained firsthand experience from Bosnia to Afghanistan and beyond, mostly as soldiers, diplomats, contractors, or nonprofit employees, and a number of them wrote influential books and articles. Nathaniel Fick's *One Bullet Away* and

Carter Malkasian's *War Comes to Garmser* offer vivid insights at the ground level. The daily writings of talented war-tested journalists, including Pamela Constable, Dexter Filkins, the late Anthony Shadid, David Kirkpatrick, Neil MacFarquhar, Jim Glanz, Liz Sly, Deb Amos, and more, chronicled both weaknesses and ways forward.

At the United Nations there were similar efforts, including the Brahimi report and the High-level Panel on Threats, Challenges and Change in 2003–2004, which included former National Security Council head Brent Scowcroft. Of the ten threats that it identified, seven dealt with the kind of violence that generated U.S. and international interventions.

Notably, many calls for reform came from the government itself.[4] Secretaries of State Powell and Rice saw the weakness, spoke of transformational diplomacy, and created the Office of the Coordinator for Reconstruction and Stabilization (S/CRS) as part of a response that was overwhelmed by daily events in Iraq and Afghanistan. In 2010, Secretary Clinton initiated the State Department's first-ever Quadrennial Diplomacy and Development Review (QDDR). Modeled after a long-standing Defense Department practice, the charge laid out the challenge:

> People, money, and ideas can move around the world so quickly that conflict, even in distant countries, has become a far greater threat to the United States. Weak governments and failing states create safe havens for terrorists, insurgencies, and criminal syndicates. Conflict near major economies and supply routes can shock distant markets. Tensions that may escalate to mass atrocities undermine America's deepest values, especially democracy and human rights.[5]

The review would conclude,

> For the past two decades, the U.S. government has recognized that U.S. national security depends upon a more effective approach to fragile states. Yet we have struggled with how to understand these challenges and how to organize our civilian institutions to deal with them. . . . Many of the capabilities and skills we need for conflict and crisis prevention and response exist at State, USAID, and other federal agencies, but these capabilities are not integrated and focused on the problem in a sustained way.[6]

The process was intense but most of those involved did an excellent job of protecting their existing approaches and bureaucracies. A major result of the 2010–2011 Washington tong war over the shape and nature of the U.S. civilian response to conflict was the creation of a new Bureau of Conflict and Stabilization Operations (CSO) at the State Department. Hopes that it would finally bring coherence and effectiveness to America's extensive conflict centered commitments were genuine, though one wag wrote, "The elephant (QDDR) gave birth to a mouse (CSO)."[7]

Those of us charged with bringing the new bureau to life did not feel that way. We saw an opportunity to drive a messy process in a fresh direction, use the convening authority of the State Department, and objectively direct funding to the greatest needs, while promoting innovative practices.

The final QDDR offered up the new CSO bureau and left the shaping to its first leaders. We believed that the new structure could gain traction and drive a convergence of policy and practice in conflict settings. We knew that cultural changes mattered and took inspiration from transformative stories all over America.[8] We set about starting something new.

10

FULFILLING OUR LEADERSHIP POTENTIAL

I.

In my first week as the assistant secretary of state designate for the proposed Bureau of Conflict and Stabilization Operations (CSO), my colleague Karin von Hippel and I went to Capitol Hill without a single talking point. The State Department never sent anyone anywhere without explicit instructions and yet, here we were, freestyling in separate meetings with the staff members of the four key appropriation and authorization committees. The secretary's office thought that this was our best chance. It was good to have some leeway.

We met skeptics in our two days on the Hill in October 2011, but they were willing to test our proposal. Irrespective of party, most wanted to support Secretary Clinton's reform effort, for they too had tired of the civilian bumbling in conflict and crisis places. My prior work in starting USAID's Office of Transition Initiatives in the mid-1990s, by now seen as a uniquely successful effort to elevate fast, direct political development assistance to countries emerging from distress, also helped.

Still, there were many questions: Do you really think that you can make something new at the State Department stick? How will you deal with the geographic bureaus that dominate life at State? Why do you believe that CSO will succeed when its predecessor office, the Secretary's Office of Coordinator for Stablization (S/CRS) has not gained influence? Why will this not be duplicative of others?

We answered that the support of Secretary Clinton was sincere and made a difference in the department; also, that a rigorous focus on a handful of countries that mattered to the United States would prevent geographic sprawl. We vowed to reach out to our colleagues in every part of the government to develop integrated strategies and to work closely with ambassadors in the target countries. With luck, CSO could become honest brokers of resources, directed to those most capable in each situation. The Hill staffers accepted these promises as necessary and new.

It helped to quote my former boss at USAID, Doug Stafford, who had advised, "Never, ever, ever, did I say ever, take a job as a coordinator." I adhered to his view and stated that CSO must be more than a gatherer of tribes—that it would need to bring resources to crises in order to matter.

Impatience with the results of the prior eight years was still strong and we offered to start with "a proof of concept" year. As we parted the final meeting with the Senate appropriators, our most vital partner of the four committees, the senior Republican staffer, a committed reformer, said, "You are in our sights" as he made a gesture of looking down the barrel of a gun.

With the Hill willing to wait and see, we set about transforming an existing operation (SCRS) of nearly 200 people into a new bureau with a redirected mission. It turned out to be a big job.

Right away, we set a new direction: making a difference in four to five high priority countries in the coming year, building a trusted and respected team, and advancing creative new practices in practical ways.

Each goal required considerable effort. The existing portfolio of SCRS countries was heavy on Afghanistan, South Sudan, and Africa, lacking influence and purpose. As U.S. policies in Afghanistan transitioned to withdrawal and South Sudan's central government began to act like its longtime adversaries in Khartoum, it seemed like a good moment to rethink the targets of opportunity.

Having put a great deal of effort into a Civilian Reserve Corps modeled after the military's standby reserve forces, SCRS had emphasized agreements with other federal agencies and numbers versus knowledgeable and experienced talent in conflict settings. Much of the work was an extension of that which is most familiar at State, reports and studies, with a field presence.

If CSO was to be serious, it would need to offer more than money and enthusiastic people. We set about building a portfolio of countries that would matter to the Secretary of State, the White House and our colleagues at State, and others. In order to be more than an extension of the most vulnerable geographic bureaus, we met with each of the six regional assistant secretaries and asked, "What worries you most in your region? Why? Are you doing everything that you would like to during this current or expected crisis?"

From those personal discussions came the following challenges in every part of the world: In Kenya, because we sought to prevent a repeat of the violent 2007 election—a disaster for the country and the international community, which uses Nairobi as an operating base for the region. In Burma/Myanmar, because its transition from military to civilian leadership was fragile and unprepared to deal with long-standing, ethnic-minority conflicts. In north Central America, because of widespread violence and huge numbers of people flooding the United States. And Syria.

The meeting with Jeff Feltman, the assistant secretary for the Middle East and North Africa (MENA), was instructive. Overwhelmed by the Arab Spring and its aftermath, Feltman had concerns in most of his 19 countries. They ranged from terrorist attacks and diplomatic safety to collapsing regimes. We went to see him in late 2011 thinking that the critical opportunities in MENA were Egypt, Libya, Yemen, and Syria. Each presented a special challenge. Egypt already had an enormous, multibillion-dollar, U.S. presence and the likelihood of influencing policy and practice would be limited. The administration's posture on Libya was that in the postwar period, the Europeans and the United Nations would take the lead—leaving little room to operate. Yemen was in the process of evacuating the embassy because of physical danger and the intelligence community dominated the strategy. That left Syria.

It was a more hopeful moment in Syria. The peaceful street demonstrations amounted to a revolution, with thousands of unheralded, mostly younger citizens speaking out about a more open society and new order. With entire areas liberated from Assad's ruthless dictatorship, including most of Aleppo, the largest city and commercial capital of the country, conventional wisdom offered that the government would be defeated within months.

Each of these opportunities would require substantial back and forth with those who had always controlled the countries, including geographic bureaus, ambassadors and embassies, USAID in Washington and mission directors, National Security Council staff, functional bureaus with existing programming (from terrorism to drugs and thugs), and congressional champions. In order to be accepted, we needed to evidence a sophisticated understanding of the place and be creative about a suggested course of action—without threatening the U.S. government landlords.

At a talk in Washington, an audience member said, "Fifty percent of your diplomatic work will be inside of the U.S. government." It was a clever line and I used it in presentations to gain knowing winks from insiders. Only when I was leaving in October 2014 did someone correct me: "You are hopelessly naïve—you must mean 90 percent." It would have helped to understand the parameters of my job: it was 90 percent internal bureaucratics and 90 percent the challenges of turning countries in conflict around. Tough math.

In those first months, we built an entire senior team,[1] selected middle managers from the existing rosters, negotiated our way out of financial commitments to a range of federal agencies, closed offices in the suburbs of Washington, and helped dozens to find other places to work. We sought to turn the abused culture of our predecessor organization into a winning team. The immensity of starting something new in a recalcitrant parent institution showed up on a daily basis. Many of the choices freed up funding and the newfound liquidity gave us operational chances.

After a few months, Secretary Clinton invited me to present the plan and activities of CSO to the Monday senior staff meeting. I started by saying that most everyone we met with in the department offered the same two words, but with quite different emphases. Some wished us an upbeat and straightforward "good luck," while others commiserated with a freighted and weighted "good luck."

A friend whose entire career had been in another federal department heard me and set up a meeting with a consultant team to help. I described the challenge of creating a new bureau inside of America's oldest government department, "It is a start-up, turn-around, merger, hostile takeover in a resistant organization, during fiscally constrained times with a year to show results." The response surprised me: "Was somebody setting you up for failure?"

No part of that sentence had ever entered my mind. Perhaps it has to do with being the youngest of three sons, within four years of age. Ingrained in the first ten years of uninterrupted losses is a persistence and the expectation that you will start winning soon. After each childhood defeat I would say, "Let's play again." That attitude cut through most of the obstacles that appeared daily at CSO.

Even as we kept finding willing allies and eager embassies, the job of starting something new at State challenged us.

I commiserated with a fellow assistant secretary of state who told me of the various difficulties that other "new" bureaus were presenting. "They seem to be unsure of what we are doing, why this bureau was created, or how we fit into their world," she said. This all sounded familiar, though her bureau was 25 years old.

Her responsibilities included some of the major issues of the time: climate change, oceans, and science. Furthermore, they were top priorities of the president and the two secretaries of state that were our bosses. It reassured me that CSO's treatment was neither personal nor unique. Still, while misery may love company, this did not feel promising.

As I left my colleague's office, the sense of the difficulty of instituting change grew. There on the wall were formal photos of her predecessors, including several of the most distinguished and honored career leaders of recent history. I thought, if even these titans could not integrate this necessary and relevant bureau into the State Department, what would we have to do to gain traction?

Making something new stick in America's oldest bureaucracy is a struggle. Tradition and practice often conspire to slow the department's adaptation within a dynamic world. Reminders and legends are everywhere. Next to the 23rd Street entrance, a plaque celebrates the State Department's standing as the first cabinet office. A clear vision and a relentless pursuit of change are the only ways to move ahead in an environment like State. Bulldoggish determination is mandatory or familiar inertia will prevail.

We settled on proof of performance as our measure. As initiatives took hold in target countries and our teams delivered innovative work, critical alliances with career ambassadors grew. Congressional visits to Turkey, Burma, and north Central America affirmed CSO's value.

On a follow-on visit to the Senate appropriation staff, the Republican staffer told me: "You are no longer in our sights [like a gun], you are now in our sight [scanning the horizon]." We had institutional roots but not full acceptance.

For real progress, beyond the practices laid out throughout this book, three macro changes are required: expand risk tolerance; institutionalize a one team, one direction, and one leader crisis management model; and bring the public role forward.

2.

In Secretary of State John Kerry's first senior management retreat, the most animated discussion of the day centered on the question of acceptable risk. Respected career diplomats felt that we had retreated into a defensive crouch. They wanted a department that valued reaching out and taking occasional long shots and believed that there is a degree of physical danger in diplomatic work.

Risk tolerance is vital to making peace. The United States has steadily moved away from this fact to our own disservice. If safety is "Job One" for our military, then wouldn't they be safer in Kentucky than most overseas posts? If we want to make a strong impression in a country, do our walled embassies, armored caravans, and gated communities on the outskirts of cities do that? When a courageous and well-informed ambassador dies in Benghazi, should we effectively pull out of Libya? If we want to know something about a place, shouldn't our people mix it up on the streets and in the stores of our hosts?

Dozens of similar questions torment us. If our operations are so constrained, what is keeping us from changing? I believe that our culture is so risk averse as to border on irrelevance. No one will argue for recklessness, but these should not be the two choices.

In speaking to groups at the State Department, including one gathering of more than 100 people, I tested our culture. Not to be threatening, I offered a "virtuous scale," with "Native Caution" on the left end and "American Ingenuity" on the right. I asked people to place the State Department on the scale and I made clear that both qualities were excellent. "Native Caution" suggested wisdom and avoiding stupid choices; "American Ingenuity" spoke to original thinking and creative solutions. All good things.

The results of these informal polls were distressing: 95 percent answered that State was all about "Native Caution"; the remaining 5 percent said that State was off the scale, beyond "Native Caution." The concept of equilibrium between the two ends seemed humorous, unreachable.

To take on the toughest problems on earth, where chaos is prevalent and people are killing each other, some degree of risk acceptance is mandatory. These are not situations that will be "managed" from a shining embassy on the outskirts of a capital or remotely by a button-downed, Washington-based organization or by the technology of a drone. No, it will take real knowledge, personal relationships, comfort with unpredictability, and an organization and people with positive, ingrained practices. Even then, bad things will happen. Risk is a given for work in violence-prone places. Recruits may not sign up to "give my life for our country," but civilian service is hazardous.

"Expeditionary diplomacy" was Secretary of State Condoleezza Rice's phrase and the United States needs to build a cadre of leaders and future officers who recognize the inherent attraction and importance of this work. We will also need to come up with improved incentives—including customized employment contracts, increased life insurance, relaxed leave policies, and special family arrangements. To do anything less will doom us.

Too many of the hurdles thrust in your way within the national security community are unnecessary, gratuitous, or insulting. The scourge of secretiveness, classifications, and security hamper the collection and sharing of information as well as the hiring of talented people and lively regular interchanges. Three million people in and around the U.S. government now hold "secret" or higher security clearances. With grotesque overclassifying of even the most mundane materials, these millions of employees must keep trillions of secrets. If history shows that two people can barely hold a secret for a week, what kind of system are we creating?

High-level reviews suggest that 95 percent of America's official secrets should be open and public.[2] Overclassification is a decades-long problem. At times CSO teams would observe a development in Syria, share it by unclassified cable or e-mail, and then find that our report was now contained in a secret report. By rule, that would make the original finding classified. Items that appeared routinely in the press, such as drones in Pakistan, might be official secrets. The absurdities persisted, slowing communications, limiting those with access to useful insights, and clogging exchanges. Too often, secrecy becomes a cover-up for dysfunctionality.

Equally damaging are drawn out and costly security clearance procedures. Today's reviews are expensive, contracted out to investigators with limited international exposure, and not helpful. I have seen the obvious raised up to alarm levels, young people with histories of travel delayed out of positions, and talent punished because they stood up for basic rights. In one case, I almost lost one of our best Balkan hands because of a prior arrest for civil disobedience—the exact skill set we needed to stand up to dictators in the region.[3] We had already alerted the investigators to his "record" and yet they came back to us, breathless with the news—and a charge of thousands of dollars for the review.

In an era of flat State Department funding, the most consistent budget growth is in diplomatic security. We cannot continue to spend more on that item and less on the people and programs if the United States wants to have influential embassies.

Excessive caution shows up in smaller daily annoyances as well. There are times when you walk through the dull corridors of the State Department that it feels like the Soviets must have won. The concrete walls, linoleum floors, and random-colored hallways feature locked offices that require another pass or code. Despite well-guarded main entrances and hard-earned personal identifications, extra security is the norm. Prior violations, such as a stolen laptop computer from an office near to a past secretary of state, become reasons for a never-ending smorgasbord of rules.

When we contrast the rigidity of the government's model with the design of Apple's new headquarters in California, we see stark differences. Steve Jobs felt that his geeks needed to mix it up more, exchange ideas, and develop joint solutions to problems—and designed a campus that would encourage those behaviors. After a few years, he still thought it was deficient—that his introverted techies were still finding too many ways to avoid each other. His solution: close the bathrooms in the extremities of the building so that Apple's employees would congregate near the center, where the only remaining bathrooms were located.

At CSO, we closed suburban offices and brought the team into a single floor across the street from State, gave everyone a roommate, opened the hallway doors to enliven discussions, and encouraged people to find unclassified ways to speed the exchange of information. We received warnings about violating rules. Each time I asked for a copy of the regulation. They never came. Apparently, if I was willing to take responsibility then it was okay.

So often in big organizations, people will cite a rule as a way to stifle change. My preferred guidance: "If it is unconstitutional, we will never do it; if there is a law, please do not violate it; if it is a regulation, let's be respectful; and if it is a practice or habit, let's make sure it makes sense." Most of the oppressive restraints fall into the latter category and, thus, present real opportunities. I have always insisted that no one who ever works for me will go to jail.

While State faces the most fascinating challenges on earth, the work often becomes lowest-common-denominator paperwork, and then cleared by dozens. Serious problems are subject to interminable delays and desultory responses. Creativity is stifled by a muddling middle.

A 2017 survey of 35,000 State and USAID employees reinforced these impressions. Citing a "nothing is easy" culture that requires constant work-arounds, respondents spoke about an inability to get things done.

> In this process a picture emerges in which accountability has been displaced by unclear decision rights, diffused authority (as opposed to shared ownership), absence of a single authority on most issues, and compartmentalized/standalone work units in lieu of unified and harmonized processes and workflows. Such a condition thwarts expediency, reduces effectiveness, saps individual motivation, and masks redundancies. To get things done at State and USAID, individuals must seek multiple approvals from various entities.[4]

There is no standard in the United States that says we must find the most difficult way to accomplish something. Breaking out of these bad habits and the obese institutions that have grown up around them is a challenge we must overcome to be better peacebuilders.

"No one, starting over, would design something like this," Bill Burns, a former deputy secretary of state, said. Those who love the civilian mission must lead the acceptance of risk debate and other vital changes. Threatened by know-nothing reform and mindless defensiveness, we must revitalize the diplomatic instruments that advance interests and resolve "problems with foreigners with minimal violence."[5]

Diplomats and development professionals have averted conflict from the Israel-Egypt peace treaty, to the collapse of the Soviet empire, the end of the Bosnian war, and nuclear agreements.[6] They took risks and our nation's prosperous existence reflects their fine work. To expand peace we will need to lean in ever more.

3.

Consuming, global emergencies require months-long, 24/7 leadership, integrated teams and clear direction. Each time there is a new international crisis, there is a reinvention of organization and leadership. While people from a variety of agencies quickly gather, we seldom come together with clear authorities and flexible resources. This challenge remained after the 2010 QDDR and a number of us offered a solution.

My own experience at the United Nations and in the U.S. government confirmed that a "one team, one direction, and one leader" model produced successes. Following the Rwanda crisis, President Clinton selected USAID Administrator Brian Atwood to pull together a government-wide effort and it worked. Later in Kosovo, Atwood asked me to lead a similar integrated team inside of USAID. While there were bureaucratic grumblings, having a daily manager with primary responsibility produced coherence.[7]

In contrast, too many large crises end up with groups of dedicated agency representatives meeting on a regular basis, but without the necessary cohesion. Right now, after 17 years in Afghanistan or even six in Syria, it is still unclear who is in charge of the U.S. operation. Several years into the Iraq and Afghanistan wars, the George W. Bush White House set up a coordinators office with General Douglas Lute in charge. That hub helped, but the role is rarely empowered enough for situations that require rapid decision-making and the redirection of people and money.

When I ask those most involved, "Who is in charge?" the answer is too often, "The president!" Please. No matter how talented our chief executive, with so many other responsibilities, he or she is in no position to run a crisis enterprise, with daily decision-making. President John Kennedy may have done that for days during the Cuban Missile Crisis, but it was a short-lived exception. The same is true for the National Security Council, which lacks the depth or breadth of talent to lead or arbitrate the constant, longer-term challenges of a crisis.

The larger strategic questions will always need the input and approval of the senior-most levels of government, but the nature of a crisis requires that a single person be in charge. With real authority over people and resources, a leader's career should rise and fall on the skill and success of the team. I feel the same way about our military commanders in major engagements.

Given that background, I joined with a handful of others and sent a memo to the secretary of state's front office recommending a "Center of Gravity" model. Within three days of a crisis declaration, the secretary of state would identify a full-time leader. The recommendation of up to three candidates would come from a senior team of the undersecretary for political affairs (responsible for all of the geographic bureaus), the undersecretary for Civilian Security, Democracy and Human Rights (responsible for all of the functional bureaus), and the deputy administrator of USAID (number two there).

The crisis manager should reflect special experience for the kind of crisis, be it war, tsunamis, or Ebola. That single leader should have a deputy from one of the other parts of the civilian side and should have the authority to direct resources across agencies, meet with the Hill, and speak for the department. A range of bureaus and others should serve as a board of advisors to the leader and provide staffing right away. Those parts of the government with the most flexible personnel and funds, State's CSO and Population Refugees and Migration (PRM), USAID's Office of Foreign Disaster Assistance (OFDA) and Office of Transition Initiatives, would be core team members. Too often, special envoys become bureaucratic orphans, with fine titles and even offices, but little else. This would avoid those traditional weaknesses.

We felt that if the secretary of state provided such an organizational nucleus, that it would be easier for the rest of the government to join in. This parallels the striking clarity of American ambassadors in a country, where they have chief executive status and lead country teams. Until large numbers of U.S. troops arrive, the ambassador is the decision maker. Without overplaying that advantage, it makes sense to replicate a clear leadership structure in Washington, where bureaucratic wars often seem greater than the wars we are seeking to resolve overseas.

The Syria conflict brought out myriad actors, all with different levels of enthusiasm. We would joke at CSO that we did not volunteer for Syria, we just did not step back when everyone else did. During my tenure, at least five major parts of the State Department were engaged in Syria, with perhaps an equivalent number at USAID and untold numbers at the Defense Department. The intelligence agencies were active.

Regular meetings provided updates, but we lacked direction and decision-making. Throughout the Syrian conflict, it was never clear that a single entity below the president had the authority to convene, coordinate, strategize, and move money, programs, and people. With a shuttered embassy in Damascus, the Washington desk and the geographic bureau took over but there was no single, empowered leader, common playbook, or shared priorities.

Syria falls under the Bureau of Near Eastern Affairs, which manages the Middle East and North Africa, from Iran to Morocco. While the region has long been tumultuous, changes in power structures and governments were rare. The bureau was thus ill prepared to analyze and adapt to the rapid pace of the Arab Spring. Suddenly, Egypt, Libya, and Yemen were on fire and Tunisia, Lebanon, and others were still scalding.

Our ambassador, Robert Ford, was back in Washington from Damascus and knew the most about the situation. An idealist without illusions, Ford was easy to work with and modest about his exposure to any kind of revolutionary movement or civil war. He was also the lead figure on negotiating with the Syrian opposition, shaping the peace talks in Geneva, and a range of other activities that took him out of Washington for weeks at a time. In constant demand, Ford had meetings in the region and in Europe for weeks every month, plus regular briefings for the Secretary of State, White House, and the Hill.

CSO pushed him and his colleagues to clarify the Washington leadership, so that we would not go weeks without decisions. We were fast, agile, analytic, and able to operate because of people and funds—but lacked deep knowledge of or experience in Syria or the region. Others had that.

He too saw the benefits of a new model, recognizing that the thinking was too limited and constrained and that decision-making was slow and rutted. He once told me, "I have worked in this region for decades and I have no prior exposure to this kind of change." He valued the expertise of those who had worked on multiple wars and transitions and recognized the need for full-time leadership.

Ford spoke to his acting assistant secretary. The response lacked awareness of the need for a central, 24/7 leader and reflected bureaucratic concerns—a deadening combination. "When you are not here Robert, I am, from 7 a.m. to 10 p.m. every day." Ford pointed out the crushing responsibility for 20 or so other countries in the midst of the Arab Spring, but that did not matter.

Creating something of a meritocratic process and having a dozen preselected leaders from the whole of government would help. There is a chronic shortage of seasoned and trusted leaders for emergency operations in almost every part of the civilian side of the government and the United Nations.

One of the most admired public officials in Washington was the late James E. Webb. Recognized for his ability to build organizations, Webb's noteworthy career peaked as the first administrator of NASA.[8] In the development of that complex, science-based organization, Webb knew that he would need capable, agile, and committed humans to fly the first generation of imperfect spacecraft. There would need to be able people in the capsules when things went wrong; those same individuals would become the spokespersons of the effort; and public enthusiasm and confidence would be greatest through those human beings. The Mercury and Apollo astronauts were the response.

Many more stories come to mind, but the need for a leadership class that could pilot our conflict efforts, much like Webb's at NASA, continues to be paramount. Any secretary of state or president should be able to identify a skilled crisis manager within days of an event. This means that State, USAID, DOD, and others will need to create a pool of a dozen or so individuals who have the temperaments and the exposure to work in a pre- or post-violence setting, help to focus the effort, build a team, and communicate the progress to a global public on a daily basis.

Is it too great a luxury to take a dozen of our most talented mid-career leaders from every part of the U.S. government, train, and place them in a standby role? With the arrival of a new crisis every few weeks, I suspect that the greater problem will be an almost immediate shortage of talent. A dozen will only take us through less than a year! At the least, those who are not immediately engaged in running their own team will be shadowing someone who is, helping them to prepare, and identifying talent around the U.S. government for their own teams once that challenge arrives. As crises brew, small groups can develop alternative strategies or red-team existing problems—always in the search for a better way.

These crisis leadership assignments in the U.S. government would be compelling, high-profile roles, not unlike the original astronauts, but it must be given priority.

Integrated teams and solid leadership are scarce. An internal caste system compounds the problems. At State in Washington, there is a 25-person political class at the top. Since most political appointees feature subject expertise, or Hill or academic experience, few have run substantial organizations. They come and go and seldom stay for more than a handful of years. Many represent and defend their organizations.

Foreign Service Officers are next and they rotate every couple of years. Abbreviated stays in difficult places, cautious careerism, and a dearth of leadership skills result. Senate confirmation holds and Hill vagaries, plus "up or out" personnel rules, reinforce timidity. Management accomplishments are of secondary import, though recent evaluation forms are more solicitous of those skills. Limited mid-career recruiting and appropriate job assignments for those few new people guarantee a change-resistant environment.

This means that the top two layers of a 90,000-strong organization[9] are running a complex global operation with slight leadership preparation—and little sense that engaging in institutional reform or human resource issues will lead to any rewards.

Civil servants, with lifetime positions, are the third level in Washington and a source of continuity. Given the inattention of the upper layers to how things work, they have genuine influence but suffer the frustrations of living through leadership gaps and changes. In many offices, there are quota-like divisions that save certain jobs for foreign service officers and others for civil service. Often, there is a fourth level of support staff, playing vital roles with IT and management issues, somewhat outside of the foreign policy guild.

Contractors appear in most levels of the system and bring special knowledge of a country, language skills, or other talents in a timely fashion. Labeled, even on the e-mail system, they are artificially apart and constrained by limited authorities.

These divisions are profound and un-American. Not only do they keep the United States from operating in an integrated and team-like way, they undermine our claims to be a pluralistic and egalitarian society. Often inflexible, the personnel system is not agile, nor does it produce a culture of leadership—qualities we need in conflict countries. I felt less of this at embassies and USAID missions, where foreign nationals and local staff are often at the heart of a well-run country team.

In order for the United States to become more effective in a violence-prone world, it will need to organize itself more cleanly and deal with self-defeating internal constraints. A shortage of crisis-related leaders and an inability to surge people or funds make the civilian side of government often irrelevant.

4.

The lack of broad, public engagement is a major failure of America's recent global interventions. Since the fall of the Berlin Wall in 1989, the United States has militarily intervened in 20 countries.[10] The United Nations currently has 16 further ongoing peacekeeping missions across the world that the United States supports financially.[11] Every one of these situations is demanding, but the absence of congressional approvals and direct citizen responsibility damages our official role.

Just before Labor Day 2013, a window opened. Having just been charged with the use of chemical weapons, Syria's Assad faced the threat of U.S. military might. Certain of disaster, Assad and his allies prepared for the worst—and showed a willingness to negotiate. It appeared that Assad would back down.

In an unscripted press conference comment, Secretary of State John Kerry said that the only way to avoid a U.S. attack would be for the Syrian government to give up all of its chemical weapons. Russia, our adversary on Syria at the United Nations, seized the moment and pressed the Assad regime. This concession would mark the high point of cooperation with Russia. The negotiations over chemical weapons showed that success was possible—with substantial persistence and the threat of greater action.

Meanwhile, President Obama's bold stroke, to seek congressional support for a limited military action, was stillborn. He knew that America's citizens required preparation and wanted Congress to put its skin on the line alongside his own.

While Obama's choice was unexpected, I saw it as wise and necessary. An affirmative action by the House of Representatives would have produced greater thoughtfulness and public involvement than we had seen at the outset of other recent interventions. A full-fledged debate among U.S. leaders, fulfilling their constitutional roles, would have deepened the average American's understanding and engagement. It also offered an opportunity to expand the range of ideas and to settle appropriate next steps for the United States.

When Hill support did not appear to be forthcoming, Obama should have forced the issue. If there is an "obligation to act against evil,"[12] then let the public debate begin. All public officials must be on the record in matters of war and peace. If we should take care of our own before venturing forth elsewhere, then make our elected representatives vote. If we need better ideas, let us look to civic engagement.

Intervening in the Middle East deserves citizen involvement and a thorough debate. Presidents since World War II led America into many engagements with limited discussion, making it easier for those who sit on the sidelines to throw stones and deepening Americans' disillusionment and misunderstanding.

The history of democracies winning "three out of every four wars they have fought since 1815" was due to a heightened "political accountability: democratically elected leaders are more careful to choose wars they can win because costly and unpopular wars will get them thrown out of office."[13] That historic virtue is now at risk.

Congress needs to assert its role and the president should expect and encourage a public debate. When multibillion-dollar war campaigns proceed without new taxes, ownership flags. When the public drifts away from all-volunteer armies, awareness dims. When "military mechanization"[14] brings impersonal destruction, winning over the populations lags. Without greater citizen buy-in, both here and in the places we seek to make more peaceful, our interventions will continue to underperform.

5. LESSONS APPLIED

So many times, we are our own worst enemy. Without clear leadership and integrated teams, or the authorities to move resources, shift people, and accept risks, the difficult becomes nearly impossible. Too often, we find the hardest way to do something. Seldom do we call upon the American people, as we must.

It reminds me of the famous blues line: "Life ain't easy, but does it have to be this hard?"

Here then are the three major changes we need to make so that our national security culture does not eat our strategies and our people for lunch.[15]

I. Accept Risk Expansion

Inherently dangerous places require greater risk tolerance. Rigid interpretations of guidelines and defensive practices make it impossible to get to know a people or place or to encourage local solutions.

We still must be careful to avoid reckless behaviors. While an obsession with helping others often provides a high level of energy, I believe that a sense of balance is critical to offering the best assistance and for gaining the full confidence of those you seek to help. There is such a fine line between being paternalistic, self-indulgent, enabling, or truly valuable, and one way to fulfill your mission is to maintain your own equilibrium.

Certain destructive and dangerous behaviors concern me: messianic instincts; indispensability divas and divos; and know-it-all delusions. Fueled by adrenaline highs that feed off risk and the importance many visitors feel when in these tormented places, these attitudes are harmful to self and those we seek to help.

How do we temper risk? I believe that the first step must be an open dialogue within the civilian agencies. The current gulf between the views of security people, lawyers, those who work in troubled places, elected representatives, and the public is enormous. A dedicated conversation will bring forward a range of improvements, from family assignments to greater insurance to the length of rotations, special leaves, and bonus pay.

II. Put Someone in Charge and Give That Person Real Authority

Conflict countries are 24/7 concerns that must be dealt with in the right moment with creativity. To do this, make sure that there is one full-time leader and one team with clear, defined responsibility. These moments should define leaders' careers, so give them ownership. That means the ability to move people and money as needed.

Be comfortable with the delegation of authority. Those on the ground should drive many elements of diplomacy and programming. Accept that structure as necessary in order to capitalize on fast-breaking developments. Recognize that changes and course corrections are a given. Greater coherence is possible.

A better organizational structure would not have reversed the Syrian tragedy, but it would have helped. When a fast-breaking crisis cuts across geographic bureaus, a single leader and team can exploit the different strengths of each organization.

The structures that took shape on Syria emphasized coordination without direction. The result at State was eight separate working groups, lots of talk, and the massive commitment of human resources without much resulting. A colleague called it "designed inactivity." A single team, with a clear and capable leader, would make better use of the talent and funding that flows to a challenge like Syria.

The complexity of conflicts requires us to bring a simplicity of design to deal with it. Can the president get a clear answer to who is in charge? Does that person have well-understood responsibilities? Is that individual working full time or do they have additional jobs? Is the leader open to and inclusive of others?

There is a need for someone whose career rises and falls with the success and failure of the venture, that we provide the necessary support to give that individual a chance to succeed, and that everyone inside of the U.S. government recognize this is the president's full-time point person.

For a variety of reasons, the idea has not yet progressed. I remain hopeful and committed. While it would require a hitherto unknown level of collaboration, the "one leader, one team" concept addresses a core flaw in a balanced way. At the least, it could start with a pilot test in a current or upcoming crisis. A move to a responsible leader with the ability to succeed will reduce confusion and chaos.

In shaping two new institutions, I came to realize that much is required. Having a clear sense of needs and of how to accomplish anything inside of a large, tradition-bound bureaucracy is the first step. Often, leaders get hung up on reorganizations or refining a structure. That inevitably leads to delays and nervous people digging in.

Much better to "ready, fire, aim" and get going on addressing challenges in real time. Experiments, pilots, and tests work—an approach that deals with culture and structure simultaneously.

III. Respect Democratic Practices

Our own democracy is the lynchpin of our global engagement. When we fail to respect it fully at home, the seeds of our own destruction grow roots.

The superficial involvement of the U.S. public over the past few decades is dangerous. After the argument for engagement, the follow-on remains distant and impersonal. That will not work.

As the people's representatives, the U.S. Congress must take on a fulsome role. Passing blanket legislation that allows the executive to run amok and the Congress to play the role of a chronic whiner will not suffice. From the Gulf of Tonkin Resolution in the Vietnam War to the 2001 Authorization for Use of Military Force (AUMF) following the Twin Towers attacks, Congress defaulted to the executive.

Those same failings show up in the analysis of our work in conflict countries. When America did not follow its own rule "that strong democratic governments are built on a balanced distribution of power between national and local leaders,"[16] we failed.

Changing our national security institutions is tough work. Be prepared to give blood every day: the need for constant transfusions is endless. Personnel issues are frequent, complaints are routine, and thought-police, security, and paperwork regulations are relentless. It can be oppressive, and the nonsense wears out good people.

Take comfort that most colleagues believe in "expeditionary diplo-macy" and the great potential of America's contributions to a more peaceful world. Recognize that making a difference in war-torn places matters. Celebrate a growing cadre of talented analysts and practition-ers, innovators in peacebuilding. They are all intent on getting out of our own way.

The responsibilities of this kind of service far exceed balance sheets or producing commercial products. You may get to address a societal divide or save a life or just hold a hand in a time of need. These are special opportunities, and our institutions should make sure that we have empowered our people to make the most of these moments.

11

EXPANDING AMERICA'S PEACEFUL CORE

I.

From my earliest days as a member of an American diplomatic family, I have known that America enjoyed an *advantageous* position. More than our size, wealth, markets, military strength, cultural dominance, or lingua franca, the United States earned a recognition as a serious, caring and creative nation, capable of sacrifice. I saw that as a kid in Spain, as a U.S. delegate on international missions, in work at the United Nations, and sitting behind our country's placard at global conferences. America is a global force, with great prospects.

That does not make us indispensable, almighty, or privileged. We are in a position to make a difference, help others, and expand a more peaceful world. Few others have that advantage, as nations or as individuals.

At times, we stumble. In 2007, I had a chance to visit South Carolina, Iowa, Minnesota, and New Hampshire as part of the Smart Power Commission. My opening question in conversations was, "How do you think the U.S. is seen in the world?" In 35 meetings in the four states, I heard one word. At a later gathering of several hundred in Houston, I asked the audience what that word might be. Almost in unison, dozens said, "Arrogant." It was an expression of dissatisfaction with our role in Afghanistan and Iraq and a feeling that "too often, we are going it alone." Still, Americans recognized that our potential is great and valued other ways we contributed.

In his 2008 campaign for the presidency, I felt that Barack Obama captured that feeling of wasted promise. It was the majoritarian zeitgeist. When I became one of America's representatives at the United Nations in New York, other nations welcomed the arrival of the Obama administration. Nevertheless, expectations remained. It was not enough that the United States was back in an engaged and constructive form. Did we come with ideas, talent, and even solutions to the mega problems that we all face? I felt that at times we stepped up, but too often showed up in familiar ways.

Now we are in another rough patch. Americans are broadly alienated from our foreign efforts, nervous about the complexity of the threats we face, and searching for improvements. President Trump offers a range of generalized promises, many premised on the notion that America will do better on its own. Purposeful distancing from friends and potential allies is isolating.

Backing off the expansion of freedom shows a dramatic disregard for America's distinctive and compelling brand. At our best, America puts people first. We bring curiosity versus a willful ignorance to our efforts. These are our sacred principles and help us to find practical ways to solve problems.

Erratic behavior combined with bombastic language is making Washington "the epicenter of political instability in the world."[1] It used to be when America sneezed Canada caught pneumonia. With President Trump, we may be stirring a global pandemic of directionless recklessness. The president's instincts are throwbacks to a simpler time—including the militarization of solutions—and will lead to harm.

With luck, President Trump's unpredictable words and actions may force many of our closest friends to become more responsible. That will not be enough. America's advantageous position, grounded in the trust of so many, will be required to address the kinds of challenges we will face.

The complexity of today's problems is daunting. My friend and guide, the late Ambassador Jonathan Moore, wrote,

> Peace-building is a microcosm of the world today. Its countries, both in their inner turmoil and in the impact they have on the world outside, epitomize our moral and material dilemmas. They are havens of resentment and injustice, crucibles of enduring ethnic hatreds; they are the clash-points of rich and poor, of traditional and

modern; they are the seedbeds of terrorism, disease, drug trafficking, and environmental degradation; they are the beacons of survival and hope. Their numbers are likely to grow; their problems are likely to spread. Waiting for the benefits of globalization, they threaten the harmony of interdependence. Peace-building challenges the world to be more connected and less separate.[2]

Moore wondered why we did not spend more time on the heart and soul of conflicts.

Progress will require the American advantage. We remain a country that has the choice of being in or out, often called for by others, and welcomed upon arrival. Our openness to and acquisitiveness of talent from all over is recognized and respected. The diversity of our people is a part of that: Bosnians in St. Louis, Haitians in Miami, and Hondurans in Washington, DC—plus the full range of the rest of the world. In Kenya, there was a wry joke after the Luo tribe candidate lost yet another presidential election. "Where is the only place on earth where a Luo can be elected president?" The answer, "The United States. Obama's father was a Luo."

A story from a close UNHCR friend shows how the United States matters. As she finished law school in Liberia, Joyce Mends Cole spoke out about the killing of her nation's leadership. In those harrowing days when a low-ranked officer in the army, Samuel Doe, took over Liberia, terror ruled. Like her friends, it was just a matter of days before Joyce might face torture or death. Despairing, Joyce went to Monrovia's cathedral—and prayed with such fervency that she shook. When she opened her eyes, next to her in the pew was U.S. ambassador Bill Swing. When he asked what was wrong, Joyce blurted out her tale of impending doom. The ambassador asked Joyce to stop by the embassy the next day—and her path of escape and recovery began. These kinds of stories are common for the United States, but few others.

Our recognition that international rules and institutions make us safer and more prosperous is also to our advantage. Six decades of large-nation peace dividends confirm the wisdom articulated by President Franklin D. Roosevelt. "We have learned that we cannot live alone at peace, that our own well-being is dependent on the well-being of other nations, far away."[3] That core belief informs America's ongoing role, even if we are reluctant to embrace new treaties and institutions that we led on.

Important to our success is a "can do" attitude. America's willingness to lean into problems and be part of the solution has catalyzed global action. When needed, we offer the idea, the financial boost, or even the young soldiers to address the challenge. Without our catalytic presence, problems will fester.

Today, America itself is not in equilibrium—and that makes our global role more difficult. We seem too self-absorbed for leadership. As we reflect, it might be worth remembering the words of my great-grandfather, William E. Barton, "The human stomach can digest any-thing except introspection." We must start with an honest self-appraisal.

If we stop to look at ourselves and America's performance in break-ing cycles of violence, much is wanting. This book details that we must reflect the spirit of "America the Beautiful" and "confirm thy soul in self-control"—that our role is catalytic and people centered. It makes clear that we need to know places better, integrate our strategies and teams, build off local initiatives, measure progress, and communicate tirelessly. And escape what Justice Brandeis described as "organization-al elephantiasis." None of those changes will be easy—yet they are foundational to America expanding global peace. As Thoreau said in *Walden*, "If one advances confidently in the direction of his dreams, and endeavors to live the life which he has imagined, he will meet with a success unexpected in common hours."[4] That is America's peaceful promise and our advantage to share with those in turmoil.

America has accumulated vast experience in building peace and of-ten ignored it. On those few occasions when humans made real progress against war, mutual respect and feeling for the other tri-umphed. On a family research trip to Chicago, I read about a sermon that our great grandfather the Reverend William E. Barton delivered in Oak Park in the weeks before the end of World War I. It was a turbu-lent moment, dominated by strong feelings. Forgiveness was not at the forefront, but he argued for a "generous peace" with the Germans. He recognized that the winners could design the peace while the van-quished would live with it. Barton felt that an inclusive and forgiving postwar would improve Germany's chances for recovery—and make Europe and the United States more stable. The argument was not pop-ular and did not prevail—and Germany tailed into World War II. We applied those lessons after the next Great War.

Success requires forgiveness and persistence, which are additional elements of modesty and acceptance of past failures. For the decisive role America played and the sacrifices we made in two world wars, the United States secured an advantageous global position that has now lasted a century. At times, we have overplayed or squandered our beneficial position—so there are no guarantees. Still, the volatility of today's world will call for America's improved engagement. I believe that the basic values of American society will reemerge and help others to build a better peace.

2.

In order for the United States to succeed, four critical trends must inform and animate our thinking.

First, we must recognize that mutual assured destruction (MAD) will define the 21st century. This idea dominated the late-20th-century discussions about nuclear weaponry and many believed kept the world's superpowers from doing anything too stupid. If you used an atomic bomb, it could result in one destroying you. Equilibrium resulted, even if we seemed to be on the precipice.

In this century, the nature of our societies, structures, and problems suggests a new kind of MAD. Many countries, even teenagers, can now mount cyberattacks on others, crippling a range of public utilities, individual autos, or air traffic control systems. Counterattacks are not attractive because of the vast array of targets. Was it the North Koreans or a computer lab at a technical high school or an informal network that includes U.S.-based geeks?

Similar complications arise in global climate change, health threats, terrorism, and, of course, nuclear arms. How each of us behaves has direct consequences on others. The consequences now feel more personal: witness the recurring fears of diseases or random attacks arriving in the United States.

The acts of individuals, the nature of communications, and our technological and social interdependence make the building of walls ineffective. "Protected" societies can be shocked at any moment by the miniaturization of weaponry or the anonymity of highly destructive actions.

Awareness of this shared risk will require us to be more expansive in how we understand these threats and in how we contain them.

Second, we must pay attention to the "silenced majorities." In conflict countries, the political marketplace usually excludes women, youth, minorities, and even many businesses, religions, and other fixtures of society. Insular decision-making expects the body politic to respond favorably to the proffered dictums.

When faced with growing activism, traditional leaders move to repress new voices. Right now there is a worldwide movement against the expansion of civil society: "120 laws constraining the freedoms of association or assembly have been proposed or enacted in 60 countries" since 2012, many of these countries being U.S. partners.[5]

The political protest "We are being left out" is thriving in most of the world's stable democracies. America's 2016 presidential campaign, the Brexit vote, and numerous other examples are reminders that our vaunted societal connectivity is threatened.

For America to renew its global leadership, we must listen to and constructively direct these surges of political energy. How we guide large new populations of motivated citizens to peaceful, democratic change will determine the quality of the next 50 years.

Developing new partnerships and capturing the public's imagination in foreign lands will be more important than the fealty of a single leader and other familiar outreach. Our choices should reflect that.

Third, we must practice asymmetric approaches. We have witnessed the effectiveness of "lone wolf" attacks, suicide bombers, self-appointed arbiters of political thought, and egocentric political leaders. "In a revolutionary era of surprise and innovation, you need to think and act like a revolutionary."[6]

Just as America's Special Forces and drones have become favored tools of 21st-century military interventions, so must we consider the asymmetric application of diplomacy and economic actions. A focus on bilateral relations and large embassies—in places like Kabul and Baghdad, Paris and Beijing—will have to give way to hundreds of smaller outposts, massive high school exchange programs, heightened social media interactivity, and focused sanctions.

International conventions and multilateral institutions must become more relevant to the threats and challenges of the time. America's inherent caution, often using the rules-based model to constrain others, will have to expand to meet the dynamism of today's markets. The United States has played contradictory roles for some time: as the greatest supporter of the current system and often as a resistant force to change.

Thinking of ourselves as an agile and innovative force will transform America's influence and effectiveness.

Fourth, we must mobilize the excess capacity in our system. Our institutions are huge—even obese—from banks, insurance companies, health care, and cable television systems to our national security establishment. Yet, few will argue that they are efficient or even make the most of the talent that they employ.

We have seen entire industries surface in the past decade, from Car2Go and Lyft to Airbnb and online reservation systems. Using excess capacity is their core principle. Collecting information and converting it into data is informing millions of decisions and choices. Such opportunities exist within the U.S. government and in how we analyze and solve large problems.

While the standard response to humanitarian crises is to raise as much money as possible, mobilize an international team, and seek to manage the situation, there may be better choices. The devastating 2005 earthquakes in Pakistan were so destructive that the only viable response was to give the victims cash to move on their own, find relatives and friends, and initiate a personal recovery. Even in the chaos of Somalia, 70 percent of assistance is now in cash.[7] In many crises, people are able to address their own initial challenges if the help is well directed and catalytic.

Each of these four trends is humbling. The threats are real and intimidating, often from unexpected or unknown places. The last three trends point to an abundance of opportunities—if we are willing to change our ways. That too will be difficult.

In order to improve our success rate we will have to be more acute about the circumstances of the time, more attentive to the large numbers who feel left out, more agile in our approaches, and willing to look for surplus capacities. We are capable of doing all of this.

3.

America's lessons are both at home and abroad.

A few days after 9/11, in Dallas, a white supremacist, Mark Stroman, shot a Bangladeshi American store clerk, Rais Bhuiyan, in the face. As part of a revenge attack on Muslims, Stroman shot and killed two others. Targeted, Rais survived. Soon thereafter, the authorities caught, convicted, and scheduled Stroman for the death penalty.

Despite a long and painful recovery, Rais dedicated himself to becoming a force for healing. He committed himself to "a world without violence and victims" and sought out every opportunity to spread his message. It was not easy. Quoting the Koran, he said, "God will not place a burden on shoulders that cannot bear it." His book, *The True American*, promoted the importance of not letting hate fill your heart.[8]

Included in his forgiveness was Mark Stroman. At Principia College's International Perspectives Conference in 2016, I heard Rais speak to how he reached out and sought to have Stroman's death penalty commuted. Among the most compelling scenes was a video of a tearful Stroman thanking Rais for his expansive humanity. It was clear that Rais's "world without hate" led Stroman to a place of peace—even as Texas moved ahead with his execution.

Rais followed the guidance of Maya Angelou, who said, "Touch someone's heart."[9] It was transformative.

For many of us who do peacebuilding work, we feel the great honor, yet accept incrementalism. Have we made any difference? There are those who look for transformative powers, but that seems unattainable. Messianic approaches are inadvisable. Could we increase our impact and influence? Only sometimes do good things happen, yet we persevere. Why?

It starts with loving the work. That must be outsized to offset the daily beat down of violent events. After a van struck him as he walked on a rural Maine road, the author Stephen King went through a grueling recovery. Multiple medical procedures left him with painful pins in various parts of his body. He lost a third of his weight and could not get around. He spoke about the "end of my endurance." Unable to sit still, he could not write. One lazy afternoon in his cottage in western Maine, King found himself in his favorite spot and started to type. Joy returned, pain receded, and he found himself lost in the words. He knew that most would be well.[10]

Those blessed to be peacebuilders must have King's passion for our work. Since positive news does not always follow our best efforts, we must care until it hurts. Millions of Americans already do. Hundreds of thousands have served as soldiers, diplomats, and humanitarians in conflict lands. Others have followed their faith or cherished causes. Whenever there is an emergency, the outpouring of American generosity inspires. We recognize the opacity of the situations, yet we lean in. The world is better for our efforts—even as we work to improve.

The dedication and fine work of colleagues at State, USAID, and the United Nations, along with partners in our military, White House, foreign governments, and nongovernmental organizations, stand out. Despite focusing on dangerous places, we never had a shortage of talented people. Their steadfast and inspired work overcame frequent obstacles—and made a difference in violent situations.

To be peacebuilders we all must dig deeper. It is inspiring to remember former Notre Dame president Theodore Hesburgh, at the cornerstone-laying ceremony for the new United States Institute of Peace (USIP) building in Washington, saying, "Peace is always good." A favorite boss, Doug Stafford, would often end a day by asking, "Have we saved a life today?" Doug knew that tending to the organizational termites could distract even the best people from their central mission.

For me, it is the sense that I might make a difference somewhere in the world. There is no universal formula, to give or to receive, but rather a healing process, the subtle guidance of substantial local human energies, and finding new ways to increase our contributions to a more peaceful world.

In every instance, there are individuals with hopes and needs. Their motivations drive their communities for better and worse. When we find those people and make a connection, America has an impact.

4.

A small story sticks in my heart. On a visit to the refugees of embattled West Africa in 1999, we stopped in the "Parrot's Beak" area of Guinea, a fertile, forested region stuck between Sierra Leone and Liberia. With both neighbors in states of war, more than 300,000 recent arrivals filled a number of massive new UNHCR camps and others were squatting in dozens more—many without the most basic protection.

The morning's U.N. flight from the busy, run-down, seaport capital of Conakry took us over much of the country and we landed in the sleepy eastern hamlet of Kissidougou. As the deputy high commissioner of the U.N. refugee agency, there were protocol requirements and we met local officials and savored Coca Colas in a one-room shed by the runway. Shortly, we were off in a small caravan with U.N. and host-government figures, wending our way through country roads.

A half hour later, we approached something I had never seen before. Lining both sides of the road into a huge refugee camp in the state seat of Gueckedou were several thousand Sierra Leoneans, cheering our arrival. They knew that a senior official from Geneva was coming and I felt the pressure of their hopefulness. How would my visit really matter?

The throng grew larger and as we got out of the car, elders, a band, dancers and thousands of refugees engulfed us. Dozens of women wore brand new Martina Hingis t-shirts, featuring the smiling face of Switzerland's top-ranked woman tennis player over their more familiar West African dresses.

It was a carnival with a purpose: do not forget us.

While the presence of so many new people creates massive pressures, it was also apparent that the area was thriving. Because the international support for the refugees did not provide the necessary daily nutrition or other critical survival needs, most of the residents of the camps needed work. Each day, they would leave their mud and twig huts, some featuring UNHCR's trademark blue plastic sheeting, and walk miles to assist local farmers.

With the influx of a huge pool of hardworking and inexpensive labor, the production of bananas and other fruits was soaring with more land cleared. Everywhere, we passed produce-laden trucks on the roads back to Conakry. At a meeting that night, the local governor confirmed that the economy was bustling and that, as a result, the region had taken on a greater importance for the national government.

As we walked around the camps, it became apparent that hundreds of Sierra Leonean teachers were holding classes. In a school-like court-yard, a European NGO had provided soccer balls and a couple of gym teachers and for a moment, you could have been in a playground any-where on earth: kids running about, smiles everywhere, and screams when a goal pierced the makeshift goal. At a later meeting, the head of the national teachers' union said that the only Sierra Leonean teachers receiving pay and students going to school were in UNHCR camps in Guinea.

We drove on to a Liberian camp, where longer-lasting displacement and institutionalized suffering produced a less festive celebration. Yet another memorable reminder of the human spirit awaited us.

After a welcoming event, my wonderful UNHCR aide, Yacoub el-Hillo, asked me to go with him to a small medical clinic a few yards away. There, we met a young Liberian mother, who had given birth to triplets that morning. Lying on a simple cot, the two tiny girls and frail young boy clung to their mother. All three babies looked as if they would fit in my palms. The mother said, "We have named our son Barton."

The entire tableau touched my heart. Here was a young family, in extreme circumstances, hanging on for dear life—with a mother doing everything she could to improve their chances. Despite the exhaustion of giving birth just hours before, that Liberian refugee mother had dug deep once more and called upon her native ingenuity to thrust her son forward.

These moments lift us all up, for they say so much about humanity. Just miles away, there may be warlords and young marauders murder-ing, raping, pillaging, and chasing people from their homes by the hun-dreds. Yet, in the middle of nowhere, innocent survivors are coming together, building communities, and imagining dreams. They are mak-ing the impossible addressable.

If we start with a core respect for the people of a place, recognize their wrenching human experiences, and accept that our role is to be-lieve in their potential, the United States will be a more effective peace-builder. Trust, the mortar of societies, will grow and we will all be safer.

America will help to expand peace.

NOTES

INTRODUCTION

1. The Netflix documentary on their work won the 2017 Academy Award for Best Documentary (Short Subject). Orlando von Einsiedel and Joanna Natasegara, *The White Helmets*, Netflix, 2016, https://www.netflix.com/title/80101827.

I. IS THE WORLD GOING TO HELL?

1. http://cco.ndu.edu/PRISM-6-3/Article/1020271/an-interview-with-stanley-mcchrystal/.

2. http://www.economist.com/news/21589143-whereprotest-likeliest-break-out-ripe-rebellion. According to the *Economist* Intelligence Unit, 65 countries (43 percent of those studied) were at a high or very high risk of social unrest in 2014. Compared with 2009, 19 more countries are now in the high-risk categories, including two-thirds of the countries in the Middle East–North Africa; also, http://fundforpeace.org/fsi/2017/05/14/fsi-2017-factionalization-and-group-grievance-fuel-rise-in-instability/.

3. https://reliefweb.int/report/worl/global-peace-index-2017.

4. http://www.cfr.org/global/global-conflict-tracker/p32137#!/; http://issuu.com/fundforpeace/docs/fragile_states_index_-_annual_repor_f3648acb0f45d8/1?e=2498657/13585266.

5. Charles T. Call, "The Lingering Problem of Fragile States," *Washington Quarterly*, Winter 2017.

6. Michael Miklaucic, *Commanding Heights: Strategic Lessons from Complex Operations*, p. xi.

7. United Nations, U.S. Departments of Defense and State, and USAID, several think tanks, and so forth.

8. United States Department of State and United States Agency for International Development. *Quadrennial Diplomacy and Development Review: Leading through Civilian Power*, http://www.state.gov/documents/organization/153142.pdf, p. 121.

9. Douglas Rutzen, "Civil Society Under Assault," *Journal of Democracy*, October 2015. http://www.icnl.org/news/2015/05_26.4_Rutzen.pdf.

10. David Brooks column, *NYTimes*, October 24, 2014. https://www.nytimes.com/2014/03/25/opinion/brooks-the-republic-of-fear.html.

11. Personal aside to author in informal exchange. The restaurant in our Belfast, Northern Ireland, hotel featured a newspaper article with the headline: "Europe's Most Bombed Restaurant." A curious promotion.

12. Greg Beck, https://www.youtube.com/watch?v=6vyLnYkrPgw.

13. See Trump inaugural speech. https://www.whitehouse.gov/briefings-statements/the-inaugural-address/.

14. Steven Pinker, *The Better Angels of Our Nature: Why Violence Has Declined*, 2011, p. xxvi. First published in 2011.

15. http://www.benjamin-franklin-history.org/pennsylvania-volunteer-militia/.

16. A positive side: "The historian Alexander Keyssar traces the growth of voting rights in the United States from the Revolution through subsequent wars. Göran Therborn notes that national wartime mobilization seems to have hastened suffrage expansions in Denmark in 1849, Germany in 1871, Norway in 1898, Finland against the tsar in 1906, and Austria in 1907, and that World War I prodded the extension of the franchise in Italy, Canada, Belgium, and Britain." John Ferejohn and Frances McCall Rosenbluth, *Forged Through Fire: War, Peace, and the Democratic Bargain*, Norton, 2017, p. 1.

17. Ibid., p. 315–16.

18. Ibid.

19. http://voicesofdemocracy.umd.edu/fdr-the-four-freedoms-speech-text/.

20. Roy Licklider, "Obstacles to Peace Settlements," in *Elgar Handbook of Civil War and Fragile States*.

21. See CSIS Pakistan report: Israel, Egypt, and Jordan. Debt reduction, budget support, military, development. Craig Cohen. *A Perilous Course: U.S. Strategy and Assistance to Pakistan*, CSIS 2017.

22. https://www.youtube.com/watch?v=n9y2qtaopbE.

23. Owen Bennett Jones, *Pakistan: Eye of the Storm*, p. xiv.

24. Steven Pinker, *The Better Angels of Our Nature*, p. 360.

25. An Air Force general had suggested it was more than $4 billion. We were never able to confirm that number.

26. See the CSIS Publication: Craig Cohen, *A Perilous Course*, https://csis-prod.s3.amazonaws.com/s3f3-public/legacy_files/files/media/csis/pubs/071214_pakistan.pdf. The consensus notion of U.S. spending in Pakistan was that it was $750 million per year—when it had risen to $2 billion. As we spoke to those who knew Pakistan in Washington, we heard a range of numbers. One Air Force general told us that the combined public and covert spending might be closer to $4 billion. We did not have access to the "dark" fund information, so settled on detailing the overt funds.

27. Craig Cohen, *A Perilous Course*, p. viii.

28. Ibid., pp. vi, vii.

29. When Pakistan developed nuclear weapons, the USAID mission went from "more than 1,000 staff members . . . to almost nothing . . . overnight. The September 11 attacks precipitated a major U.S. reengagement." Ibid., p. 2.

30. Biden-Lugar, then Kerry-Lugar became two pieces of proposed legislation that began to redirect America's assistance to Pakistan.

31. CSIS Post Conflict Reconstruction Project's special report, *Early Warning? A Review of Conflict Prediction Models and Systems*, available at https://csis-prod.s3.amazonaws.com/s3fs-public/legacy_files/files/publication/080201_early_warning.pdf.

32. The National Intelligence Council's *Mapping the Global Future: Report of the 2020 Project*, http://webapp1.dlib.indiana.edu/virtual_disk_library/index.cgi/6112953/FID2670/Bin/NIC_2004-13.pdf.

33. Personal conversation with author at Ditchley Conference in 2002.

34. Personal communication with author in 2017.

35. CMM: http://www.usaid.gov/our_work/cross-cutting_programs/conflict/

36. Micah Zenko, https://warontherocks.com/2015/11/millennium-challenge-the-real-story-of-a-corrupted-military-exercise-and-its-legacy/.

2. WHY SHOULD WE ACT AND WHEN?

1. U.S. Secretary secretary of state John Kerry, "Remarks at Yale College Class Day" (Yale University, New Haven, CT, May 18, 2014).

2. Frank M. Coffin, *Witness for AID*.

3. Ibid.

4. Ibid., p. 268.

5. George Washington's Farewell letter, 1796, https://en.wikisource.org/wiki/Washington&27s_Farewell_Address.

6. Thomas Jefferson's First Inaugural Address, 1801, http://avalon.law. yale.edu/19th_century/jefinau1.asp.

7. John Quincy Adams, July 4, 1821, http://www.theamericaconservative. com/repository/she-goes-not-abroad-in-search-of-monsters-to-destroy/.

8. Warren Zimmerman outlined this in his *First Great Triumph* and William Pfaff described it in *The Irony of Manifest Destiny*.

9. Mark Twain, October 6, 1900, http://www.historywiz.com/ primarysources/marktwain-imperialism.htm.

10. Adam Gopnik, *New Yorker*, January 6, 2014, https://www.newyorker. com/magazine/2014/01/06/two-ships.

11. Joshua Cooper Ramo, *The Age of the Unthinkable: Why the New World Disorder Constantly Surprises Us and What to Do about It.*

12. Leslie Gelb and Richard K. Betts, *The Irony of Vietnam*, p. 353, Washington, Brookings, 1979.

13. He produced revealing data on the links between various issues, much as the World Bank's *Voices of the Poor: Crying Out for Change* by Deepa Narayan and Paul Collier's *Bottom Billion* did years later.

14. David Halberstam, *War in a Time of Peace*, p. 30.

15. Karin von Hippel, *Democracy by Force: US Military Intervention in the Post–Cold War World,* 2000, p. 2. She cited 98 armed conflicts between 1990 and 1996, with only seven between states.

16. Joseph Nye, *Soft Power*, p. xi.

17. James Fallows, "The Fifty-First State," *Atlantic* (November 2002).

18. Charles Blow, "War-Weariness," *New York Times*, August 31, 2013.

19. Henry Kissinger in *World Order.*

20. Zbigniew Brzezinski, Foreign Affairs, January/February 2002, https:// www.scribd.com/document/77129930/Zbigniew-Brzezinski-Balancing-the-East-Upgrading-the-West-U-S-Grand-Strategy-in-an-Age-of-Upheaval.

21. Barbara Salazar Torreon, Congressional Research Service, October 12, 2017, https://fas.org.sgp/crs/natsec/R42738.pdf: Afghanistan, Albania, Bosnia and Herzegovina, Colombia, Congo (DR), Croatia, Haiti, Iraq, Kuwait, Liberia, Libya, Macedonia, Pakistan, Panama, Philippines, Somalia, Sudan, Syria, Yemen, Yugoslavia. This does not include special operations.

22. http://www.un.org/en/peacekeeping/operations/current.shtml; the United States pays on average about 25 percent of all costs.

23. Karin von Hippel, *Democracy by Force: US Military Intervention in the Post–Cold War World*, p. 12.

24. Edward Peterson, *The American Occupation of Germany*, p. 10, quoted in Karin von Hippel *Democracy by Force: US Military Intervention in the Post–Cold War World.*

25. Toshio Nishi, *Unconditional Democracy: Education and Politics in Occupied Japan, 1945–1952*, 1982, p. 34, quoted in Karin von Hippel *Democracy by Force: US Military Intervention in the Post–Cold War World.*

26. John Dower, lecture November 6, 2000, https://vimeo.com/37754928.

27. John Dower video lecture.

28. Ian Buruma, *Inventing Japan: 1853–1964*, p. 134.

29. Cited in Karin von Hippel, *Democracy by Force: US Military Intervention in the Post–Cold War World*, p. 17.

30. John Dower, lecture, November 6, 2000, https://vimeo.com/37754928.

31. Ian Buruma, *Inventing Japan: 1853–1964*, p. 136.

32. Ibid.

33. Ibid., p. 133.

34. Ibid., p. 134.

35. Ibid., p. 133.

36. See John Dower vimeo.

37. Bryan R. Gibby, *Will to Win*, p. 3.

38. Ibid., p. 8.

39. John Lie (University of Illinois at Urbana-Champaign), "Aid Dependence and the Structure of Corruption: The Case of Post-Korean War South Korea."

40. My earliest memories of this debate go back to Senator Mike Mansfield, who argued for our departure from Korea, Germany, and Japan. The 2016 presidential campaign surfaced the issue, though not as a central feature.

41. Kenneth Frankel, President, Canadian Council for the Americas, "The Colombian Peace Agreement," *Globe and Mail* op-ed. June 17, 2014, http://www.ccacanada.com/why-colomias-voters-kept-the-peace-process-alive-by-kenfrankel-globe-and-mail/#.WmJ6S6inH-g.

42. Michael Shifter, "Plan Colombia," *Americas Quarterly* (Summer 2012).

43. I visited a major government initiative in Macarena around 2008 and saw the commando's operation.

44. Professor Chuck Call, Skype interview with Princeton class, February 15, 2016.

45. For example, the United States is not expected to pursue secret U.S. indictments of the FARC.

46. http://www.people-press.org/2013/12/03/public-sees-u-s-power-declining-as-support-for-global-engagement-slips/.

47. According to the Center for Global Development, "At the aggregate level, only 16 percent of U.S. assistance has been focused on what Africans definitively cite as their most pressing problems. On average, less than one third of U.S. assistance has been aligned with people's top three concerns in 11 African nations over time." http://www.cgdev.org/.

48. Robert Lamb, Post-Conflict Reconstruction Project, CSIS, July 2013.

49. Karin von Hippel, *Democracy by Force: US Military Intervention in the Post–Cold War World.*

50. Former secretary of state Colin Powell offered this while the NSA advisor in 1990, https://en.wikipedia.org/wiki/Powell_Doctrine.

51. https://warontherocks.com/2014/02/a-second-look-at-the-powell-doctrine/.

52. Quoted by Frank Hoffman in ibid.

53. Secretary of State Albright at Harvard commencement, https://1997-2001.state.gov/statements/970605.html.

.54. https://en.wikipedia.org/wiki/Atrocities_Prevention_Board.

· 55. Pilgrim leader John Winthrop's oft-quoted idealization of America.

56. John Ferejohn and Frances McCall Rosenbluth, *Forged Through Fire: War, Peace, and the Democratic Bargain*, p. 17.

A NEW HOPE IN THE 1990S

1. Carnegie Commission, *Preventing Deadly Conflict*, p. xvii.

2. Sadako Ogata, *The Turbulent Decade*, p. 17.

3. Ibid., p. 18.

4. Ibid., pp. 25, 267–68 and informal conversation with author.

5. David Halberstam, *War in a Time of Peace*, p. 262.

6. Richard Holbrooke credited in ibid., p. 265.

7. Madeleine Albright and William Woodward, *Madam Secretary*, p. 155. Albright also described a United Nations that could play world night watchman: monitor and raise the alarm, but not guarantee a response.

8. https://history.state.gov: Unburdened by the Cold War international framework that structured U.S. foreign policy for nearly 50 years, the Clinton administration sought to outline new objectives for U.S. foreign policy, including novel uses for military power. Ambassador to the United Nations Madeleine Albright outlined a U.S. policy of "assertive multilateralism," with an increased role for the United Nations. National Security Advisor Anthony Lake emphasized the role of economic power in the new world order, and argued for a U.S. role in the "enlargement" of the community of free nations. The new administration, however, faced multiple challenges in the former Yugoslavia, Somalia, North Korea, and Haiti that complicated their attempts to implement the broad strategies and objectives defined by the administration's leaders.

9. Mary Anderson, quoted in Kimberly Maynard, *Healing Communities in Conflict*.

10. Benjamin Barber, *Jihad vs. McWorld*.

11. Scott Anderson, *The Man Who Tried to Save the World*, p. 30.

12. Ibid., p. 119.

13. Ibid., pp. 113, 120.

14. Ibid., p. 31.

15. "Notwithstanding authority" provides a waiver of regular rules in extreme situations that threaten U.S. national security. While seldom used, its availability and the threat of its use produces action from recalcitrant bureaucratic partners.

3. BOSNIA

1. Laura Silber and Allan Little, *The Death of Yugoslavia*, p. 28.

2. See Richard West, *Tito and the Rise and Fall of Yugoslavia*, 1994.

3. Laura Silber and Allan Little, *The Death of Yugoslavia*, pp. 28–29.

4. A travel agent before the war. Special thanks also to Bob Gelbard, Ambassador John Menzies, John Fox, and John Fawcett for their guidance and help during the early days in Bosnia.

5. Ray Jennings, field report to OTI headquarters.

6. Ibid.

7. Laura Silber and Allan Little, *The Death of Yugoslavia*, p. 391.

8. We found the work of James Surowiecki, both his *New Yorker* columns and *The Wisdom of Crowds*, to be most helpful.

9. See Jennings report mentioned above.

10. In each case, the United States was embroiled in a conflict and needed a better understanding of the dynamics. In Mozambique, Gersony's research proved that many of the most grotesque abuses came from America's allies. In Liberia, a mass murder was investigated. In Nicaragua, Gersony developed a way forward for a rugged and independent region of the country, after spending half a year motoring along the coast in open boats.

11. Bob Gersony in oral report to author and others

12. Alastair Pilkington, personal communication with the author, unknown date.

13. http://www.upi.com/Archives/1999/10/22/Editor-loses-legs-in-Bosnia-car-bombing/1392940564800/.

14. See Steve York, *Bringing Down a Dictator* (San Francisco: Kanopy Streaming, 2014).

4. RWANDA

1. Philip Gourevitch, *We Wish to Inform You That Tomorrow We Will Be Killed with Our Families*, p. 57.

2. Ibid., p. 96.

3. http://www.refworld.org/docid/469f3874c.html.

4. Madeleine Albright and William Woodward, *Madam Secretary*, p. 148.

5. Of course there were heroic exceptions, such as Alison Des Forges, who sought to bring attention and assistance to individual Rwandans and to the genocide from the start, petitioning the U.S. government and international organizations.

6. https://en.wikipedia.org/wiki/Operation_Support_Hope.

7. Mark Frohart, October 9, 2017, during Skype guest visit to author's Princeton class.

8. https://www.nytimes.com/2014/06/12/opinion/all-justice-is-local.html?_r=1.

9. Ibid.

10. Buddy Shanks, WIT director in a field report.

11. UN Human Rights monitor to the author on a field visit near Kibungo.

12. Buddy Shanks, final report as he left Rwanda in April 2000

13. Ibid.

14. Ibid.

15. Ibid.

16. Buddy Shanks's farewell note to author and others, April 2000.

17. http://www.independent.co.uk/news/obituaries/aloisea-inyumba-politician-who-played-a-key-role-in-the-rebuilding-of-rwanda-8527166.html.

5. HAITI

1. Edwidge Danticat in http://www.newyorker.com/news/news-desk/haiti-us-occupation-hundred-year-anniversary.

2. Keith Crane, *Building a More Resilient Haitian State*, 2010.

3. See Amy Wilentz's *The Rainy Season*.

4. https://history.state.gov/milestones/1992000/haiti.

5. Including one in October 1993.

6. A hero of the Haiti effort was IOM's Bill Hyde, one of the giants of the humanitarian world.

7. See Bob Shacochis, *The Immaculate Invasion*, https://www.amazon.com/Immaculate-Invasion-Bob-Shacochis/dp/0802145183.

8. See Philippe Gerard's excellent review in the *Journal of Conflict Studies*, https://journals.lib.unb.ca/index.php/jcs/article/view/290/461.

9. Kirk Nielsen, "As Haiti Disbands Army, Soldiers Are Retooled for Scarce Civilian Jobs," *Christian Science Monitor*, December 11, 2015, http://www.csmonitor.com/1995/1211/11081.html.

10. We sought to work in each of Haiti's 10 departments, many of the 41 arrondissements, and some of the 133 communes or municipalities.

11. The invaluable contributions of Steve Siegler, a committed internationalist, made this come to life.

12. http://www.nytimes.com/1994/10/10/world/kelly-s-tough-new-job-reforming-haiti-s-police.html.

13. http://articles.chicagotribune.com/1994-10-17/news/9410170083_1_haitian-police-police-force-haitian-boat-people.

14. The ratio of police to citizens was a fraction of a similar effort in El Salvador after their civil war.

15. Paul Farmer, *Haiti After the Earthquake*, pp. 394, 382.

16. Daniel Patrick Moynihan, *Pandaemonium*, p. 10.

17. See James Surowiecki, *The Wisdom of Crowds*.

18. Buddy Shanks's final report, April 2000.

THE CRUCIBLE OF THE NEW CENTURY

1. President George H. W. Bush to Gorbachev after fall of USSR, December 2, 1989. Quoted in Derek Chollet's *America Between the Wars*, p. 521.

2. Derek Chollet and James Goldgeier, *America Between the Wars*, p. 329.

3. David Halberstam, *War in a Time of Peace*, p. 16.

4. Joseph Nye, *Soft Power*, p. xi.

5. *Report of the Secretary-General pursuant to General Assembly Resolution 53/35: The Fall of Srebrenica*, http://www.securitycouncilreport.org/atf/cf/%7B65BFCF9B-6D27-4E9C-8CD3-CF6E4FF96FF9%7D/a_549_1999.pdf; *Report of the Independent Inquiry into the Actions of the United Nations During the 1994 Genocide in Rwanda*, http://www.securitycouncilreport.org/atf/cf/%7B65BFCF9B-6D27-4E9C-8CD3-CF6E4FF96FF9%7D/POC%20S19991257.pdf.

6. *The Fall of Srebrenica* (see previous note, though it also refers to Rwanda report).

7. http://www.unhcr.org/cgi-bin/texis/vtx/search?page=search&docid=3ba0bbeb4&query=Kosovo.

8. http://www.un.org/en/peacebuilding/pdf/historical/hlp_more_secure_ world.pdf (along with its satirical and yet constructive twin, a junior staff effort called "The Low-Level Panel").

9. Ibid.

6. IRAQ

1. Barton et al., "A Wiser Peace: An Action Strategy for a Post-Conflict Iraq," https://csis-prod.s3.amazonaws.com/s3fs-public/legacy_files/files/media/ csis/pubs/wiserpeace.pdf.

2. "Extension of Remarks," *Congressional Record*, June 11, 2003.

3. Rajiv Chandrasekaran in Afghanistan.

4. Rajiv Chandrasekeran, *Little America: The War within the War for Afghanistan*, p. 261.

5. Anthony Shadid, *Night Draws Near: Iraq's People in the Shadow of America's War*, p. 260.

6. Ibid.

7. Ibid., p. 263.

8. Baghdad focus group led by the author in July 2003.

9. Basra, Mosul, Irbil, Najaf, Karbala, Hillah, and elsewhere.

10. Iraq's Post-Conflict Reconstruction. A Field Review and Recommendations, July 17, 2003, file:///C:/Users/barton/Downloads/Iraq_Trip_Report.pdf.

11. John J. Hamre, Frederick Barton, Bathsheba N. Crocker, Johanna Mendelson, and Robert Orr, *Iraq's Post-Conflict Reconstruction: A Field Review and Recommendations*, July 17, 2003, https://www.cfr.org/sites/default/files/ pdf/2005/08/Iraq_Trip_Report.pdf.

12. Neil MacFarquhar, "The Struggle for Iraq: Life in Baghdad; Open War Over, Iraqis Focus on Crime and a Hunt for Jobs," *New York Times*, September 16, 2003.

13. Frederick Barton, "Defining Success in Iraq and Its Implications for the Gulf," in *The Gulf: Challenges of the Future*, ed. Emirates Center for Strategic Studies and Research, p. 291.

14. See Michael Tackett, *Chicago Tribune*, April 20, 2008, for an interesting review of Aiken's talk. https://www.timesargus.com/articles/declaring-truth-and-myth-on-iraq-and-vietnam/.

15. https://csis-prod.s3.amazonaws.com/s3fs-public/legacy_files/files/ attachments/040908_progressperil_summary.pdf.

16. CSIS Post Conflict Reconstruction Project, *Capturing Iraqi Voices*, July 2004.

17. Ibid.

18. Rajiv Chandrasekaran, *Imperial Life in the Emerald City*, p. 328.

19. French military conference discussion (not for attribution).

20. Conversation with Andy Gordon, June 23, 2017.

21. Frederick Barton, Bathsheba Crocker, and Craig Cohen, http://www.nytimes.com/2005/01/19/opinion/should-we-stay-or-should-we-go.html?_r=0.

22. The author visited a handful of U.S. states in the spring of 2007 as part of the Smart Power Commission and these comments came in response to his questions.

23. http://www.globalsecurity.org/military/ops/iraq_casualties.htm and https://en.wikipedia.org/wiki/Casualties_of_the_Iraq_War.

24. http://www.huffingtonpost.com/2013/10/15/iraq-death-toll_n_4102855.html.

25. See Linda Bilmes and Joseph Stieglitz, http://www.washingtonpost.com/wp=dyn/content/article/2010/09/030AR2010090302200.html.

26. Stanley A. McChrystal on Afghanistan, Iraq, and U.S. preparation, *PRISM*, 2016, http://cco.ndu.edu/PRISM-6-2/Article/1020271/an-interview-with-stanley-mcchrystal/.

7. AFGHANISTAN

1. Stephen Biddle and J. Alexander Thier, "Defining Success in Afghanistan," *Foreign Affairs* (July 1, 2010).

2. Anwar Ahady then Governor of Da Afghanistan Bank at CSIS event in Washington around 2004.

3. See USAID review of similar projects at http://pdf.usaid.gov/pdf_docs/Pnadj142.pdf.

4. Stephen Biddle and J. Alexander Thier, "Defining Success in Afghanistan."

5. Morgan L. Courtney, Frederick Barton, Bathsheba N. Crocker, and Hugh Riddell, *In the Balance: Measuring Progress in Afghanistan: A Report of the CSIS Post-Conflict Reconstruction Project*, Washington, DC: CSIS Press, Center for Strategic and International Studies, 2005.

6. Researchers collected 6,000 qualitative data points, including 1,000 structured conversations with Afghans in 13 provinces, and more than 200 interviews with 27 U.S., 12 international, 20 multinational, and 55 Afghan sources from 10 research institutions, 40 government agencies, 20 international organizations, 19 NGOs and civil society organizations, 15 private businesses and contractors, and various cross sections of Afghan society.

7. *Breaking Point: Measuring Progress in Afghanistan*, March 2007, https:/
/csis-prod.s3.amazonaws.com/s3fs-public/legacy_files/files/media/csis/pubs/
070329_breaking.pdf.

8. Seema Patel, Frederick Barton, Karin von Hippel, Steven Ross, and
CSIS Post-Conflict Reconstruction Project, *Breaking Point: Measuring
Progress in Afghanistan*, March 2007, http://www.csis.org/media/csis/pubs/
070329_breakingpoint.pdf.

9. Representatives of many NATO and alliance countries (France, Germany, United Kingdom, Canada, Holland, Italy, Australia, New Zealand, Singa-
pore, etc.), all parts of the U.S. government (including multiple meetings at
DOD, State, and USAID, etc.), and multinationals were interviewed.

10. This represented the personal responses that the author heard as he
shared the findings with those who ran programs in Afghanistan.

11. Carter Malkasian, *War Comes to Garmser: Thirty Years of Conflict on
the Afghan Frontier*, p. xvi.

12. Ibid., p. 100.

13. Ibid., p. 101.

14. Ibid.

15. Ibid., p. 71 and more.

16. Ibid., p. 76.

17. Ibid.

18. Ibid., p. 77.

19. Ibid., pp. 80–81.

20. Ibid., p. 81.

21. Ibid., p. 92.

22. Rajiv Chandrasekaran, *Little America: The War within the War for Afghanistan*, p. 184.

23. Ibid., p. 185.

24. Bob Woodward, *Obama's Wars*.

25. Stanley A. McChrystal, *My Share of the Task*, p. 317.

26. Ibid.

27. Ibid., p. 322.

28. Ibid., p. 334.

29. Ibid., p. 330.

30. Ibid., p. 331.

31. Ibid., p. 338.

32. Steve Coll, *New Yorker*, October 11, 2017.

33. Bob Woodward, Appendix, *Obama's Wars*.

34. Douglas Ollivant, New America Foundation, quoted in Thomas Gibbons-Neff, *Washington Post*, October 16, 2016.

35. Thomas Gibbons-Neff, *Washington Post*, October 16, 2016.

36. The reported plan at the end of June 2017.

37. Erin Cunningham, *Washington Post*, November 1, 2016.

38. https://www.sigar.mil/pdf/quarterlyreports/2017-01-30qr.pdf.

39. Quoted in the *New York Times* review of her book, February 22, 2015.

40. Rod Norland, *New York Times*, September 24, 2014.

41. "Kunduz Residents Live in Fear of Taliban's Return," *New York Times*, February 7, 2016.

42. Rod Norland, *New York Times*, September 24, 2014.

43. Quoted in the *Washington Post* review of his book, *88 Days to Kandahar*, February 22, 2015.

44. Quoted in *New York Times* review, February 15, 2015.

45. Frances Z. Brown, "Afghanistan's Need for Reform: We Have Seen the Enemy, and It Is Our Anecdotes," *Foreign Policy*, October 30, 2012.

46. Phrase used by Rajiv Chandrasekaran, author/journalist, to describe efforts in Afghanistan, *PBS Newshour*, July 11, 2012.

47. United States and Office of the Special Inspector General for Iraq Reconstruction, *Learning from Iraq*, SIGIR final report, 2013.

48. Josh Boak, *Washington Post*, January 4, 2011.

49. Rory Stewart and Gerald Knaus, *Can Intervention Work?*, pp. xxii–xxiii.

50. Jean-Marie Guéhenno, *The Fog of Peace*, pp. xvi–xvii.

51. Stanley A. McChrystal on Afghanistan, Iraq, and U.S. preparation, *PRISM*, 2016, http://cco.ndu.edu/PRISM-6-3/Article/1020271/an-interview-with-stanley-mcchrystal/.

52. Ibid.

53. Quoted in column, https://counterpunch.org/2016/07/04/in-hopeless-occupation-war-becomes-its-own-end/.

54. Personal comment from audience made at author's talk at Woodrow Wilson School around 2007.

55. Kenneth Cukier and Viktor Mayer-Schoenberger, "The Rise of Big Data: How It's Changing the Way We Think About the World," *Foreign Affairs* 92, no. 3 (May/June 2013), https://www.foreignaffairs.com/system/files/pdf/articles/2013/92305.pdf.

56. Ibid.

57. Personal conversation with author.

58. http://publications.gc.ca/collections/collection_2008/dfait-maeci/FR5-20-1-2008E.pdf.

59. Ibid., p. 30.

CURRENT AND FUTURE CHALLENGES

1. Maria Stephan, memo, November 7, 2012.

8. SYRIA

1. Michael Shear, Helene Cooper, and Eric Schmitt, "Obama Administration Ends Effort to Train Syrians to Combat ISIS," *New York Times*, October 6, 2015, https://www.nytimes.com/2015/10/10/world/middleeast/pentagon-program-islamic-state-syria.html; Eric Schmitt and Ben Hubbard, "US Revamping Rebel Force Fighting ISIS in Syria," *New York Times*, September 6, 2015, https://www.nytimes.com/2015/09/07/world/middleeast/us-to-revamp-training-program-to-fight-isis.html.

2. Mike Mahdesian, e-mail to author, July 21, 2017.

3. U.N. Security Council Resolution 2139, press report and full text, February 22, 2014, https://www.un.org/press/en/2014/sc11292.doc.htm.

4. https://history.state.gov/milestones/1945-1952/berlin-airlift.

5. Sadako Ogata, *The Turbulent Decade*, p. 56.

6. Tod Wilson, interview, May 7, 2017.

7. Maria Stephan, memo, November 7, 2012.

8. Author's notes, State Department meeting, early 2012.

9. Interview with Chris Corpora and Jonas Wechsler. April 21, 2017.

10. Jonas Wechsler and Chris Corpora interview, Spring 2017.

11. See Michael D. Shear, Helene Cooper, and Eric Schmitt. "Obama Administration Ends Effort to Train Syrians to Combat ISIS," *New York Times*, October 9, 2015, https://www.nytimes.com/2015/10/10/world/middleeast/pentagon-program-islamic-state-syria/html; Alex Gorka, "US Mission to Train Syrian Opposition Forces Goes Awry," *Strategic Culture Foundation*, August 7, 2016, https://www.strategic-culture.org/news/2016/07/08/us-mission-train-syrian-opposition-forces-goes-away.html.

12. Named after Sen. Patrick Leahy, the Vermont Democrat who has made upholding human rights standards a hallmark of his career. It is thus of deep concern to Capitol Hill that the government follow these requirements.

13. We received this information from the Public Diplomacy part of the State Department, though the information was imprecise.

14. http://www.defenddemocracy.org/media-hit/holding-civil-society-workshops-while-syria-burns/.

15. Omar Alhalabi.

16. John Jaeger, CSO representative in Turkey, collected this data as the stations expanded throughout Syria. Because of the ongoing conflict, it was difficult to be exact.

17. John Jaeger, interview, May 8, 2017.

18. The eloquent words of a CSO colleague who worked in Turkey.

19. Derek H. Chollet, *The Long Game: How Obama Defied Washington and Redefined America's Role in the World*, 2016, p. 129.

20. Dennis Ross, "Trump Leads from Behind in Syria," *Wall Street Journal*, December 5, 2017.

21. Interview with Corpora and Wechsler, April 21, 2017.

22. Quoted by Stephen M. Walt in his *New York Times* op-ed, May 12, 2017.

23. https://www.nytimes.com/2017/04/06/world/middleeast/us-said-to-weigh-military-responses-to-syrian-chemical-attack.html?_r=0.

24. Jonas Wechsler and Chris Corpora, interview, April 21, 2017.

25. Interview with CSO team member in spring 2017.

26. John Jaeger, interview, May 8, 2017.

27. http://www.cnn.com/2013/08/27/world/meast/syria-civil-war-fast-facts/.

28. Louisa Loveluck, "In Shattered Aleppo, Convoys Carry the Devastated and Defeated from the Last Rebel Zones," *Washington Post*, December 15, 2016.

29. Editorial, *Washington Post*, December 15, 2016.

30. David Ignatius, *Washington Post*, December 16, 2016.

31. Missy Ryan, "U.S. Officials Say Assad Can't Win Civil War, despite Russian Claims," *Washington Post*, December 9, 2017.

32. Meeting with author in Istanbul, early 2014.

9. WHAT MIGHT WE SEE IN THE YEARS AHEAD?

1. http://cop-k.org/Who%20We%20Are.html.

2. Roundtable luncheon with CSO staffers in 2017.

3. A visit to Royal Dutch Shell's headquarters confirmed that oil was no longer an attractive product for them in the Delta because of widespread tapping. Also, Shell's investment in their anchor campus diminished.

4. See George Packer piece in the *New Yorker*.

5. In a visit to his Delta home, I found President Johnson to be deeply introverted and awkward, but more engaged and informed than credited by others.

6. Earlier in Indonesia (1999), USAID/OTI had worked with Garin Nugroho, the country's foremost documentary filmmaker, to shape a series of

television commercials that challenged the population to find a peaceful way forward. It was at a time of riots and attacks on the local Chinese population, an Asian financial crisis, and the transition from the Suharto regime. The threat of national instability was great.

7. http://www.stakeholderdemocracy.org/anigerdeltalegacy/story-of-the-impact/dawn-in-the-creeks/.

8. http://www.stakeholderdemocracy.org/anigerdeltalegacy/story-of-the-impact/dawn-in-the-creeks/episodes/ provides a link to the entire Delta Legacy story and episodes of the show's two seasons.

9. Igarape Institute, quoted in "A Place Too Used to Death," *New York Times*, July 16, 2017.

10. "A 2015 study found that 174,000 Hondurans, 4 percent of the country's households, had abandoned their homes because of violence." Sonia Nazario, *New York Times*, August 14, 2016.

11. Ibid.

12. Remark made at a meeting with author in early 2012.

13. The annual rate of 4,500 murders was cut in half during the truce.

14. Mari Carmen Aponte's recess appointment and return to Washington after a year, followed by a successful confirmation battle in the Senate, was one of the great Washington stories of 2011.

15. James Bosworth, https://www.wilsoncenter.org/sites/default/files/LAP_single_page.pdf, p. 62.

16. "Honduras's homicide rate is around 80 per 100,000—nearly eight times greater than what is considered to be an epidemic. In some communities, the actual murder rate could be more than double the national average." Creative Associates, http://www.creativeassociatesinternational.com/projects/honduras-alianza-joven/.

17. Sonia Nazario, *New York Times*, August 14, 2016.

18. Ibid.

19. Ibid.

A BETTER TOMORROW

1. Robert Lamb, U.S. Policy Responses to Potential Transitions, March 2013, CSIS https://csis-prod.s3.amazonaws.com/s3fs-public/legacy_files/files/publication/130307_Lamb_PolicyResponses_Web.pdf.

2. Carnegie Commission on Preventing Deadly Conflict, *Preventing Deadly Conflict: Final Report with Executive Summary*, Washington, DC: Carnegie Corporation of New York, 1998.

3. See the work of the first PCR Project co-directors Scott Feil, Michele Flournoy, Johanna Mendelson, and Bob Orr, *Play to Win*, The Commission on Post-Conflict Reconstruction, CSIS and the Association of the U.S. Army, January 2013.

4. See, for example, http://www.worldpoliticsreview.com/articles/print/13378; http://cco.dodlive.mil/files/2014/02/prism3-18_bowen.pdf; http://www.usglc.org/report-on-reports/; https://www.stimson.org/content/diplomacy-time-scarcity.

5. United States Department of State and United States Agency for International Development, *Quadrennial Diplomacy and Development Review: Leading through Civilian Power*, http://www.state.gov/documents/organization/153142.pdf, p. xii.

6. Ibid., p. 122.

7. See Dan Serwer's blog on QDDR. https://www.peacefare.net/about/

8. To fulfill its promise, the United States will have to embrace the more sociological change described by a range of current writers. Malcolm Gladwell, Atul Gawande, Daniel Kahneman, James Surowiecki, and others provide new frames that expand the possibilities for fresh U.S. approaches. Many of those works feature creative American initiatives that are working in a globalized economy and that could have resonance in our government institutions. We will also need to apply crime reduction successes in Sicily and Medellin and other violent settings.

10. FULFILLING OUR LEADERSHIP POTENTIAL

1. Ambassador Patricia Haslach, Karin von Hippel, Jerry White, Dolores Brown, Tod Wilson, Chuck Call, Ben Beach, and later Erin Barclay.

2. See studies and Senator Daniel Patrick Moynihan's role and view, https://en.wikipedia.org/wiki/Moynihan_Commission_on_Government_Secrecy.

3. Ray Jennings, hanging off the State House in Alaska, protesting oil policies.

4. Insigniam, *Listening Report: For the U.S. Department of State and U.S. Agency for International Development*, June 2017.

5. Ambassador Chas W. Freeman, quoted in Stephen Walt, "Rex Tillerson Is Underrated," *Foreign Policy*, November 20, 2017.

6. See "The Shriveling State Department," *New York Times* editorial, November 19, 2017.

7. Deputy Administrator Harriet Babbitt oversaw the entire effort.

8. See W. Henry Lambright, *Powering Apollo: James E. Webb of NASA* (Baltimore: Johns Hopkins University Press, 1995).

9. The approximate number of State and USAID employees, with the vast majority being national staff members.

10. Via http://academic.evergreen.edu/g/grossmaz/interventions.html: Afghanistan, Albania, Bosnia and Herzegovina, Colombia, Congo (DR), Croatia, Haiti, Iraq, Kuwait, Liberia, Libya, Macedonia, Pakistan, Panama, Philippines, Somalia, Sudan, Syria, Yemen, Yugoslavia. This does not include special operations.

11. http://www.un.org/en/peacekeeping/operations/current.shtml; the United States pays on average about 25 percent of all costs.

12. Leon Wieseltier, *Washington Post*, December 18, 2016.

13. John Ferejohn and Frances McCall Rosenbluth, *Forged Through Fire: War, Peace, and the Democratic Bargain.*

14. Ibid., p. 16; they cite the "substitution of equipment for men is the use of unmanned aerial vehicles (drones) in Afghanistan, Iraq, and Pakistan, up from 25,000 flight-hours in 2002 to 625,000 in 2011."

15. Credited to the late management guru Peter Drucker, now popularized by others.

16. Roger B. Myerson, University of Chicago, "The Post-Conflict Gap in American Military Strategy," 2016.

11. EXPANDING AMERICA'S PEACEFUL CORE

1. Strobe Talbott, quoting a high-level Asian diplomat on Susan Glasser's podcast, http://www.politico.com/magazine/story/2017/06/19/tom-malinowski-man-who-argued-with-dictators-215278.

2. Jonathan Moore, "Peace-Building in an Inseparable World," *New England Journal of Public Policy*, p. 132, https://scholarworks.umb.edu/cgi/viewcontent.cgi?article=1143&context=nejpp.

3. Fourth Inaugural Address, January 20, 1945, https://avalon.law.yale.edu/20th_century/froos4.asp.

4. https://www.goodreads.com/quotes/290603-if-one-advances-confidently-in-the-direction-of-his-dreams.

5. Douglas Rutzen, "Civil Society Under Assault," *Journal of Democracy* 26, no. 4 (October 2015). National Endowment for Democracy and Johns Hopkins University Press, http://www.icnl.org/news/2015/05_26.4_Rutzen.pdf.

6. Joshua Cooper Ramo, *The Age of the Unthinkable*, p. 11.

7. Skype conversation with Peter deClercq, head of U.N. humanitarian effort for Somalia, in November 2017.

8. Author's notes from remarks at Principia College's International Perspectives Conference, fall 2016, https://content.principia.edu/sites/ipc2016/rais-bhuiyan/.

9. As quoted by Rais at the International Perspectives Conference, 2016.

10. See King's reflections on bouncing back in *On Writing* by Stephen King, New York, Scribner, 2000.

BIBLIOGRAPHY

Acemoglu, Daron, and James A. Robinson. *Economic Origins of Dictatorship and Democracy*. New York: Cambridge University Press, 2009.

Aday, Sean, United States Institute of Peace, George Washington University, and Harvard University. *Blogs and Bullets: New Media in Contentious Politics*. Washington, DC: United States Institute of Peace, 2010.

Albright, Madeleine K., and William S. Cohen. *Preventing Genocide: A Blueprint for U.S. Policymakers*. Washington, DC: American Academy of Diplomacy, United States Holocaust Memorial Museum, and the United States Institute of Peace, 2008.

Albright, Madeleine, and William Woodward. *Madam Secretary*. New York: Miramax Books, 2005.

Anderlini, Sanam Naraghi. *Women Building Peace: What They Do, Why It Matters*. Boulder, CO: Lynne Rienner, 2007.

Anderson, Scott. *The Man Who Tried to Save the World: The Dangerous Life and Mysterious Disappearance of Fred Cuny*. New York: Random House, 2000.

Annan, Kofi A., and Nader Mousavizadeh. *Interventions: A Life in War and Peace*. London: Penguin Books, 2013.

Armitage, Richard Lee. *CSIS Commission on Smart Power: A Smarter, More Secure America*. Washington, DC: CSIS Press, 2007.

Barber, Benjamin R. *Jihad vs. McWorld*. New York: Ballantine Books, 1995.

Barton, Frederick, and Bathsheba Crocker. *A Wiser Peace: An Action Strategy for a Post-Conflict Iraq*. Washington, DC: CSIS Press, 2003.

Barton, Frederick, Bathsheba N. Crocker, and CSIS Post-Conflict Reconstruction Project. *Progress or Peril? Measuring Iraq's Reconstruction*. Washington, DC: Center for Strategic and International Studies, 2004.

Barton, Frederick, Mehlaqa Samdani, Karin von Hippel, and CSIS Post-Conflict Reconstruction Project. *A New Course for Pakistan: PCR Project Research Visit*. Washington, DC: CSIS Press, 2008.

Barton, Frederick, Steve Seigel, Morgan L. Courtney, and Center for Strategic and International Studies *Engaging Youth to Build Safer Communities: A Report of the CSIS Post-Conflict Reconstruction Project*. Washington, DC: CSIS Press, 2006.

Barton, Frederick, Karin von Hippel, and Center for Strategic and International Studies *Afghanistan and Pakistan on the Brink: Framing U.S. Policy Options*. Washington, DC: Center for Strategic and International Studies, 2009.

Barton, Frederick, Karin von Hippel, Sabina Sequeira, and Mark Irvine. *Early Warning? A Review of Conflict Prediction Models and Systems*. Washington, DC: Center for Strategic and International Studies, 2008. https://www.csis.org/analysis/early-warning.

Bass, Gary J. *The Blood Telegram: Nixon, Kissinger, and a Forgotten Genocide*. New York: Vintage Books, 2014.

———. *Freedom's Battle: The Origins of Humanitarian Intervention*. New York: Vintage Books, 2009.

Bendaña, Alejandro. *Constructing Alternatives*. Managua, Nicaragua: Centro de Estudios Internacionales, 2005.

Benjamin, Daniel, and Steven Simon. *The Next Attack: The Failure of the War on Terror and a Strategy for Getting It Right*. New York: Owl Books, 2006.

Berkeley, Bill. *The Graves Are Not Yet Full: Race, Tribe and Power in the Heart of Africa*. New York: Basic Books, 2003.

Biddle, Stephen, and J. Alexander Their. "Defining Success in Afghanistan." *Foreign Affairs* (July 1, 2010).

Binnendijk, Hans, and Patrick M. Cronin. *Civilian Surge: Key to Complex Operations*. Washington, DC: Published for the Center for Technology and National Security Policy by National Defense University Press, 2009.

Bird, Annie R. *US Foreign Policy on Transitional Justice*. New York: Oxford University Press, 2015.

Birdsall, Nancy, and William D. Savedoff. *Cash on Delivery: A New Approach to Foreign Aid*. Washington, DC: Center for Global Development, 2012.

Bjornlund, Eric C. *Beyond Free and Fair: Monitoring Elections and Building Democracy*. Washington, DC: Woodrow Wilson Center Press, and Baltimore: Johns Hopkins University Press, 2004.

Boot, Max. *The Savage Wars of Peace: Small Wars and the Rise of American Power*. New York: Basic Books, 2014.

Boutros-Ghali, Boutros. *Unvanquished: A U.S.-U.N. Saga*. New York: Random House, 1999.

Bowen, Stuart W. United States, and Office of the Special Inspector General for Iraq Reconstruction. *Hard Lessons: The Iraq Reconstruction Experience*. Washington, DC: Department of Defense, 2017.

Brainard, Lael, and Derek Chollet, eds. *Too Poor for Peace? Global Poverty, Conflict, and Security in the 21st Century*. Washington, DC: Brookings Institution Press, 2007.

Brennan, Richard R. and National Defense Research Institute (U.S.). *Ending the U.S. War in Iraq the Final Transition, Operational Maneuver, and Disestablishment of United States Forces-Iraq*. Santa Monica, CA: RAND National Defense Research Institute, 2013.

Brinkerhoff, Derick W. *Governance in Post-Conflict Societies: Rebuilding Fragile States*. Abingdon, UK: Routledge, 2008.

Brooks, Rosa. *How Everything Became War and the Military Became Everything: Tales from the Pentagon*. New York: Simon and Schuster Paperbacks, 2017.

Brown, Michael Edward. *Nationalism and Ethnic Conflict*. Cambridge, MA: MIT Press, 2001.

Brzezinski, Zbigniew. *The Choice: Global Domination or Global Leadership*. New York: Basic Books, 2005.

———. *Out of Control: Global Turmoil on the Eve of the Twenty-First Century*. New York: Touchstone Books, 1995.

Buruma, Ian. *Inventing Japan: 1853–1964*. New York: Modern Library, 2003.

Call, Charles. "The Lingering Problem of Failed States," *Washington Quarterly*, Winter 2017.

———. *Why Peace Fails: The Causes and Prevention of Civil War Recurrence*. Washington, DC: Georgetown University Press, 2012.

Call, Charles, Vanessa Wyeth, and International Peace Institute. *Building States to Build Peace*. Boulder, CO: Lynne Rienner, 2008.

Campbell, John. *Nigeria Dancing on the Brink*. Lanham, MD: Rowman & Littlefield, 2013.

Campbell, Kurt, and Michael O'Hanlon. *Hard Power: The New Politics of National Security*. New York: Basic Books, 2007.

Caplan, Richard. *Exit Strategies and State Building*. Oxford: Oxford University Press, 2012.

———. *International Governance of War-Torn Territories: Rule and Reconstruction*. Oxford: Oxford University Press, 2008.

Carnegie Commission on Preventing Deadly Conflict. *Preventing Deadly Conflict: Final Report with Executive Summary*. Washington, DC: Carnegie Corporation of New York, 1998.

Carothers, Thomas. *Critical Mission: Essays on Democracy Promotion*. Washington, DC: Carnegie Endowment for International Peace, 2004.

Carr, Rosamond Halsey, and Ann Howard Halsey. *Land of a Thousand Hills: My Life in Rwanda*. New York: Plume, 2000.

Castillo, Graciana del. *Rebuilding War-Torn States: The Challenge of Post-Conflict Economic Reconstruction*. Oxford: Oxford University Press, 2008.

Chandrasekaran, Rajiv. *Imperial Life in the Emerald City: Inside Iraq's Green Zone*. New York: Alfred A. Knopf, 2006.

———. *Little America: The War within the War for Afghanistan*, New York: Alfred A. Knopf, 2012.

Chayes, Sarah. *The Punishment of Virtue: Inside Afghanistan after the Taliban*. New York: Penguin Press, 2007.

Chesterman, Simon. *You, the People: The United Nations, Transitional Administration, and State-Building*. Oxford: Oxford University Press, 2009.

Chollet, Derek H. *The Long Game: How Obama Defied Washington and Redefined America's Role in the World*. New York: PublicAffairs, 2016.

Chollet, Derek H., and James M. Goldgeier. *America Between the Wars: From 11/9 to 9/11; The Misunderstood Years Between the Fall of the Berlin Wall and the Start of the War on Terror*. New York: Perseus Books, 2015.

Chollet, Derek H., Mark Irvine, and Bradley Larson. *A Steep Hill: Congress and U.S. Efforts to Strengthen Fragile States*. A Report of the CSIS Post-Conflict Reconstruction Project. Washington, DC: Center for Strategic and International Studies, 2008.

Chua, Amy. *World on Fire: How Exporting Free Market Democracy Breeds Ethnic Hatred and Global Instability*. New York: Anchor Books, 2004.

Clark, Wesley K. *Waging Modern War: Bosnia, Kosovo, and the Future of Combat*. New York: Public Affairs, 2002.

Cockburn, Andrew, and Patrick Cockburn. *Out of the Ashes: The Resurrection of Saddam Hussein*. New York: Harper Perennial, 2000.

Coffin, Frank M. *Witness for AID*. Boston: Houghton Mifflin, 1964.

Cohen, Craig. *A Perilous Course: U.S. Strategy and Assistance to Pakistan*. A Report of the Post-Conflict Reconstruction Project, Center for Strategic and International Studies. Project, co-directors Frederick Barton and Karin von Hippel. Washington, DC: Center for Strategic and International Studies, 2007. https://csis-prod.s3.amazonaws.com/s3fs-public/legacy_files/files/media/csis/pubs/071214_pakistan.pdf.

Cohen, Eliot A. *The Big Stick: The Limits of Soft Power and the Necessity of Military Force*. New York: Basic Books, 2018.

Collier, Paul. *Bottom Billion*, New York: Oxford University Press, 2007.

Commission on Global Security, Justice, and Governance. *Confronting the Crisis of Global Governance: Report of the Commission on Global Security*. The Hague: The Hague Institute for Global Justice, and Washington, DC: The Stimson Center, 2015.

Commission on Human Security. *Human Security Now: Protecting and Empowering People*. New York: United Nations, 2013.

The Commission on Post-Conflict Reconstruction, *Play to Win*, CSIS and the Association of the U.S. Army, January 2013.

Commission on Weak States and National Security and Center for Global Development. *On the Brink: Weak States and US National Security*. Washington, DC: Center for Global Development, 2004.

Connable, Ben. *Embracing the Fog of War: Assessment and Metrics in Counterinsurgency*. Santa Monica, CA: RAND Corporation, 2012.

Connable, Ben, and Martin C. Libicki. *How Insurgencies End*. Santa Monica, CA: RAND Corporation, 2010.

Cooke, Jennifer G. and J. Stephen Morrison. *U.S. Africa Policy beyond the Bush Years: Critical Challenges for the Obama Administration*. Washington, DC: CSIS Press, 2009.

Cortright, David, Melanie C. Greenberg, and Laurel Stone. *Civil Society, Peace, and Power*. Lanham, MD: Rowman & Littlefield, 2017.

Courtney, Morgan L. Frederick Barton, Bathsheba N. Crocker, and Hugh Riddell. *In the Balance: Measuring Progress in Afghanistan: A Report of the CSIS Post-Conflict Reconstruction Project*. Washington, DC: CSIS Press, Center for Strategic and International Studies, 2005.

Cousens, Elisabeth M. Chetan Kumar, and Karin Wermester. *Peacebuilding as Politics: Cultivating Peace in Fragile Societies*. Boulder, CO: Lynne Rienner, 2001.

Covey, Jock, Michael J. Dziedzic, and Leonard R. Hawley, eds. *The Quest for Viable Peace: International Intervention and Strategies for Conflict Transformation*. Washington, DC: United States Institute of Peace, and Arlington, VA: Association of the United States Army, 2006.

Crane, Keith. *Building a More Resilient Haitian State*. Santa Monica, CA: RAND Corporation, 2010.

Crocker, Chester A., Fen Osler Hampson, and Pamela Aall. *Grasping the Nettle: Analyzing Cases of Intractable Conflict*. Washington, DC: United States Institute of Peace, 2007.

————. *Turbulent Peace: The Challenges of Managing International Conflict*. Washington, DC: United States Institute of Peace, 2006.

CSIS Post-Conflict Reconstruction Project. *Capturing Iraqi Voices*. Washington, DC: Center for Strategic and International Studies, 2004.

Cukier, Kenneth, and Viktor Mayer-Schoenberger. "The Rise of Big Data: How It's Changing the Way We Think About the World." *Foreign Affairs* 92, no. 3 (May/June 2013): 28–40. https://www.foreignaffairs.com/system/files/pdf/articles/2013/92305.pdf.

Dambach, Charles F. *Exhaust the Limits: The Life and Times of a Global Peacebuilder*. Baltimore: Apprentice House, 2010.

DARA (Development Assistance Research Associates). *The Humanitarian Response Index (HRI) 2009: Whose Crisis? Clarifying Donor's Priorities*. London: Palgrave Macmillan UK, 2016.

Davidson, Janine. *Lifting the Fog of Peace: How Americans Learned to Fight Modern War*. Ann Arbor: University of Michigan Press, 2011.

Davis, Paul K., Claude Berrebi, Christopher S. Chivvis, Sarah Olmstead, Julie E. Taylor, Veronique Thelen, Stephen Watts and Elizabeth Wilke. *Dilemmas of Intervention: Social Science for Stabilization and Reconstruction* Santa Monica, CA: RAND Corporation, 2011. https://www.rand.org/pubs/monographs/MG1119.html.

De Waal, Alex. *Advocacy in Conflict: Critical Perspectives on Transnational Activism*. London: Zed Books, 2015.

Diamond, Jared M. *Guns, Germs, and Steel: The Fates of Human Societies*. New York: W. W. Norton, 2017.

Diamond, Larry. *Developing Democracy: Toward Consolidation*. Baltimore: Johns Hopkins University Press, 1999.

————. *Squandered Victory: The American Occupation and the Bungled Effort to Bring Democracy to Iraq*. New York: Henry Holt, 2006.

Diamond, Louise, and John W. McDonald. *Multi-Track Diplomacy: A Systems Approach to Peace*. West Hartford, CT: Kumarian Press, 2013.

Dobbins, James. *America's Role in Nation-Building from Germany to Iraq*. Santa Monica, CA: RAND Corporation, 2003.

————. *The Beginner's Guide to Nation-Building*. Santa Monica, CA: RAND National Security Research Division, 2007.

————. *Europe's Role in Nation-Building: From the Balkans to the Congo*. Santa Monica, CA: RAND Corporation, 2008.

————. *Overcoming Obstacles to Peace: Local Factors in Nation-Building*. Santa Monica, CA: RAND Corporation, 2013.

————. *The UN's Role in Nation-Building: From the Congo to Iraq*. Santa Monica, CA: RAND Corporation, 2005.

Dobbins, James, and Carnegie Corporation of New York. *After the War: Nation-Building from FDR to George W. Bush.* Santa Monica, CA: RAND National Security Research Division, 2008.

Dower, John W. *Embracing Defeat: Japan in the Wake of World War II.* New York: W. W. Norton, 2000.

Durch, William J. *The Brahimi Report and the Future of Peacekeeping Operations.* Washington, DC: Henry L. Stimson Center, 2003.

Durch, William J., and Tobias C. Berckman. *Who Should Keep the Peace? Providing Security for Twenty-First-Century Peace Operations.* Washington, DC: The Henry L. Stimson Center, 2006.

Edwards, Michael. *Future Positive: International Co-Operation in the 21st Century.* London: Earthscan, 2004.

Egel, Daniel, Charles Ries, Ben Connable, Todd C. Helmus, Eric Robinson, Isaac Baruffi, Melissa A. Bradley, Kurt Card, Kathleen Loa, Sean Mann, Fernando Sedano, Stephan B. Seabrook, and Robert Stewart. *Investing in the Fight: Assessing the Use of the Commander's Emergency Response Program in Afghanistan.* Santa Monica, CA: RAND Corporation, 2016.

Emirates Center for Strategic Studies and Research. *The Gulf: Challenges of the Future.* Abu Dhabi: Emirates Center for Strategic Studies and Research, 2005.

Esposito, Dina, and Bathsheba Crocker. *To Guarantee the Peace: An Action Strategy for a Post-Conflict Sudan.* A Report for the Secretary of State's Africa Policy Advisory Panel. Washington, DC: Center for Strategic and International Studies, 2004.

European Centre for Conflict Prevention and Swedish Peace Team Forum. *Preventing Violent Conflict and Building Peace: On Interaction between State Actors and Voluntary Organizations.* Stockholm: Swedish Peace Team Forum, 2002.

Evans, Gareth J. *The Responsibility to Protect: Ending Mass Atrocity Crimes Once and for All.* Washington, DC: Brookings Institution Press, 2008.

Fallows, James M. *Blind into Baghdad: America's War in Iraq.* New York: Vintage Books, 2006.

———. "The Fifty-First State." *Atlantic* (November 2002).

Farmer, Paul, Abbey M. Gardner, Cassia van der Hoof Holstein, and Joia Mukherjee. *Haiti after the Earthquake.* New York: PublicAffairs, 2012.

Feldman, Noah. *What We Owe Iraq.* Princeton, NJ: Princeton University Press, 2004.

Ferejohn, John, and Frances McCall Rosenbluth. *Forged Through Fire: War, Peace, and the Democratic Bargain.* New York: W. W. Norton, 2017.

Flanagan, Stephen J., and James A. Schear. *Strategic Challenges America's Global Security Agenda.* Washington, DC: Potomac Books, 2014.

Fleischner, Justine, Karin von Hippel, and Frederick Barton. *Homebound Security: Migrant Support for Improved Public Safety in Conflict-Prone Settings: A Report of the CSIS Post-Conflict Reconstruction Project, October 2009.* Washington, DC: Center for Strategic and International Studies (CSIS), 2009.

Forman, Shepard, and Stewart Patrick. *Good Intentions: Pledges of Aid for Postconflict Recovery.* Boulder, CO: Lynne Rienner, 2000.

Fowler, Michael C. *Amateur Soldiers, Global Wars: Insurgency and Modern Conflict.* Westport, CT: Praeger, 2005.

Fromkin, David. *A Peace to End All Peace: The Fall of the Ottoman Empire and the Creation of the Modern Middle East.* New York: Henry Holt, 2009.

Garrels, Anne. *Naked in Baghdad.* New York: Picador, 2004.

Gelb, Leslie, and Richard K. Betts. *The Irony of Vietnam.* Washington, DC: Brookings, 1979.

Ghani, Ashraf, and Clare Lockhart. *Fixing Failed States: A Framework for Rebuilding a Fractured World.* Oxford: Oxford University Press, 2009.

Gibby, Bryan R. *Will to Win.* Tuscaloosa: University of Alabama, 2012.

Gladwell, Malcolm. *Blink: The Power of Thinking without Thinking.* New York: Back Bay Books, 2013.

———. *Outliers: The Story of Success.* New York: Back Bay Books, 2013.

————. *The Tipping Point: How Little Things Can Make a Big Difference*. New York: Back Bay Books, 2002.

Glantz, Aaron, and Iraq Veterans Against the War (Philadelphia). *Winter Soldier, Iraq and Afghanistan: Eyewitness Accounts of the Occupations*. Chicago: Haymarket Books, 2008.

Gordon, Michael R., and Bernard E. Trainor. *Cobra II: The Inside Story of the Invasion and Occupation of Iraq*. New York: Vintage Books, 2007.

————. *The Endgame: The Hidden History of America's Struggle to Build Democracy in Iraq*. New York: Pantheon, 2012.

Gourevitch, Philip. *We Wish to Inform You That Tomorrow We Will Be Killed with Our Families*. New York: St. Martins Press, 1998.

Gribbin, Robert E. *In the Aftermath of Genocide: The U.S. Role in Rwanda*. New York: iUniverse, 2005.

Guéhenno, Jean-Marie. *The Fog of Peace: A Memoir of International Peacekeeping in the 21st Century*. Washington, DC: Brookings Institution Press, 2015.

Guttieri, Karen, and Jessica Piombo. *Interim Governments: Institutional Bridges to Peace and Democracy?* Washington, DC: United States Institute of Peace, 2007.

Hachigian, Nina, and Mona Sutphen. *The Next American Century: How the U.S. Can Thrive as Other Powers Rise*. New York: Simon and Schuster, 2008.

Halberstam, David. *War in a Time of Peace: Bush, Clinton, and the Generals*. New York: Scribner, 2001.

Hamre, John J., Frederick Barton, Bathsheba N. Crocker, Johanna Mendelson, and Robert Orr. *Iraq's Post-Conflict Reconstruction: A Field Review and Recommendations, July 17, 2003; Iraq Reconstruction Assessment Mission June 27–July 7, 2003*. New York: Council on Foreign Relations, 2003. https://www.cfr.org/sites/default/files/pdf/2005/08/Iraq_Trip_Report.pdf.

Hauss, Charles. *Security 2.0: Dealing with Global Wicked Problems*. Lanham, MD: Rowman & Littlefield, 2015.

Hayner, Priscilla B. *Unspeakable Truths: Confronting State Terror and Atrocities*. New York: Routledge, 2002.

Helton, Arthur C., and Council on Foreign Relations. *The Price of Indifference: Refugees and Humanitarian Action in the New Century*. Oxford: Oxford University Press, 2007.

Hideō, Sato. *Containing Conflict: Cases in Preventive Diplomacy*. Tokyo: Japan Center for International Exchange, 2003.

Hoffman, Peter J., and Thomas George Weiss. *Sword and Salve: Confronting New Wars and Humanitarian Crises*. Lanham, MD: Rowman & Littlefield, 2006.

Holt, Victoria K., and Tobias C. Berkman. *The Impossible Mandate? Military Preparedness, the Responsibility to Protect and Modern Peace Operations*. Washington, DC: The Henry L. Stimson Center, 2006.

Holt, Victoria K., Glyn Taylor, Max Kelly, United Nations Department of Peacekeeping Operations and Office for the Coordination of Humanitarian Affairs. *Protecting Civilians in the Context of UN Peacekeeping Operations: Successes, Setbacks and Remaining Challenges*. New York: United Nations, 2010.

Hunt, Swanee. *This Was Not Our War: Bosnian Women Reclaiming the Peace*. Durham, NC: Duke University Press, 2011.

————. *Worlds Apart: Bosnian Lessons for Global Security*. Durham, NC: Duke University Press, 2011.

Huntington, Samuel P. *The Clash of Civilizations and the Remaking of World Order*. New York: Touchstone, 2003.

Hurwitz, Agnès, and Reyko Huang. *Civil War and the Rule of Law: Security, Development, Human Rights*. Boulder, CO: Lynne Rienner, 2008.

Ignatieff, Michael, Amy Gutmann, and Kwame Anthony Appiah. *Human Rights as Politics and Idolatry*. Princeton, NJ: Princeton University Press, 2003.

Ikenberry, G. John. *After Victory: Institutions, Strategic Restraint, and the Rebuilding of Order after Major Wars*. Princeton, NJ: Princeton University Press, 2001.

Ikenberry, G. John, Anne-Marie Slaughter, Princeton Project on National Security, and Woodrow Wilson School of Public and International Affairs. *Forging a World of Liberty under Law: U.S. National Security in the 21st Century: Final Report of the Princeton Project on National Security*. Princeton, NJ: Woodrow Wilson School of Public and International Affairs, Princeton University, 2006.

Insigniam. *Listening Report: For the U.S. Department of State and U.S. Agency for International Development*. June 2017.

Iraq Study Group (U.S.), James Addison Baker, Lee Hamilton, and Lawrence S. Eagleburger. *The Iraq Study Group Report*. New York: Vintage Books, 2006.

Jenkins, Kate, and William Plowden. *Governance and Nationbuilding: The Failure of International Intervention*. Cheltenham, UK: Edward Elgar, 2007.

Johnston, Douglas M. *Religion, Terror, and Error: U.S. Foreign Policy and the Challenge of Spiritual Engagement*. Santa Barbara, CA: Praeger, 2011.

Jolly, Richard, Louis Emmerij, and Thomas George Weiss. *UN Ideas That Changed the World*. Bloomington: Indiana University Press, 2009.

Jones, Bruce, Carlos Pascual, and Stephen John Stedman. *Power and Responsibility: Building International Order in an Era of Transnational Threats*. Washington, DC: Brookings Institution Press, 2009.

Jones, Owen Bennett. *Pakistan: Eye of the Storm*. New Haven, CT: Yale University Press, 2009.

Jones, Seth G., and International Security and Defense Policy Center, eds. *Securing Tyrants or Fostering Reform? U.S. Internal Security Assistance to Repressive and Transitioning Regimes*. Santa Monica, CA: RAND Corporation, 2006.

Jones, Seth G., and Safety Rand Infrastructure and Environment (Organization). *Establishing Law and Order after Conflict*. Santa Monica, CA: RAND Corporation, 2005.

Kahneman, Daniel. *Thinking, Fast and Slow*. New York: Farrar, Straus and Giroux, 2015.

Kaplan, Robert D. *Balkan Ghosts: A Journey through History*. New York: Vintage Books, 1996.

Kelly, Terrence K., and RAND Corporation. *Stabilization and Reconstruction Staffing: Developing U.S. Civilian Personnel Capabilities*. Santa Monica, CA: Rand Corporation, 2008.

Kennedy, Paul. *Preparing for the Twenty-First Century*. London: Harper Collins, 2002.

Kent, R. C., John Ratcliffe, CSIS Post-Conflict Reconstruction Project, Humanitarian Futures Programme, *Responding to Catastrophes: U.S. Innovation in a Vulnerable World*. Washington, DC: Center for Strategic and International Studies, 2008.

King, Stephen. *On Writing*, New York: Scribner, 2000.

King's College London and Security and Development Group Conflict. *A Review of Peace Operations: A Case for Change*. London: King's College, 2003.

Kissinger, Henry. *World Order*. New York: Penguin, 2014.

Kleinfeld, Rachel. *Advancing the Rule of Law Abroad: Next Generation Reform*. Washington, DC: Carnegie Endowment for International Peace, 2012.

Korpivaara, Ari, Raphaelle Castera, Aryeh Neier, Open Society Institute, and Fondation connaissance et liberté of Port-au-Prince. *Beyond the Mountains: The Unfinished Business of Haiti*. New York: Open Society Institute, 2004.

Krasno, Jean E., Donald C. Daniel, and Bradd C. Hayes. *Leveraging for Success in United Nations Peace Operations*. Westport, CT: Praeger, 2003.

Krause, Joachim, Charles K. Mallory, Aspen European Strategy Forum, Conferencia, and Aspen Institute Berlin, eds. *International State Building and Reconstruction Efforts Experience Gained and Lessons Learned*. Opladen, MI: Barbara Budrich, 2010.

Kriesberg, Louis, and Bruce W. Dayton. *Constructive Conflicts: From Escalation to Resolution*, Lanham, MD: Rowman & Littlefield, 2017.

Kuperman, Alan J. *The Limits of Humanitarian Intervention: Genocide in Rwanda*. Washington, DC: Brookings Institution Press, 2001.

Lake, Anthony, and Selig S. Harrison. *After the Wars: Reconstruction in Afghanistan, Indochina, Central America, Southern Africa, and the Horn of Africa*. New Brunswick, NJ: Transaction, 1991.

Lamb, Robert. "US Policy Responses to Potential Transitions: A New Dataset of Political Protests, Conflicts, and Coups." CSIS Post-Conflict Reconstruction Project. Washington, DC: March 2013.

Lambright, W. Henry. *Powering Apollo: James E. Webb of NASA*. Baltimore: Johns Hopkins University Press, 1995.

Lederach, John Paul. *Building Peace: Sustainable Reconciliation in Divided Societies*. Washington, DC: United States Institute of Peace, 2010.

Levy, Adrian, and Cathy Scott-Clark. *Deception: Pakistan, the United States, and the Secret Trade in Nuclear Weapons*. New York: Walker and Co., 2007.

Lewis, Norman. *Naples '44: A World War II Diary of Occupied Italy*. New York: Open Road Media, 2013.

Licklider, Roy. "Obstacles to Peace Settlements." In *Elgar Handbook of Civil War and Fragile States*.

Lie, John. "Aid Dependence and the Structure of Corruption: The Case of Post–Korean War South Korea," *International Journal of Sociology and Social Policy* 7, no. 11/12 (1997): pp. 48–89.

Linder, Rebecca, Frederick Barton, Karin von Hippel, Nick Menzies, Viktoria Schmitt, Steve Seigel, and Center for Strategic and International Studies. *Wikis, Webs, and Networks: Creating Connectivity for Conflict-Prone Settings*. Washington, DC: Center for Strategic and International Studies, 2006.

Lippmann, Walter. *U.S. Foreign Policy: Shield of the Republic*. New York: Johnson Reprint Corp., 1972.

Malkasian, Carter. *War Comes to Garmser: Thirty Years of Conflict on the Afghan Frontier*. Oxford : Oxford University Press, 2016.

Malone, David. *The International Struggle over Iraq: Politics in the UN Security Council, 1980–2005*. Oxford: Oxford University Press, 2007.

Mann, James. *Rise of the Vulcans: The History of Bush's War Cabinet*. New York: Penguin Books, 2004.

Marks, Susan Collin. *Watching the Wind: Conflict Resolution during South Africa's Transition to Democracy*. Washington, DC: United States Institute of Peace, 2002.

Marston, Daniel, and Carter Malkasian. *Counterinsurgency in Modern Warfare*. Oxford: Osprey Publishing, 2010.

Maynard, Kimberly. *Healing Communities in Conflict*. New York: Columbia University Press, 2002.

McAllester, Matthew. *Beyond the Mountains of the Damned: The War inside Kosovo*. New York: New York University Press, 2003.

McChrystal, Stanley A. *My Share of the Task*. New York: Portfolio/Penguin, 2014.

McChrystal, Stanley A., Tantum Collins, David Silverman, and Chris Fussell. *Team of Teams: New Rules of Engagement for a Complex World*. Penguin Publishing Group, 2015.

McMaster, H. R. *Dereliction of Duty: Lyndon Johnson, Robert McNamara, the Joint Chiefs of Staff, and the Lies That Led to Vietnam*. New York: Harper, 2017.

McNerney, Michael J., Jennifer D. P. Moroney, Peter G. Mandaville, Terry Hagen, RAND Corporation, National Security Research Division, United States Department of State, and Bureau of Political Military Affairs. *New Security and Justice Sector Partnership Models: Implications of the Arab Uprisings*. Santa Monica, CA: RAND Corporation, 2014.

Mead, Walter Russell, *Special Providence: American Foreign Policy and How It Changed the World*. New York: Alfred A. Knopf, 2002.

Mehler, Andreas, and Claude Ribaux. *Crisis Prevention and Conflict Management in Technical Cooperation: An Overview of the National and International Debate*. Wiesbaden, Germany: Universum, 2000.

Miklaucic, Michael, National Defense University, Center for Technology and National Security Policy, and Center for Complex Operations. *Commanding Heights: Strategic Lessons from Complex Operations*. Washington, DC: National Defense University Press, 2010.

Minow, Martha. *Between Vengeance and Forgiveness: Facing History after Genocide and Mass Violence*. Boston: Beacon Press, 2009.

Mitchell, George. *Making Peace*. New York: Alfred A. Knopf, 2013.

Montgomery, Tommie Sue. *Peacemaking and Democratization in the Western Hemisphere*. Coral Gables, FL: North-South Center Press, University of Miami, 2000.

Moore, Jonathan. "Peace-Building in an Inseparable World." *New England Journal of Public Policy* 19, no. 2 (2005).

Moynihan, Daniel Patrick. *Pandaemonium: Ethnicity in International Politics*. Oxford: Oxford University Press, 1994.

Muscat, Robert J. *Investing in Peace: How Development Aid Can Prevent or Promote Conflict*. Armonk, NY: M. E. Sharpe, 2002.

Narayan, Deepa. *Voices of the Poor: Crying out for Change*. Washington, DC: World Bank, Poverty Group, 2000.

Narayan, Deepa, and International Bank for Reconstruction and Development. *Can Anyone Hear Us? Voices of the Poor*. New York: Oxford University Press, 2002.

National Intelligence Council. *Mapping the Global Future: Report of the 2020 Project*. Washington, DC: Government Printing Office, 2004.

Neuffer, Elizabeth. *The Key to My Neighbor's House: Seeking Justice in Bosnia and Rwanda*. New York: Picador, 2002.

Nye, Joseph S. *The Paradox of American Power: Why the World's Only Superpower Can't Go It Alone*. Oxford: Oxford University Press, 2003.

———. *Soft Power*. New York: PublicAffairs, 2009.

Oakley, Robert B., Michael J. Dziedzic, and Eliot M. Goldberg. *Policing the New World Disorder: Peace Operations and Public Security*. Honolulu: University Press of the Pacific, 2002.

Ogata, Sadako, *The Turbulent Decade: Confronting the Refugee Crises in the 1990s*. New York: W. W. Norton, 2005.

Ondaatje, Michael. *Anil's Ghost*. London: Bloomsbury, 2011.

Orlando, Leoluca. *Fighting the Mafia and Renewing Sicilian Culture*. New York: Encounter Books, 2010.

Orr, Robert Cameron, and Center for Strategic and International studies and Association of the United States Army. *Winning the Peace—An American Strategy for Post-Conflict Reconstruction*. Washington, DC: CSIS Press, 2004.

Packer, George. *The Assassins' Gate: America in Iraq*. New York: Farrar, Straus and Giroux, 2006.

Patel, Seema, Frederick Barton, Karin von Hippel, Steven Ross, and CSIS Post-Conflict Reconstruction Project. *Breaking Point: Measuring Progress in Afghanistan*. A report of the Center for Strategic and International Studies. Washington, DC: CSIS Press, 2007.

Patrick, Stewart. *Weak Links: Fragile States, Global Threats, and International Security*. Oxford: Oxford University Press, 2011.

Patrick, Stewart, and Kaysie Brown. *Greater than the Sum of Its Parts? Assessing "Whole of Government" Approaches to Fragile States*. New York: International Peace Academy, 2008.

Peace Operations: Developing an American Strategy. Washington, DC: National Defense University Press, 1995.

Perito, Robert. *Where Is the Lone Ranger When We Need Him? America's Search for a Postconflict Stability Force*. Washington, DC: United States Institute of Peace, 2004.

Pfaff, William. *The Irony of Manifest Destiny: The Tragedy of America's Foreign Policy*. New York: Walker and Co., 2010.

Phillips, David Lawrence. *Losing Iraq—Inside the Postwar Reconstruction Fiasco*. New York: Westview Press, 2005.

Pierre, Andrew J., Georgetown University, Institute for the Study of Diplomacy, and American Academy of Diplomacy. *Coalition Building and Maintenance: The Gulf War, Kosovo, Afghanistan, and the War on Terrorism*. Washington, DC: Georgetown University, Institute for the Study of Diplomacy, 2002.

Pinker, Steven. *The Better Angels of Our Nature: Why Violence Has Declined*. New York: Penguin, 2012.

Pollack, Kenneth M., Brookings Institution, and Iraq Policy Working Group. *A Switch in Time: A New Strategy for America in Iraq.* Washington, DC: Saban Center for Middle East Policy at the Brookings Institution, 2006.

Ponzio, Richard J. *Democratic Peacebuilding: Aiding Afghanistan and Other Fragile States.* Oxford: Oxford University Press, 2011.

Power, Samantha. *Sergio: One Man's Fight to Save the World.* New York: Penguin Books, 2010.

Power, Samantha, and Derek H. Chollet. *The Unquiet American: Richard Holbrooke in the World.* New York: PublicAffairs, 2011.

Priest, Dana. *The Mission: Waging War and Keeping Peace with America's Military.* New York: W. W. Norton, 2004.

Ramo, Joshua Cooper. *The Age of the Unthinkable: Why the New World Disorder Constantly Surprises Us and What to Do about It.* New York: Back Bay Books, 2010.

Report of the Independent Inquiry into the Actions of the United Nations During the 1994 Genocide in Rwanda. New York: United Nations, 1999. http://www.securitycouncilreport. org/atf/cf/%7B65BFCF9B-6D27-4E9C-8CD3-CF6E4FF96FF9%7D/POC%20S199 91257.pdf.

Report of the Secretary-General pursuant to General Assembly Resolution 53/35: The Fall of Srebrenica. New York: United Nations, 1999.

Reychler, Luc, and Thania Paffenholz, eds. *Peacebuilding: A Field Guide.* London: Lynne Rienner, 2001.

Rieffel, Alexis. *Restructuring Sovereign Debt: The Case for Ad Hoc Machinery.* Washington, DC: Brookings Institution Press, 2003.

Rohde, David. *Beyond War: Reimagining American Influence in a New Middle East.* New York: Viking, 2013.

Rubin, Barry M. *The Long War for Freedom: The Arab Struggle for Democracy in the Middle East.* Hoboken, NJ: Wiley, 2006.

Rubin, Trudy. *Willful Blindness: The Bush Administration and Iraq.* Philadelphia: Philadelphia Inquirer, 2004.

Rutzen, Douglas. "Civil Society Under Assault." *Journal of Democracy* 26, no. 4 (October 2015), National Endowment for Democracy and Johns Hopkins University Press.

Scahill, Jeremy. *Dirty Wars.* London: Serpent's Tail, 2013.

Schadlow, Nadia. *War and the Art of Governance: Consolidating Combat Success into Political Victory.* Washington, DC: Georgetown University Press, 2017.

Schiffer, Michael, David Shorr, and Stanley Foundation. *Powers and Principles: International Leadership in a Shrinking World.* Lanham, MD: Lexington Books, 2009.

Schirch, Lisa, Deborah Mancini-Griffoli, and Alliance for Peacebuilding. *Local Ownership in Security: Case Studies of Peacebuilding Approaches.* The Hague: Alliance for Peacebuilding, GPPAC, Kroc Institute, 2015.

Sen, Amartya. *Development as Freedom.* Oxford: Oxford University Press, 2013.

Shacochis, Bob. *The Immaculate Invasion* . New York: Grove Press, 2010. https://www. amazon.com/Immaculate-Invasion-Bob-Shacochis/dp/0802145183.

Shadid, Anthony. *Night Draws Near: Iraq's People in the Shadow of America's War.* New York: Picador, 2006.

Shifter, Michael. "Plan Colombia." *Americas Quarterly* (Summer 2012).

Silber, Laura, and Allan Little, *The Death of Yugoslavia.* New York: Penguin Books, 1997.

Simkhada, Shambhu Ram, Daniel Harry Warner, and Politics PSIO Workshop on Religion Conflict and Humanitarian Action, eds. *Religion, Politics, Conflict and Humanitarian Action: Faith-Based Organisations as Political, Humanitarian or Religious Actors; Proceedings of the Workshop, May 18–19, 2005, Geneva, Switzerland.* Geneva, Switzerland: Program for the Study of International Organization(s)—Graduate Institute of International Studies, 2006.

Singer, Peter W. *Children at War.* Berkeley: University of California Press, 2009.

Smith, Dane F. *U.S. Peacefare: Organizing American Peace-Building Operations.* Santa Barbara, CA: Praeger Security International, 2010.

Smith, Dane F. and Center for Strategic and International Studies, *An Expanded Mandate for Peace Building: The State Department Role in Peace Diplomacy, Reconstruction, and Stabilization*. Washington, DC: Center for Strategic and International Studies, 2009.

Soderberg, Nancy E., and Brian Katulis. *The Prosperity Agenda: What the World Wants from America—and What We Need in Return*. Hoboken, NJ: John Wiley and Sons, 2008.

The Stanley Foundation. *Capturing the 21st Century Security Agenda: Prospects for Collective Responses*. Muscatine, IA: The Stanley Foundation, 2004.

Stedman, Stephen John, Donald S. Rothchild, and Elizabeth M. Cousens. *Ending Civil Wars: The Implementation of Peace Agreements*. Boulder, CO: Lynne Rienner, 2002.

Stephan, Maria J. *Civilian Jihad: Nonviolent Struggle, Democratization, and Governance in the Middle East*. Basingstoke, UK: Palgrave Macmillan, 2010.

Stewart, Rory, and Gerald Knaus, *Can Intervention Work?* New York: W. W. Norton, 2012.

Stromseth, Jane E., David Wippman, Rosa Brooks, and American Society of International Law. *Can Might Make Rights? Building the Rule of Law after Military Interventions*. Cambridge: Cambridge University Press, 2010.

Surowiecki, James. *The Wisdom of Crowds*. New York: Anchor Books, 2011.

Traub, James. *The Freedom Agenda: Why America Must Spread Democracy (Just Not the Way George Bush Did)*. New York: Farrar, Straus Giroux, 2008.

United Nations High Commissioner for Refugees. *The State of the World's Refugees 2000: Fifty Years of Humanitarian Action*. Oxford: Oxford University Press, 2000.

United Nations High-Level Panel on Threats, Challenges and Change. *A More Secure World: Our Shared Responsibility*, Report of the Secretary General's High-Level Panel on Threats, Challenges and Change. New York: United Nations, 2004. http://www.un.org/en/peacebuilding/pdf/historical/hlp_more_secure_world.pdf.

United States and Office of the Special Inspector General for Iraq Reconstruction. *Learning from Iraq*. Washington, DC: U.S. Government Printing Office, 2013.

United States Department of State and United States Agency for International Development. *Quadrennial Diplomacy and Development Review: Leading through Civilian Power*. Washington, DC: U.S. Department of State and U.S. Agency for International Development, 2010. http://www.state.gov/documents/organization/153142.pdf.

von Hippel, Karin. *Democracy by Force: US Military Intervention in the Post–Cold War World*. Cambridge: Cambridge University Press, 2000.

Walt, Stephen M. *Taming American Power: The Global Response to U.S. Primacy*. New York: W. W. Norton, 2010.

Walter, Barbara F. *Committing to Peace: The Successful Settlement of Civil Wars*. Princeton, NJ: Princeton University Press, 2002.

Waslekar, Sundeep, Ilmas Futehaly, and Strategic Foresight Group. *Cost of Conflict in the Middle East*. Mumbai: Strategic Foresight Group, 2009.

Weaver, Mary Anne. *Pakistan: In the Shadow of Jihad and Afghanistan*. New York: Farrar, Straus and Giroux, 2013.

Weinstein, Jeremy M. *Inside Rebellion: The Politics of Insurgent Violence*. Cambridge: Cambridge University Press, 2009.

West, Richard. *Tito and the Rise and Fall of Yugoslavia*. London : Sinclair-Stevenson, 1994.

Wilentz, Amy. *The Rainy Season*. London: Vintage, 1994.

Women on the Frontlines of Peace and Security. Washington, DC: National Defense University Press, 2014.

Woodrow Wilson School of Public and International Affairs and CSIS Post-Conflict Reconstruction Project, *Securing Peace: An Action Strategy for Sri Lanka*. A Report. Washington, DC: Center for Strategic and International Studies, 2004.

Woodward, Bob. *Bush at War*. Volume 3. New York: Simon and Schuster, 2006.

———. *Obama's Wars*. New York: Simon and Schuster, 2014.

World Bank. *World Development Report 2011: Conflict, Security, and Development*. Washington DC: World Bank, 2003.

Wright, Thomas J. *All Measures Short of War: The Contest for the 21st Century and the Future of American Power*. New Haven, CT: Yale University Press, 2017.

Zartman, I. William. *Governance as Conflict Management: Politics and Violence in West Africa*. Washington, DC: Brookings Institution Press, 1997.

Zeeuw, Jeroen de. *From Soldiers to Politicians: Transforming Rebel Movements after Civil War*. Boulder, CO: Lynne Rienner, 2008.

Zeeuw, Jeroen de, Krishna Kumar, and Nederlands Instituut voor Internationale Betrekkingen "Clingendael." *Promoting Democracy in Postconflict Societies*. New Delhi: Lynne Rienner, 2008.

Zenko, Micah. *Red Team: How to Succeed by Thinking like the Enemy*. New York: Basic Books, 2015.

Zimmermann, Warren. *First Great Triumph: How Five Americans Made Their Country a World Power*. New York: Farrar, Straus and Giroux, 2004.

Zumwalt, Elmo R. *On Watch: A Memoir*. New York: Quadrangle, 1977.

INDEX

ABOUT THE AUTHOR

With direct experience in more than 40 conflicts, **Ambassador Rick Barton** has worked with local people to bring innovative practices and pragmatic ideas to the world's most violent places. A builder of organizations and developer of talent, Barton co-founded two pathbreaking US government creations: USAID's Office of Transition Initiatives and the State Department's Bureau of Conflict and Stabilization Operations. Barton served as Deputy High Commissioner for Refugees at the United Nations in Geneva, America's representative to the Economic and Social Council of the United Nations in New York, and Assistant Secretary of State in Washington. He teaches at Princeton's Woodrow Wilson School, where he is the co-director of the Scholars in the Nation's Service Initiative with his wife of 43 years, Kit Lunney. Their daughter, Kacy, is a teacher.